T R A S H

A true story by Laurie Anne Hoover

 **FriesenPress**

Suite 300 - 990 Fort St
Victoria, BC, Canada, V8V 3K2
www.friesenpress.com

Copyright © 2015 by Laurie Anne Hoover
First Edition — 2015

Cover illustration by Laurie Anne Hoover.

ISBN
978-1-4602-6272-6 (Hardcover)
978-1-4602-6273-3 (Paperback)
978-1-4602-6274-0 (eBook)

1. Biography & Autobiography, Personal Memoirs

Distributed to the trade by The Ingram Book Company

For Kara

ACKNOWLEDGEMENTS

I WOULD LIKE TO THANK ALL OF THE FAMILY AND FRIENDS who have stood by me, believed in me, and supported the writing of this book. I particularly want to thank my sister, Angela Hoover-LaPointe for her wisdom, nurturing, continuous encouragement, and making me believe that everything I do is a brilliant work of art.

My special gratitude also extends to my dear friends Anita Alton, Jennifer Wolfreys, and Wendy Bonnell for their enthusiastic support and the thoughtful readings and insights provided as I moved from chapter to chapter.

And finally, it is difficult to adequately find the words to thank my love, Kara McGaw, who persuaded me to persevere with this book when I was resigned to storing it in a drawer forever and who continues to inspire fearlessness in creativity.

DISCLAIMER

THIS IS A TRUE STORY. SOME DETAILS HAVE BEEN CHANGED TO protect the innocent, the guilty, the living, and the dead. A few details have been embellished for the sake of dramatic effect; however, every aspect of this story has an element of truth. All names are fictitious and are from the author's imagination. Any relationship of these names to actual people is purely coincidental. The author is aware that stories often change in the telling and acknowledges that this can further blur the line that separates reality from fantasy. Any misrepresentation of actual persons or events is unintentional. The author's intent is not to hurt any member of the family presented in this book. The author's intent is to present a survival story that is as authentic as possible and recounts true experiences as told from the main character's point of view, which may vary significantly from the recollections of the actual people upon which the other characters are based.

Trigger Warning

This story contains scenes of domestic, verbal, physical, and sexual violence; alcohol and drug abuse; and parental neglect. Reader discretion is advised.

That's the way it is with stories. You come to appreciate them for their good intentions, aware that they don't always tell the truth. They shape people, towns, landscapes, and cheat you into believing certain things about yourself. They select, discard, and amend plots that become history. That's how we invent ourselves.

L.L. Tostevin, *Frog Moon*

I have a tale to tell.
Sometimes it gets so hard to hide it well.

Madonna, *Live to Tell*

PROLOGUE

I KEEP THESE PHOTOGRAPHS AND SNAPSHOTS IN A RATTY plastic bag. They are in no particular order. I have not done what I was asked to do with them. I was supposed to arrange them into a visual record for my parents, but years continue to pass and I still have not honoured their request. Not one of these pictures has been lost, even though I have been rather careless with them as I have moved from place to place. Many of them are bent, folded, and dog-eared. I have kept them, like my old letters and cards, because there is something in them that I refuse to let go—in these pictures are my truths and inventions, and losing one of them would be like losing a part of myself, so full of ego. Maybe that's why I haven't given them back to my parents. They have become mine. I have stolen them. I have stolen our history, as if it is a history I would want to remember. It's more like a history to be learned from like the Nuremburg Trials. I imagine I will still be carrying these pictures as an old woman, probably in the same old plastic S&R Department Store bag, showing them to friends and telling the stories of each one, eliminating some details and embellishing others, distorting the truth.

I will not put these pictures in order. I will not impose a chronology, even if it were possible. I am usually fanatic about proper times and proper places, having studied art history at university and now, myself, a teacher of that subject. I recall how there, in the large lecture halls at Queen's, I would write gruelling slide tests. With my head filled with a jumble of names and dates, I would sit in the dark waiting for the first slide. The screen would invariably fill with a picture. On one occasion it was a portrait, not completely unlike some of those in my plastic bag. Every time I see this painting, it reminds me of one photograph in particular. I remember:

The painting appears on the screen, larger than life. In it a man and a woman stand stiffly in their bedroom chamber. They do not stand very close to each other, but their hands touch. It is a celebration of texture. The man wears an enormous broad rimmed hat and a fur-trimmed cloak; the woman wears a delicate white headdress and a velvety green gown, also trimmed with fur.

It is this woman who commands my attention. Her head is bowed slightly and her hands are delicate and elongated—vulnerable. It does not take long to notice that her small body is thick at the belly. This is one of the painting's symbolic secrets. There is no child swimming within her flesh under her gown. Not yet. The swollen contour formed by the robe alludes to her future child bearing. I know this from a lecture on Flemish art. On my test paper I write: 'Arnolfini Wedding Portrait by Jan Van Eyck, 1434'.

After identifying the work, as I puke out all that I know about it in an attempt to impress the professor—the media, the symbolism, the wonder of the convex mirror in the background reflecting the world of the bedroom chamber and count-less other details—I wonder if I have really learned anything about Flemish art. One easily overlooked detail I notice is the small broom hanging from one of the bedposts. The woman's role is clear: Clean the house and make babies. Is this my own interpretation or did the prof say that? How much of our insight is borrowed?

I have heard these photographs call to me a thousand times, and a thousand times I have taken them out of their plastic dwelling to look at them. I spend a lot of time observing one picture. It always makes me think of the *Arnolfini Portrait*. It is a black and white; the year is 1964. There are six people seated at the dinner table. It must be dinner, not lunch or breakfast—the roast beef carcass in the center of the table provides this clue. The table is littered with post-meal debris, like dishes with particles of food, forks, and knives scattered on plates, a glass of milk three quarters empty or one quarter full, depending on how one chooses to look at it. A woman I do not know is seated at the left. She stares at the photogra-pher, expressionless, with tightly closed lips. On her face she wears horn-rimmed glasses and on her body, a striped cotton housedress.

I mention her only because she is seated beside my parents. Were they friends? The stranger appears to be at least twenty years older than they, and is probably a friend or neighbour of my grandparents, who are seated directly on the right side of my mother and father. If this stranger was a friend of my parents, it is well explained why I do not know her. I do not know her because she came to know my parents, and that is enough.

My black and white mother sits on the lap of my black and white father. Their faces are young, fresh, and smiling. They are the reason the picture is being taken; they are the focus. My mother has a dark Jackie Kennedy hairdo. Brows plucked pencil-line thin. White lipstick. My father has a navy brush cut and sharply protruding parts, like his Adam's apple and his ears.

My other parents, my grandparents, are the ones who put on this meal in their small Princess Street apartment in Kingston. I recognize the table, the painted-over light switches, the mix and match dishes and cutlery certainly purchased from Woolworth's across the street. My grandmother appears to sit comfortably beside my father; she looks healthy, robust, with a full head of jet-black hair. This is a time when the cancer cells remained dormant in her body, before her body became a war zone. My grandfather sits beside her with his arms crossed on the table. He is the only one who doesn't look at the photographer. He looks, with obvious tenderness and pride, at my mother. He appears as I have always known him: a long, wiry, gentle man with thick black glasses, an enormous nose, nicotine stained fingers, and dressed in a white tank style undershirt, the kind that my teenage students call a wife beater.

As I look at him looking at my mother, I wonder if he is considering the fact that she is not his true daughter, not of his blood. When mother was made, Grandmother was making love to Grandfather's friend while Grandfather was making war in France. It is one of the truths hidden in this picture.

I am in this photograph too, concealed beneath my mother's flesh and her polyester blouse with the large floral print. I am connected to the events, to the lives, captured by the photographer, part of this and part of what is to come, part of the secrets, the lies, and the truths.

These photographs are important to me, not only for what can be observed, but also for what lays hiding within them. They hold the truth of this story.

* * * * *

It was while growing up in conservative Kingston, Ontario, and attending Catholic schools that I learned there were no crimes that could not be forgiven, especially in families. It was my first experience with Catholic guilt topped with a healthy dose of bullshit. The truth is that there are atrocities committed in families, war crimes, the kind that Jesus Christ himself might find difficult to stomach, let alone forgive. There seems to be a modern need to moan about miserable childhoods. Until now, I have chosen to keep much of my history buried deep within my gut. I still don't know if I have the courage to tell it. Lying is easy; telling the truth is a tough deal. This story won't appeal to everyone and it will be important to even less. Only when I see my sister or my two brothers does the past tend to rear itself, usually after diving into a bottle. My parents have chosen to put their heads into a bucket of sand. They cannot afford these memories or to face the wreckage of their war. They would prefer that I did not have a story to tell or that I would choose to not have a memory, especially not a memory that paints them black. Now it is too late.

I have often thought of writing this story for the few people who would care. Why write it now? There are reasons. I'm going to tell it because I am sick. Sick in my head. Though I'm packed full of Prozac, I have a difficult time sleeping and somehow I think that releasing all of the ghosts will purge me, like a good brainwash. This story will also provide a record for my sister and brothers. Each has had their demons to wrestle, like relationship failures, bouts with mental illness, substance abuse, or trouble with a SWAT team. They must realize that we were both born and made.

The truth is that many bizarre, devastating, and tragic events took place within our family. My parents came to treat their children like shabby baggage, refuse, hostages that could be sacrificed. I know they will not approve of me telling this story, but as I said, it is too late. It has also become necessary. I don't want this to become the usual sob story. Simply, I need to sleep.

I

A SNAPSHOT. SNAPSHOTS ARE LESS POLISHED AND POSED THAN photographs. They catch people off guard, unawares. In this one, my father stands in a doorway of the earliest family home I can remember. At least I can remember this place without worrying that I might be lying about it. If I try to relay any of our earlier history, I would only have vague shadows, glimpses of colour, fleeting sounds. If I chose to write about events before Montreal Street, I would have to believe the stories my parents told me, and that would not be wise. They are not a reliable source.

My father has a gentle, surprised smile in this picture, a smile that hides the truth of his fearsome nature. He is a master of illusion. He manages to hide himself even in a snapshot. His shining young baby face, his tidy haircut, and the perfect knot in his tie conceal that he is a colossal alcoholic who could fly into a murderous rage in a split second. Right beside his head is a black dial telephone mounted to the grease-stained wall, the phone that he would later yank from its roots and use as a weapon against my mother.

This is 414 Montreal Street in Kingston. In 1970, it was a dingy link in a chain of two-storey semi houses for low-income families. Each of these dwellings had a dusty, tired appearance and sat almost directly on the sidewalk with front yards no larger than a postage stamp. Though good bones could be found in the skeletons of these structures, the skin was a cheap layer of heaving faux-brick asphalt shingles. The walls did not leak, but the roof did. Rainy days found my mother's tin cookware well used as the ceilings wept water and nicotine. The wallpaper was peeled and torn in irregular scabs to reveal the garish history of several interior design ideas. Worn, tissue-thin linoleum covered the floors that would never come clean, despite my mother's best effort. Our scant furnishings were completely utilitarian, mismatched, crippled, scraped and punctured, a mixture of fake wood veneer, pressboard and cheap fabric. We called this home for three years.

By this time, my parents, Margaret and Wade Hellers, had completed their family with four children; my mother was only twenty-four years old and father

1

was twenty-three. They had all four of us within five years. There are few people today who would not regard that as a disaster waiting to happen. In the 1950s and 60s, it was par for the course, especially in Catholic families. Catholic women had two choices: get married to a man and have children or enter a convent to become a nun. She could give her life to a man, or to God. Choosing a man meant choosing children—as many as possible. Good Catholic girls could not have one without the other. The successful migration of the male seed to the female egg was of utmost importance. The issue that the Vatican and observing Catholics chose to ignore was the physical, mental, and financial cost for women. My mother almost died giving birth to her last two children, my brothers. She later described bleeding "like a stuck pig" and being "delirious with toxaemia".

Her mother-in-law encouraged her to self-abort her fourth child with a hot mustard bath. My grandmother was in the habit of giving short speeches about the inordinate power of condiments.

She said, "Margaret, it's easy. A tub full of hot water and some dry mustard and the problem is over. If that doesn't work, we can sterilize a fucking coat hanger."

Mom laughed. She thought it was a joke, but my grandmother wasn't laughing. She said, "Think about it. Can you and Wade afford any more kids? Can your body afford any more kids? This method is fairly painless and effective. It's like having a bad stomach cramp. I'll fix you a stiff rye and coke and you'll be over it in no time. It'll be easier than childbirth, like having a really good shit."

Fortunately for my youngest brother, Mother chose to ignore Grandmother Ida's remedy. Mother relishes telling the story of Sean's difficult birth and how the doctors said, "Margaret, we're at a crucial point. You must decide who we should save— you or the baby." Mother replied, "The baby. Oh, please save the baby!"

Mother not only enjoys repeating this story, she enjoys any story in which she is a martyr.

She, though, was the one in those early years who tried to make something familial out of what we were living. She was the one who tried to provide regular meals for her children while my father got irretrievably smashed at the Plaza Hotel in downtown Kingston. This place held an air of mystery for me, as I had never seen it but it was a significant topic during my parents' frequent arguments. Father became quite fond of the section called "Ladies and Escorts," an area women could enter only if in the company of a man; yet, he never took my mother there. He would go to the Plaza after working his usual day as a mechanic at Canadian Tire, clearly feeling that he was owed this privilege after doing brake jobs all day. His mind was never occupied by the lack of formula, milk, or diapers while Mother tended to the four young children at home. She would wait for hours, telling us that he was going to walk through the door at any second with some food and milk. My infant brother's hungry screams still haunt me. My mother would try to soothe him with a little corn syrup on her thumb. On one occasion, she prompted my father's teenage sister to telephone the Plaza and ask for him with hysterical screams about a home emergency and impending doom. When he came to the phone, Aunt Tanya told him that she was calling from the neighbour's house. She screamed, "Wade, the upper floor of the house is on fire and not everyone has managed to get out yet!" She was convincing. He raced home and discovered the foil. Before he even entered the row house, he put his fist through the glass of the front door. Then he put his bloodied fist into my mother's face.

It was there, on Montreal Street, that the seeds of my hatred for my father were planted and grew voraciously. I'm not sure when my parents started their brutal war against each other, but I know that neither seemed to mind taking their children with them.

I I

I REMEMBER: *IT'S NOVEMBER. DAD GOES DEER HUNTING. IT'S the two weeks of the year that we children have come to anticipate and treasure. There is peace in the house. Mom buys us colouring books and crayons, and she brings home special sugar treats and some popcorn. We worship this time with her. She laughs with us, reads stories, and colours pictures in each of our books. It feels like a real family. The best part is seeing her face so relaxed. She is beautiful. She shows me how to layer crayon colours to make winter trees in my book. I am filled with love for her as I watch her hand glide back and forth over the page. That hand has done hard work. The skin is leather dry and chapped and her pink nail polish is chipped. I couldn't love her any more than I do at this moment.*

"The moment that the shit hit the fan." That's how my mother summed it up much later. His name was Joey Rowens. He lived down the street and was a good friend of our neighbour, Alice. She introduced Joey to my parents at a barbeque and beer fest that spilled out onto the street. My father despised him immediately. I thought he looked a bit like Elvis, if The King had a bad case of acne and got hit by a truck. Joey was always sniffing after my mother like a dog in heat. When Dad wasn't looking, he would try to pull her down on his lap. Mom and Alice would giggle like some of the silly girls in my class whenever a boy smiled at them.

"Oh, he wants your ass, Margie," Alice whispered.

"Shut up!" Mom replied. "If Wade gets even a hint of this, I'll be goddamned and dead."

When Dad entered the room with his bottle of beer, everyone changed the subject and Joey went outside to wrestle with one of his friends, the thick folds of his greasy hair shining in the sun. I watched my mother watch Joey through the window. I was five or six years old and somehow, I knew she was playing with fire.

My father went deer hunting. The air was crisp and cool and I wondered how he could enjoy sitting in the cold woods. Killing the deer, I understood. He wasn't happy unless he was conquering something. Before he went, I vowed

4

that if he killed a deer, I wouldn't eat any part of it. "You don't know what you're missing," he said.

No, it was he who didn't know what he was missing. As soon as he left with his truck-load of friends, Mom turned the music up and poured herself a beer. She put on her favourite blouse with the beige diamonds on a brown background. It had a belt at the waist and she always got compliments when she wore it. She fixed her makeup, adding more eyeliner and another coat of pale lipstick. Alice came over with one of her friends and Joey followed, practically panting like a wild animal. I knew there was going to be trouble. I felt like puking. The four of them sat at the metal kitchen table with the fake marble top, drinking beer and laughing between puffs on their cigarettes. Though I was very young, I could sense Joey's eagerness. He had that kind of energy that reminded me of any number of the dopey kids I encountered in the schoolyard, excited over a new toy they couldn't wait to play with.

While he scratched his fingernails into the top of the table, my mother bowed her head and smiled sheepishly. At the appropriate times, she would throw her head back and explode with a burst of laughter.

Alice and her friend played the dangerous game right alongside them, elbowing my mother, making twisted faces toward Joey. Alice noticed me watching, nodded toward me and said, "Doesn't she have anything better to do, Marg?"

Mom said, "Lynn, go up to your room and play, or better yet, check on your sister and brothers."

"I don't want to," I replied. "I want to stay here."

"Get the fuck out of here!" my mother yelled. Laughter.

I felt the heat creep over my face as I blushed profusely and slowly backed out of the kitchen heading upstairs. Without my presence, I knew my mother would do things that she shouldn't. My stomach began to twist into an enormous knot.

In my room, Annie was colouring pictures in her Charlie Brown colouring book. She was working on Peppermint Patti and Lucy standing at Lucy's therapy desk. "The doctor is in: 5 cents."

"Alice and Joey are downstairs with Mom," I told her.

"Who cares?" she replied, without lifting her crayon.

"They're drinking beer. I think they're getting drunk," I said.

"What can we do about that? We're just kids."

My sister always had a way of putting things into perspective for me.

I stayed upstairs colouring with Annie and played blocks with Wally. Sean, still an infant, was asleep. Mom checked on us a couple of times and I could see that she was drunk, but managed to bring us "snot" sandwiches and water. It was really Sandwich Spread layered between the pieces of bread, a store-bought condiment made from mayonnaise and relish. It was whitish yellow with little green pieces of pickle throughout. We called it snot and it was a staple in our diet.

"Mom, do you want to colour a picture with us?" I asked.

"No, Lynn, I don't want to colour a friggin' picture. I'm actually having some fun for once."

"Is Joey still here?" I asked.

"Yeah, he is. What about it?" she questioned, with hands on her hips.

"Nothing Mom."

The evening wore on with loud but indiscernible talking as Elvis and Charlie Rich belted out the tunes on our used, newly stolen, eight-track music player. My sister and brothers had long fallen asleep. I was not so fortunate. I rolled around in my bed worrying about what was happening to my mother—a source of constant anxiety. I couldn't hear Alice's voice anymore. You couldn't mistake her voice and if you were in any place with her, there was no way you wouldn't hear her. I knew she had left.

Other than the music, everything was too quiet. My mother never let the music continue playing this late at night because she couldn't sleep. She would get pissed off at Dad for loudly singing along with the songs after everyone had gone to bed.

If the music was still playing, someone was still at the house.

Joey.

I crawled out of my bed, dreading what I might discover. My guts churned. I tasted sour fluid in my mouth. Charlie Rich was singing:

> *When we get behind closed doors,*
> *And she lets her hair hang down,*
> *And she makes me glad that I'm a man,*
> *For no one knows what goes on*
> *Behind closed doors.*

How I grew to hate that song. I walked quietly to the top of the stairs and could hear familiar sounds. They were the moans and whimpers I heard when my parents shut their bedroom door, yet I knew my father wasn't home. I slinked my body carefully down the stairs; with each step, I peered through the railing.

There they were, my mother and Joey. They were rolling around like two cats caught in a burlap bag, panting and groaning.

"What are you doing, Mom?" My voice was nervous and whiny.

Two heads instantly popped up from beneath the blanket, big eyed and terrified. "Lynn, go back to bed!" she demanded.

"I don't want to. I want to know what you're doing."

"That's none of your business! Get your ass back up to bed before I make you wish you were never born!" she screamed.

"But I already wish that, Mom."

"GO…TO…BED…NOW! SMART ASS!"

I knew it was time to surrender. I went back upstairs and cried myself to sleep. I thought that this was the most horrible thing that had ever happened in my family. The day of my father's return would soon prove me wrong.

The following morning, my mother took me aside before preparing breakfast. With a huge smile she said, "Lynn, I want to talk to you about something serious, something adult." She knew how to appeal to me. She cleverly used the word "adult" knowing that I would be thrilled to be the chosen one for her confidence. She explained, "About what you saw and heard last night… it wasn't what you might think."

"What was it, Mom?"

"Well, I had had a few drinks and I just got silly with Joey," she replied.

Wow, you must really think I'm stupid, I thought.

"The thing is, Lynnie, I want you to promise me that you won't say anything about this to your father. He wouldn't think it was very funny and he might hurt Mommy," she continued.

I don't think it's very funny either.

"Don't worry, Mom. I will never tell him."

"You're a really good girl, Lynn. How would you like some special pancakes for breakfast?"

"Sounds good!" She patted me on the back and repeated what a good girl I was.

Wade Hellers arrived home late on that cold November evening, but not before visiting Alice and her pals to throw back a few pints. They decided to apprise my father of how Joey Rowens had paid my mother a lengthy visit while he was gathering deer meat for his cave. The caveman smashed his beer bottle against the wall and stormed out.

The telephone rings. Mom picks up the phone. "Oh, hi Alice. How are ya?" There is a short pause and then, "Oh, my good Christ! When?!" After another short pause, my mother starts to cry and hangs up the phone. "What's the matter, Mom?" I ask. She is incoherent, weeping and gasping.

Finally, she manages some words. "Your father is on his way home and he's really mad. You had better go up to your room."

"I'm not leaving," I state firmly.

"Lynn, GO, you should be in bed by now anyway," she sobs.

"No! I'm not leaving!"

My father bursts through the front door. Before he is even inside the house, I can hear his rage, "You fucking whoring cunt! I'm going to break every slutty bone in your body, you cock-sucking bitch!"

Mother cries loudly. "Please, Wade, don't! Calm down and we can talk about this!" she pleads.

"Talk about WHAT? How you fucked Joey Rowens, that greasy, slimy mother-fucker?" Foamy spit flies from his mouth.

I take refuge behind a kitchen chair as he backs mother into a corner. She holds her hands up and begins to round the kitchen table. He goes straight for her. He shoves her with all his strength, sending her over a chair and ass first into the laundry basket. She sits there, pathetic and sobbing. Suddenly, he leaves the room in the direction of the front door. I hope that he is going to leave and I make a move toward my mother, still sitting in the laundry basket.

Dad returns, carrying his rifle. We sit there with gaping mouths as he loads it. In an instant, my mother scrambles, first on her hands and knees, then rises as she reaches the phone. As she picks up the handset, he flies at her with lightning speed and rips the phone from the wall with one hand while holding his gun in the other. I start screaming and don't recognize the sound of my own voice. Mom jumps away from him and begins a full run down the hall toward the front door. He flings the uprooted telephone at her and misses her by inches, denting the wall.

I run after her. I follow her out the front door and down Montreal Street. I call for her to wait for me, but she doesn't. She keeps screaming that he is going to kill her. I yell to her, "What about the kids, Mom? What if he hurts the kids?!" My sister and brothers are asleep in the house. She can't hear me or she isn't listening because she keeps running at a steady pace with me behind her.

I turn around to look behind me. He's there. He is running after us with his rifle in hand. There is a rush through my body and I only slightly feel stones under my bare feet. I follow my mother around the corner of Stephen Street, where she runs a few more paces and collapses on someone's lawn. I run up to the wooden front porch of this house and pound loudly on the door. This is our hope. These people will help us. An older man opens the door. He is wearing boxer shorts and a t-shirt; he has a bald head. I yell at him, "That man across the street is after us and he has a gun! Please let us in!" The man looks past me and sees my father, across the street, standing under a lamppost with his weapon.

The unthinkable happens. The man closes his door in my face.

I hear my mother sobbing and I slowly turn around to see her sitting on the grass. I raise my head and make eye contact with my father. He stands there, in the same spot under the lamppost, with his rifle half raised. We look at each other for what seems like years. Suddenly, just like that, he lowers the gun and walks back toward our house.

I run to my mother. "Get up, get up! We have to hide," I tell her. She goes limp and lies down on the lawn, still weeping. "Mom! Get up! He might come back!" I scream hysterically. I grab her arm and pull at her to get her moving. She stumbles to her feet, moaning with snot running from her nose. We cross Stephen Street and find refuge in the shrubbery of another yard. We squat down in the bushes, breathing heavily.

"Mom, what do you think he will do with Annie, Wally, and Sean?" I ask. "They're in the house all by themselves." I start to cry again.

"Don't worry about them," she replies. "He doesn't want to hurt you kids. He wants to hurt me." I want to believe her. I feel cold. We are both barefoot and wearing only light shirts and pants.

"My feet are really cold, Mom."

"Here, give them to me and I'll rub them," she says.

She is rubbing my feet.

Blackness.

I have no further recollection of this evening. My mother told me later that we spent the whole cold November night hiding in the neighbour's bushes.

The following morning, she walked into the kitchen wearing a black eye. I don't know when he gave it to her, whether it was during the row with the gun or once she got us back into the house. Whatever the case, she was beaten down and deflated. Her body drooped as if all the air and muscle had been removed. I watched her hands tremble as she tried to sip a cup of tea.

"Are you okay, Mom?" I asked in a whisper. She stared straight ahead and didn't answer. Tears welled up in her eyes and I had to look away when I saw one ball of water roll down her bruised cheek.

"I wasn't the one who told Dad about Joey," I said, terrified that she might think it was me who had betrayed her.

"Oh Lynn, I know you didn't. Please don't say Joey's name anymore, okay?"

"Sure, Mom. I hate him anyway." She forced a smile.

My father no longer permitted Joey Rowens or Alice to enter our house. If Mother was going to socialize, she had to find a whole new set of friends. Mom came to rely on the company of her sister, Sheila. Sisters were safe. Aunt Sheila would come over with her daughter, Patricia. She was a year and a half younger than me, but I liked her company and she always brought her tea set. My sister and I were thrilled because we didn't have a tea set. Mom would make us some real tea that we could sip out of the little cups with the pretty blue flowers all over them. She would make little peanut butter finger sandwiches that we ate off the tiny plates. I was glad that she used peanut butter instead of the usual snot. That would have been awfully embarrassing. Annie, Patricia, and I would sit with proper posture, sipping our tea, politely nibbling on our sandwiches, complaining about our imaginary husbands being such a pain in the neck. When Aunt Sheila and Patty left, we begged Mom to get us our own tea set for Christmas.

"It doesn't even have to be a fancy one," Annie said.

"Well, we'll see what Santa Claus can do about that," Mom replied.

As it turned out, Aunt Sheila was having similar problems with her husband Gord. I don't know exactly what those problems were because when she relayed them to my mother, she always did so in a tiny whisper between her sobs. Her situation became so tense that she and Patty came to live with us for a week. Annie and I were so excited to have Patty and her tea set with us for such a long time. The only trouble was that Aunt Sheila insisted on Patty wearing pretty frilly dresses with pure white knee socks—every day. When we wanted to go outside and play, Aunt Sheila would make Patty sit on the couch alone so she wouldn't get her special dresses dirty. My mother even offered to lend her some of my play clothes so she wouldn't have to worry about soiling these dresses. Sheila's response was flat but firm: "No thanks, Margaret. I want Patricia to learn what it's like to be a lady."

I couldn't bear the thought of Patty sitting there, bored, just because she had on some silly dress. When both our mothers were occupied, I grabbed her hand and led her out to the backyard. We sat on the grass and played with my brother's plastic trucks. It couldn't have been any more than fifteen minutes before Aunt Sheila's imposing body appeared at the back door. She screamed, "Patricia Ann! Get your ass into this house right now. I told you not to move off of that couch. Let me see your dress!"

Patty gave me a nervous look and moved slowly toward her mother. Sheila grabbed her arm and spun her around so hard that she fell to the ground.

"Look what you've done to your new dress! There's a grass stain on it!" she blasted as she belted Patty on her back. Patty walked slowly into the house, shaking and weeping. I felt terrible. This was my fault. I walked into the house and bravely approached my Aunt Sheila.

"Auntie Sheila?"

"What do you want!?" she shrieked.

"It was me who took Patricia outside to play," I confessed.

"I don't want to deal with you right now! I've got to get this stain out of your cousin's new dress!"

My mother said, "Lynn, go up to your room right now."

On my way up the stairs, I peered into the living room to see Patty sitting on the couch in her underwear and socks, red faced and weeping. "I'm sorry," I said as I made my way up to my room. I always loathed dresses and this experience only confirmed that my hatred was justified.

Aunt Sheila and Patty left our house even before the week was out. My father grew tired of Sheila's snivelling about Gord and made it uncomfortable for her to continue her stay. He would fill his guts with beer and make her listen to his rants about how the man of the house is always in charge and a woman needs to know her place or she'd get a fist in her gob. Sheila clearly discovered that life in our house was worse than the one she lived at home.

After the short stay, my Aunt Sheila didn't visit as often. Mom would call her and my aunt would always have an excuse for why she couldn't come over. I felt like telling my mother the truth as I saw it: Aunt Sheila won't come over anymore because you married an asshole and your kids are dirty.

Mother managed to find herself a new friend and confidante. Her name was Stacey and she lived on upper Montreal Street in a small apartment. I'm not sure how Mom met her, but I do remember meeting Stacey for the first and only time. She was pretty with shoulder length curly, dark hair. She was wearing a white t-shirt and pink short pants. We entered her kitchen, and there in a highchair, was a baby babbling happily holding onto a bottle. We sat at her tiny table and she asked us if we had lunch yet. Mom told her that we hadn't but not to worry about it; we would get something when we got home.

With the prospect of snot sandwiches facing me, I decided I would say something. "But I'm really hungry now, Mom," I said. Mom glared at me with that look that said *shut your friggin' face*.

"That settles it," Stacey replied, "I'll make us some lunch. Do you like French fries with ketchup, Lynn?"

I thought I had suddenly died and gone to heaven. This woman was a goddess. "I love them!" I exclaimed, barely containing my glee.

Not only were they fries, they were crinkle cuts! Who was this woman and when could we come to her house again? I savoured every one of the oily sticks, slick with ketchup and sprinkled with salt. I ate the whole plate of fries and Stacey said, "Wow, Lynnie, you have quite the appetite."

Mom said, "Yeah, she's a goddamn pig but skinny as a rail. I don't know where she puts it all."

After I finished my lunch, I played with Stacey's baby boy, dangling toys in front of his face while he laughed and spat gobs of drool down his shirt. Mother and Stacey were talking and laughing. It was glorious to see her relaxed and smiling again.

When it came time to leave, I didn't want to go. "This has been a great afternoon," I told Mom. "Yes, I had a good time too," she replied. As we headed for the door, I thanked Stacey for the yummy lunch. She said, "Anytime, kiddo." I flashed Stacey the peace sign as I walked out.

As Mother and I walked down Montreal Street toward home, I asked, "Where is Stacey's husband?"

"Stacey doesn't have a husband."

"Why not?"

"That's complicated, Lynn."

My cogs started turning. "Wow, then Stacey has the best life ever! She has an apartment, a cute baby, good food, and no husband! That's exactly the way I'm going to live when I grow up!" I said excitedly.

Mother looked at me with concern. "Lynn, you need to have a husband to have a baby," she said.

"Well, Stacey doesn't have a husband and she has a baby," I reasoned.

"That's because Stacey didn't want to stay with the father of her baby," she replied.

"Cool! That's what I'm going to do."

"Lynn, it's not cool. Stacey is left to do everything on her own." Mom said worriedly.

"Exactly! I can do that!" It was a revelation. I had never met anyone like Stacey, with a baby and no husband. I couldn't believe it was possible, but I learned the truth that afternoon. I was elated.

Mom warned me, "Lynn, I don't think it's a good idea for you to mention these ideas of yours to your father. He would get really upset."

"I try not to talk to him anyway."

Though my mother cautioned me, I must have wagged my tongue. We never visited Stacey again. Whenever I asked Mom about her, she told me not to talk about Stacey anymore. I was consistently told to be quiet about something. I knew that my father was behind it.

| | |

WITH MY INCREASING FEAR OF MY FATHER, MY SILENCE BEGAN
to grow. I started to hate going to my Kindergarten class at St. John's Elementary
School and would close my lips as tight as a drum when I arrived. My teacher,
Miss Martin, would ask me questions about my interests and I wouldn't answer
her. I would stare straight ahead as if catatonic. I felt bad for Miss Martin; it
wasn't her fault. She was so nice and pretty. She reminded me of Bridget Bardot
or Barbara Feldon, if Barbara had blond hair. I just felt like I was dumped off in
a big room full of babies. I didn't want to play with the plastic food and dishes
in the "kitchen", nor did I want to play house. I didn't want to touch any doll
or string beads. The only activities I enjoyed were painting at the easels and
building castles in the sandbox, always alone. Miss Martin finally gave in and
let me paint all day. I did a truckload of paintings. I loved the chalky smell of the
paint and how the colours would glide off my brush onto the newsprint. The first
mark I made was always the most exciting, to see the first colour laid down. Miss
Martin always made sure that there was an easel equipped with full jars of paint
just for me.

Whenever I finished a painting, Miss Martin would ask me to explain it to
her. She was always amazed at the detail in my paintings and pointed out that the
people actually had bodies, clothes, and facial expressions. I would tell her who
was in the painting and where the action was taking place. She would pull out
her thick blue or green marker and write everything I said at the bottom of the
painting. *This is my Grandma and Grandpa reading me a story. This is my Mom,
my sister Annie, my brother Wally, my baby brother Sean, and me. Oh and that's
Aunt Sheila.*

"Where is your father?" Miss Martin asked.

"He doesn't fit," I replied.

She didn't write that at the bottom of my painting.

*The phone rings. My mother answers, "Oh, hello, Miss Martin." Oh God, what
have I done wrong? Does she want to know why I don't put Dad into my paintings?*

There is a long pause. "Sure," Mother says, "at 4:00 in the afternoon. I'll see you then. Okay. Goodbye."

"What did Miss Martin want, Mom? I don't think I did anything wrong."

"She wants to meet with me to talk about you. She thinks you're bored at school. Are you bored?"

"Well, except for painting, there are only baby things to do at school."

"Haven't you told her that you like crossword puzzles? You and Nanny do them all the time."

"There aren't any crossword puzzles in my class, Mom," I explain. "The kids just play with toys and try to kiss each other."

Miss Martin wanted to know how to make me more interested in school. Mom told her that I loved to learn new things and that one of my favourite activities was doing the Whiz Word crossword puzzles out of the *Kingston Whig Standard* newspaper.

"What?" Miss Martin asked.

"Yes," my mother replied, "she'll work on those puzzles for hours. She can also spell and print many words and she is able to write some words using cursive writing. I taught her that."

Mom came home and told me how shocked Miss Martin was and that she was going to make some puzzles for me to do. I was so excited. My cousin Matthew was there and slapped me on the back and said, "Way to go girl!"

Matthew came over to baby-sit while Mother attended her meeting with Miss Martin. We always had a blast when he came over. He was eighteen, brought us chips and pop, was highly permissive, and slept most of the time on the couch. We loved him. Within that year, he killed himself with a shotgun. In his note, he begged for forgiveness and tried to explain his drug addiction. The entire family was devastated. I believe that was the last time I saw him.

* * * * *

I hadn't looked forward to going to school in a long time, but that Monday I was bouncing off the walls with excitement. I couldn't even finish my breakfast of pasty oatmeal and sugar. I was trying to hustle Annie to finish her crud in a bowl so that we could get to school early.

Once inside the classroom, Miss Martin approached me with a huge smile. "I've got something special for you to do today, Lynn," she said. I was about to burst. From behind her back, she revealed a large white card divided into nine squares, each containing one consonant or vowel. *What the hell is that?* I thought.

She must have noticed the quizzical look on my face because she yelped, "It's a word puzzle!"

"I don't get it," I said.

"Well, you look at each of the letters, and try to write down as many three letter words as you can. For example, here is an R, an A, and an M. Well, that would make "RAM" and we know that "RAM" isn't a word; so you have to try other combinations of letters," she explained. I thought, *you must be stupid Miss Martin, because ram is a word. It is a kind of animal and you can also use this word when you ram this retarded puzzle up your ass.*

"Thank you for doing this for me, Miss Martin, but this isn't a real crossword puzzle," I told her. Her pretty face dropped and I felt enormous remorse for what I thought and said.

"Well, what is your idea of a crossword puzzle?" she asked.

"You know, the kind where you have clues and you have to figure out the right word to fit into the squares. I also like the kind where you have to search for the words in the list and circle them in the puzzle. Finding three letter words is too easy. I like puzzles with longer words."

She gaped at me.

"Who taught you how to do this?" she asked with a serious face.

"My mom and my grandmother. Especially my grandmother, Nanny Carron. When I visit her, we do all kinds of word puzzles. She even bought me flash cards with words on them, the kind without the pictures. The ones with the pictures are too easy."

Miss Martin looked stunned. I started to think I was pretty hot shit. That's what my father called it when I said something clever or if I showed him that I could do something well. He would say, "You think you're pretty hot shit, don't you?"

In a trance-like voice, Miss Martin told me to go on over and work on a painting. "I'll have some better puzzles for you tomorrow."

The following day, Miss Martin presented me with a treasure chest of puzzles. I fell madly in love with her that very moment. It was evident that she had gone to a lot of trouble just for me. There were copies of Whiz Word from the *Whig Standard*, a booklet of crossword puzzles, a dictionary, and homemade flash cards made with her impeccable printing. She wanted to try the flash cards with me first. I noticed that only a few of the words had three letters. She would gasp with amazement at every one I said correctly. I would get flustered and blush when I couldn't read one of them. She said, "Don't worry, honey, these words are above the Kindergarten level."

She went to get the principal. Mrs. Burton came into the classroom and sat down beside me. I was terrified. Though she looked like a nice little old lady with pure white hair and horn-rimmed glasses, Mrs. Burton was known for her frequent and effective use of the strap. I felt the familiar heat creep into my face and lowered my head. Miss Martin explained, "Lynn, I want you to show Mrs. Burton some of the things we have been doing."

Mrs. Burton said, "Hello Lynn." She held out her hand and I shook it. "Miss Martin tells me that you can read quite a few words. Would you read some for me?"

Miss Martin held up the flash cards and I read the words. I even managed to read some of the words I didn't know because I remembered them after Miss Martin told me what they were. Mrs. Burton's mouth hung open. She stood up and asked Miss Martin to accompany her to the door. I could see their mouths moving, but I couldn't tell what they were saying. My teacher moved across the room and picked up some of my paintings to show Mrs. Burton. They kept looking over at me and smiling. Once I realized they weren't going to bring me into their conversation, I grabbed a Whiz Word out of the box and began my search.

Another meeting with my parents was called. Once it was over, my mother told me about it. She sat me down to lunch with a luxurious grilled cheese sandwich. Mom told me that the school administration felt I should skip one or maybe two grades. I was horrified. I didn't want to go into a new classroom, especially with older kids. "What do you think about that?" Mom asked.

"Oh please, Mom, don't make me do it." I started crying.

"Why not? They say you're too bright for the Kindergarten class."

"Oh, Mom, those older kids will beat me up!" I screamed.

"I don't think the kids would beat you up, but they are worried about how quiet and shy you are," she explained.

"That's right! I'm too shy. I would probably never speak again!"

"You said that it was boring and that you were in a class full of babies."

"I'm not bored anymore. I've got lots of fun things to do now," I said pleadingly. "I don't want to leave my class! I have friends!"

The truth was that I didn't want to leave Miss Martin. Screw the kids. Now that she understood me and I could relate to her, I was going to be torn from her. It was unbearable.

"Don't worry about it, Lynn. The school just wanted me to talk to you about it and see how you felt. If you don't want to skip a grade, they won't make you do it. They said that they could provide different activities for you that are designed for smart kids," Mom said.

I was instantly relieved. I had been brought close to a full meltdown.

"That sounds great! I can do that! Then I won't have to leave my class or Miss Martin."

So began my long, arduous journey through what is now called "enrichment" and "gifted" programming, which I think is no better today than it was then. Though I was told I wouldn't have to leave my classroom, I was removed from it a good deal of the time. I would end up stuck in some room with an educator, either alone or with some other poor sod in the same program. We would perform our tasks like good little puppets, circus freaks. We weren't able to talk to each other. I would try to complete the work as quickly as possible so that I could return to my class. Soon they were onto me and gave me more work so that I would be in the little room for the required amount of time. *Fuck that,* I thought. I was onto *them*. I started to pretend that I didn't know how to do the work or answer the questions. The educator would send me back to class. This worked for a while, until my teacher caught on that I really could do the work I was given and was sent back to the program. The educator, whose name I cannot recall, told me I should never waste my gifts. *Screw you.* At this time, my potty mouth was still only in my head.

I V

AS THE SUMMER HOLIDAYS APPROACHED AND I WAS PROMOTED into Grade One, I looked forward to spending as much time as possible with my Grandma and Grandpa Carron, who lived at 187A Princess Street in apartment 6. They lived right beside Sam the Record Man and across the street from Woolworth's. Whenever I went there for a visit, I would stop to look at the music display in Sam's big window. At that time, Gary Puckett and the Union Gap was still causing quite a stir. I thought Gary was cute but I didn't think he understood the kind of power he had. My parents bought the eight-track and got drunk to the songs. The way our eight-track player worked, the tape would play over and over unless it was removed. I learned the words to every song:

> Young girl, get out of my mind,
> My love for you is way out of line
> Better run girl,
> You're much too young, girl.

However, it was one song in particular that always sent my father into a drunken frenzy: *Woman*. That one part always did him in after more than a dozen beers:

> Oh, woman,
> Oh, woman.
> Have you got cheating on your mind?

Toward the end of any given evening, while this song played, Dad would fulfill his urge to cuff my mother in the head, sending her to bed in tears. I thought my father was a bastard, but I didn't hold it against Gary and the Union Gap. I loved their music. *Lady Willpower it's now or never, give your love to me and I'll shower your heart with tenderness, endlessly.*

Relative to this living environment, my maternal grandparents provided me with a paradise, a safe haven, a home. I adored them completely. They always spoke to each other respectfully and treated me like I was precious. Grandpa doted on Nanny and me. Though I wasn't aware of it, my grandmother had already been diagnosed with cancer and had one kidney removed.

The day that they told me about the kidney they said that it just didn't work anymore. I watched Grandpa change the dressing on the gaping wound in my Nanny's side. Before he bandaged her, I asked to take a closer look, too curious to contain myself. Nanny let me look at the puckering brown hole in her side and I started to cry. There was fluid oozing out of it.

"Doesn't that hurt, Nanny?"

"Sometimes, honey, but I take pain killers for that," she replied with a smile.

Later, Grandpa made us a superior dinner with pork chops, mashed potatoes, corn, and peas. After seeing the hole in Nanny's side, my appetite had waned. Then I smelled Grandpa's cooking. He would always say, "You're too thin. Have some more," as he plopped hot tasty seconds onto my plate.

Grandpa said he could cook anything after being an army cook. He became a cook because he couldn't perform his usual military duties. He was a drunk. Not a drunk like my father; the drink didn't make him violent and mean-spirited, at least not from what I observed. My mother tells a different story. She said he could be one cruel bastard, sticking pins in her legs if she misbehaved. I had a hard time visualizing that but I knew she wasn't making it up.

After dinner, we would watch the *Lawrence Welk Show* as Bobby and Sissy danced around the stage and beautiful Guy and Ralna sang an enchanting love song. My grandparents were captivated by every moment of this show, especially when Lawrence would conduct his big band. My favourite show, *All in the Family*, came on later. My grandparents and I didn't miss even one episode. Watching Archie Bunker make an ass out of himself made us giggle for hours, even after the show was over. I always felt sorry for Edith; she was so sweet, kind, and open-minded and Archie was always telling her to "Stifle!" The three of us enjoyed the episodes when Edith would actually stand up to Archie and tell him to make his own damn dinner.

Once we had watched *All in the Family*, Nanny and I would do a crossword puzzle and she would read me stories and prayers from her *Catholic Press Prayer Book* followed by 'Twinkle, Twinkle, Little Star' before going to bed. Grandpa always fixed the bed for me on the pullout couch with fresh, clean sheets and blankets. When I crawled into this bed, I never felt safer.

My visits to my other grandmother, my father's mother, at the notorious site of 16 James Street, stood in stark contrast. It wasn't my Grandmother Ida's fault that she preferred the company of junkies and thieves. It wasn't even completely her fault that horrible acts were played out under her roof. I think that it is up to parents to fully investigate any environment in which they leave their children; at this, my parents failed dismally—not that they would have given a shit anyway.

Nanny Ida's house was larger than Nanny Carron's apartment, but far dumpier. The smell of eggs and sulphur filled every room. The kitchen was always a mess because she had most of her adult kids still living there, and not one of them would clean up after themselves or help her. Not only that, my uncles would invite their friends and girlfriends over, smoke an Everest-sized mountain of dope, and feed them food and booze that my grandmother bought. There was always a full sink of dishes caked with food, ashtrays that spilled onto the kitchen table, beer bottles with bloated cigarette butts in them, enough crumbs to feed a family, and hardened coins of egg goop stuck to the countertops. Every time I went there, I wanted to puke.

The mess wasn't the only reason. My parents would dump us off there while they went out to the Legion 560 or did some household chore. They would leave us there even if my grandmother wasn't available at the mercy of my uncles or some of Grandmother's misfit, jailbird friends from the Millhaven or Joyceville Institutes. Annie and I would find used syringes taped under the furniture, foil tubes full of pot and hash, and used condoms. My parents would drop us off and see that there were passed out drunks and drug paraphernalia all over the place. No matter. They had places to go.

Unlike Nanny and Grandpa Carron's place, there seemed to be no safe place to sleep at 16 James Street.

My sister Annie is sitting up and rocking herself on Nanny Ida's couch. She chants, "I want Mommy, I want Daddy, I want Mommy, I want Daddy, I want Mommy, I want Daddy." She stares straight ahead each time she engages in this ritual. I begin to follow along with her, "I want Mommy, I want Daddy," until I'm exhausted and lay down on the sofa to sleep. When I wake up, someone is rubbing a stick against my bum. I feel it poking me. I don't understand. Why would somebody want to rub a stick against my arse? I look for Annie. She's not there. I move to get up to find her and a hand pulls me down. I won't turn over. I don't want to see who it is. I can smell whiskey, cigarettes, and sweat. Suddenly, I understand; that thing against my bum isn't a stick. My mind goes black.

I didn't really want to know who it was. The only person I knew it wasn't was Jack Reynolds. Jack was a homosexual. I knew what that was because my father talked about beating the shit out of them in hotel bathrooms all over Kingston. When I asked him what a homosexual was, he said it was a sick guy who liked to stick his dick up another guy's ass. Because my father hated gays, I had an immediate and everlasting empathy for them.

Jack Reynolds, too, couldn't escape abuse and humiliation down at 16 James Street. I woke up one morning to find him passed out, propped over a kitchen chair with his pants pulled down. On his ass, someone had used red lipstick and wrote, "Enter at your own risk."

I think it was my sister, Annie, who suffered the most there, yet she couldn't tell because she feared never seeing Grandmother Ida again. Shame and fear were other motivators. I learned later about her abuse at the hands of our step-grandfather, Walter, and others. At the same time I was getting my education at 16 James, she was dealing with Harry the Horseman. That's what everyone called him. He would wait until my sister was having a bath and sneak into the bathroom that never had a lock on the door. On one occasion, he put his hands on her. He lifted her up and said, "I just want to look at your pretty titties." Annie started screaming and my grandmother ran up the stairs. Grandma Ida beat on Harry and yelled at him, "Get the fuck out of my house!" Harry staggered down the stairs and out the side door. Annie was inconsolable and could barely breathe.

Grandma Ida took her aside and told her to never tell my parents; "They will never let you see Grandma again, honey."

Back at home, my bum started to feel sore and itchy. I would touch it and scratch it, getting no relief. I couldn't bear to wear undergarments. All I wanted on my body were loose nightgowns or long t-shirts. One evening, while my parents listened to music and tuned out of the world, I decided to sit on the stairs and pick at my bum in private. Our dog, Prince, paid me a visit.

Prince was a mutt, a cross between a terrier and a lab, and he was the most loving creature I have ever encountered. He was also as tough as nails. He survived distemper, during which he chewed off his tail, and being hit by a car that broke both his back legs. He would live to be nineteen years old. Prince was completely loyal and protective and I think he lived that long to keep an eye on us kids. Anyone who tried to tickle or wrestle with us was greeted with growls and his playful attacks. He even bit a couple of uncles who tried to throw us, screaming, off the dock and into the river at my grandmother's cottage. Prince died a few months after my youngest brother left home. He quietly laid himself down under a tree in my parents' backyard and slipped into his permanent nap, his life's work completed.

On the stairs that night, somehow, Prince knew I was injured. He could smell it on me. He started to force his nose between my legs and lifted me up. I was in shock and could not understand what he was doing. When I lifted myself up, he put his head under my nightgown and started to lick my bum. After an instant of confused disbelief, I was completely soothed. The irritation that I had felt for days was relieved almost immediately. I didn't want him to stop, but was terrified of being caught with the dog's head up my nightie. I let him carry on a little longer and then I stopped him, thinking that this whole thing was just wrong. The next day, my bum felt much better. I felt I had been miraculously healed. I gave Prince a huge hug.

Around the same time, my sister started to play with her "diggy." That's the word my mother taught us for that mysterious area between our legs. Annie would tell me how much her diggy hurt. "Well stop playing with it," I would tell her. She said, "I need to scratch it; it's really sore and itchy." I told her that Mom said it was a bad thing to play with our diggies. Sometimes, Annie would touch her diggy and cry.

Annie's situation worsened. My mother took her to the family doctor. He informed my parents that my baby sister had been penetrated by an object, or more probably, a penis; the abrasions left inside her little body left no doubt. Following her appointment, Annie had to withstand a serious question and answer session, carried on by my mother. In the end, she named her primary abuser—my step-grandfather, Walter Simmons. This is what I have been told. I remember that my father threatened to shoot Walter and even loaded one of his guns for the purpose.

My grandmother, Ida, talked him out of it. She was still married to him at the time. Instead, my father bludgeoned Walter's face. Somehow, he found a place within himself where he could succumb to the fear of his mother and accept the rape of his tiny daughter. I know this because Walter is still alive and never had to spend even one day in jail.

Not only did Walter live on, fairly unpunished, but my parents, more than aware of his assaults, came to break bread with him and do small repairs on his car while they shared cases of beer. While Walter was at our house, Annie would seclude herself in her bedroom and cry until he left. With beer stink oozing out of his pores, my father once went into my sister's room and actually asked her why she was crying. "Because you let Walter come in our house," she told him. "Get over it," he slurred.

I was more fortunate than my younger sister and two brothers, being allowed the reprieve of regular visits to Nanny and Grandpa Carron's home. Their names were Agnes and Earl. At any opportunity, I would call them and ask them if I could visit for the weekend. They always obliged and the requests became more frequent as I grew older. With their small apartment and Nanny's accelerating illness, they could take only one of us overnight. I was old enough that I could safely entertain myself while they had their naps. They saved their money and bought me tablets of paper, paint-by-number sets, and a treasured set of pencil crayons. They also made several books available to me, including a set of encyclopedia for young people and a copy of *Alice in Wonderland* that Grandpa found for me while shopping at the A&P. I drew colourful pictures of every character in that book. Grandpa and Nanny also provided me with almost every one of the Golden Wonder Books. I had the *Golden Book of Reptiles and Amphibians, The Golden Book of Mammals* and my precious copy of *The Golden Book of Dinosaurs*. I would tape together several sheets of paper to make mural-sized drawings of the Tyrannosaurus Rex and the Triceratops. My grandparents would proudly present these drawings to every visitor and neighbour they had. Starving for recognition, I relished the attention and the remarks about my "incredible talent" and "eye for detail".

Grandpa and Nanny's favourite drawing was the one I did of my Uncle Harland, their son, while he was deer hunting. I drew a detailed picture of him running from a bear in the woods with his gun dropping to the ground. He told us the exciting story of his near fatal encounter with a female bear protecting her cubs. I was pleased that he didn't shoot the mother bear. He said that he respected her for trying to protect her babies. Uncle Harland lived with my grandparents, but I didn't see him very often because he worked as a mechanic and, when he wasn't doing that, he was frequenting the pubs and bars. Harland was tall, with a beer belly, always dressed in blue work clothes, and was very fond of Brill Cream, the slimy goo that so many men used to paste their hair down, making it appear wet and greasy. He was long divorced from his wife and never saw his two kids. My grandparents kept a newspaper cut-out of his son pitching a winning baseball game. This was all that I ever saw of either of my cousins. I knew better than to ask Uncle Harland about them.

One of the most pleasant activities during these visits was venturing to The Smoke Shop with Grandpa. His signal for the outing was always to gently shake his closed hand toward me, filled with coins that made a wonderful tinkling sound. It was music to my ears. He laid the coins into my small hand and said, "Let's get moving, sweetheart." On the way there, we had to pass the "Hippie Park", a gravel lot with tree stumps on Princess Street that is now covered by financial offices. Grandpa always warned me not to talk to the longhaired hippies, that they were "goddamned dangerous freaks". I thought they were friendly and that they looked cool. They always had a smile, a wave, and said hi to me. Giving me one of his sternest looks, Grandpa would put my arm down when I gave them the peace sign.

"They're not so bad, Grandpa. They're a lot nicer than some people I know."

Grandpa went to The Smoke Shop to buy his tobacco and cigarette tubes for his homemade butts. While he chatted with the man who owned the shop, I had plenty of time to search for a new comic book. I loved the Looney Toon comics with Bugs Bunny, Sylvester the Cat, and Daffy Duck, but my favourites were the horror comics. I couldn't get enough of vampires, monsters that hid in old ladies' basements, or humans who could turn into big worms when there was a thunderstorm. If there wasn't a new comic book to buy, Grandpa would jingle some more change toward me for the latest copy of *Mad Magazine*. Alfred E. Newman and his antics always cracked me up. He always secretly purchased a Cherry Blossom, Treasures Bar, or Mars Bar, and hid them in his pocket to present to me later. Even though I came to know that he was doing it, I always acted surprised and was truly delighted by his choice.

On one occasion, while we walked home from the Smoke Shop, I asked why the hippies were dangerous. I knew about Kent State in Ohio and that crazy day in May 1970. I had seen John Filo's award winning photograph of a young girl with her arms outstretched, her face twisted in anguish, kneeling over the body of Jeff Miller. I could see that Jeff was a hippie. He had long hair and a headband, a baggy shirt, and scruffy jeans. There was a river of blood flowing from a hole in his face, the home of a national guardsman's bullet. I knew that the students at Kent were protesting the Vietnam War. I wanted to learn more about what happened, but couldn't read well enough at the time to do so. I relied on photographs and music:

> Tin soldiers and Nixon's coming
> We're finally on our own.
> This summer I hear the drumming,
> Four dead in Ohio

> *Ohio*, Crosby, Stills, Nash, and Young

To my question, Grandpa replied frankly. "Because they're a bunch of goddamned lazy junkies. They sit on their scrawny arses all day, shooting up, playing their music. They don't work one goddamned day and they lip off about the Vietnam War and Nixon being a warmonger. I don't see those little bastards putting their lazy asses on the line for their country; half of them are goddamned draft dodgers and they're too scared to stand up, haul ass, and fight."

"You're one of those brave guys who fought in the war, aren't you Grandpa?" I asked.

He said, "Not in the Vietnam War, honey. I fought in the Second World War. I was stationed in France."

"What happened in that war?"

"Nothing I'm going to repeat to you. It was ugly. You don't need to hear about that stuff. And let me tell you, Vietnam is no prettier."

"You must have been so brave, though," I said.

As he took me by the hand, he said, "Everyone who goes to war is brave, honey."

I wanted to talk about Jeff Miller. Though he didn't go to Vietnam, he went to a different kind of war and died too. Wasn't he brave?

Upon arrival home, Grandpa presented Nanny with a large package of Craven "A" cigarettes and a copy of the *Reader's Digest*. Then, with a puzzled look on his face, he fished through his pockets and said, "Gee, I thought I had something for you too, Lynnie." I knew better, but pretended I was disappointed, twisting my face into a convincing pout. Unable to bear it, he released the chocolate delight from the cotton prison of his pocket and laid it proudly in my hands.

"Thanks so much, Grandpa! You always know my favourites."

Moments later, he emerged from his bedroom carrying a long, narrow box. He handed it to me and told me to open it. I looked at Nanny and she smiled a broad, beautiful smile. As I opened the box, and the light hit its contents, I saw gold sparkles and stripes and patterns of glorious colour. They were my grandfather's army medals, lined up on a long pin. I had seen him wear them on his impressive, perfectly pressed uniform when he ventured out to the local Legion. I thought they were visually stunning.

"Those are the medals I got while I was in the army," Grandpa said.

"I know," I replied in awe. I couldn't believe he was letting me hold them.

"Lynn, I want you to have these after I die," he told me.

"Oh Grandpa, I don't want to think about you dying!" I exclaim.

"I know that. Your old Grandpa has a lot of days still left in him. It's just that I want these to be yours after I'm gone."

"Oh, thank you so much Grandpa! When I get them, I will guard them with my life," I told him, still unable to see my life without him in it.

Afterward, Nanny and I shared stories from our books. She asked me to read something for her only if I had a Looney Toon comic or *Mad Magazine*. She didn't like the horror comics. "Oh, Lynn, they're too creepy for me," she said. When she would relay the engaging stories from the *Reader's Digest*, I sat in amazement at how well she could read. I wanted to be just like her.

Later that very evening, as I was getting ready for bed and changing into my nightie, Nanny noticed that there was a spot on my underwear. She said, "Honey, it looks like you have blood on your underwear." I felt the furnace in my face ignite. Even though my beloved dog Prince had soothed my wounds, I had not stopped scratching at myself. As I pulled down my underwear with the little pink flowers, I noticed the stain where my bum touched them. *Think fast.*

"Oh, that happened at Nanny Ida's house. I fell on a stick," I told her.

"How on God's great Earth did that happen?" Nanny Carron asked me.

The gears of my imagination were fortunately well oiled and they started their protective spin.

"Well, I was trying to pull a branch from a tree in Nanny Ida's backyard, and as I pulled it off, I fell into a pile of brush." I actually said the word "brush" and thought it sounded awfully convincing. She had to believe me.

I continued, "It was really silly. When I landed in the brush, a stick poked me in my bum." This became the story that I chose to believe was true. There were no other alternatives. This story made sense.

She asked, "Can I take a look at it to see if you're okay?"

"NO! It's fine Nanny. I just cut myself and it doesn't hurt anymore. It would be so embarrassing to have you look at my bum hole," I replied.

Nanny laughed. "Have you told your Mom about how you hurt your bum?" she asked.

"No. It's fine, Nanny."

She said, "Okay, if you're sure. How about a nice warm bath to clean yourself up?"

"Sounds good."

My grandmother drew me a bath in the large claw foot tub in their apartment bathroom. I always loved the smell of this bathroom. It was a mixture of the scent of Grandpa's bar of shaving soap and his latest bottle of Aqua Velva or Old Spice. It was always so clean and I knew I didn't have to lock the door.

After the bathing ritual, Nanny dressed me in my nightie and took me by the hand over to the couch. She read to me from the *Catholic Press Prayer Book*. She told me that Jesus was my friend. She read:

> *O Jesus! You are my true friend, my only friend. You take part in all my misfortunes; You take them on Yourself; You know how to change them into blessings.*

> *You listen to me with the greatest kindness when I relate my troubles to You, and You have always balm to pour on my wounds.*

"Jesus was really cool, wasn't he? Why did he have to die that way?" I asked.

"Jesus died to set us free and allow us into Heaven," she replied.

"I don't understand. Why did God let his son die to get us into Heaven?"

"Well, if you don't get it sweetie, you have to look at it as one of God's mysteries."

Oh, I try to understand mysteries, Nanny.

* * * * *

26

Mother took me to the doctor. I'm not sure which of my complaints prompted the visit. Nothing was explained to me other than the fact that if I was a good girl and cooperated with the doctor, she would take me for chocolate ice cream, my favourite. On my first visit to Dr. Springer, I had my finger pricked to take blood. It hurt like hell and I cried. It felt like he stuck the blade of a knife into my finger. He checked my eyes, nose, and ears and then pressed his fingers into my stomach. I got ice cream after this visit.

The next appointment with Dr. Springer didn't run so smoothly. I laid face down on an examining table when he asked my mother to step out of the room. Again, nothing was explained to me. With a gloved hand, Dr. Springer inserted his finger up my bum. I screamed as loud as I could. I didn't scream because of the pain; I screamed with rage.

On the following visit to Dr. Springer, he approached me, in front of my mother, to prick my finger for more blood. As he reached for the metal prick on the instrument table, my right leg shot out and kicked his table on wheels clear across the room. *Take that, you bastard*, I thought.

Mom didn't take me out for chocolate ice cream. It didn't matter. I knew it was a done deal when the metal instruments flew off his cart and onto the floor.

Though she was pissed off and wearing a puckered mouth, I decided to ask my mother why I had to visit Dr. Springer so often. "Because you have a nervous stomach," she told me flatly.

It was no wonder. Every summer, I was on a continuous train that rode between the serpentine, treacherous tracks of Nanny Ida's house and the smooth, level ones of Nanny Carron's home. I begged my parents to take me to Nanny and Grandpa Carron's instead of 16 James Street, but there were times when they were off on a visit to an aunt, an uncle, or one of their twenty-one grandchildren.

Sometimes the dump off at 16 James was bearable, usually when one of our aunts was visiting. We liked our Aunt Bea, who was married to our Uncle Frederick. She adored children and treated us with the same interest, kindness, and compassion that she gave her own children, Frederick Jr. and Helen. Aunt Bea had flaming red hair, a beautiful smile that revealed her large white teeth, and one of the most infectious laughs I have ever heard. I remember:

It's late afternoon at Grandma Ida's house. My sister, brothers, and I have been dropped off again to endure the smell of sulphur and the filth, while Mom and Dad venture to some mysterious destination. Aunt Bea is there with my cousin, Frederick, who we call Freddie. Nanny Ida makes us a spectacular lunch of tuna sandwiches and macaroni salad. She is one fine cook, like Grandpa Carron. There wasn't one dish she made that we wouldn't gobble down in huge bites.

She calls my brother Wally a "hungry gutted bastard". Still chewing, he lowers his blood-red face in shame.

"*He's just hungry, Nanny,*" I tell her.

"*Hungry? He's a fucking bottomless pit,*" she says. "*Don't your mother and father feed you rug rats?*"

"*Yes, Nan. Sometimes it isn't enough, though,*" I reply.

Aunt Bea looks at me sympathetically. "*You kids go ahead and eat whatever you want. There's plenty here.*" She pours some more milk into Wally's empty glass. He instantly gulps it down as if in fear that someone might snatch it from him. His gulping is loud and Aunt Bea tells him to slow down, that it's rude to gulp like that. "*I'm sorry, Aunt Bea,*" he says. "*It's just so good.*"

Nanny Ida and Bea have some whiskey and beer with their lunch. They talk and laugh about times at the cottage while Bea plays a game of Trouble with us. We love popping the clear globe that holds the dice, making our moves over the plastic pots around the game board. Nanny doesn't play; she's busy getting pissed and packaging macaroni salad in plastic bowls. She complains about our Uncle Garrett and how she wishes he would get a fucking job before she tosses his ass out onto the street. It's big talk for her; she never once tossed any of her kids asses out onto the street.

After a while, we go into the living room to watch television while Aunt Bea and Nanny Ida continue their mini party in the kitchen. Soon there is a loud knock at the side door. This is not unusual because Nanny is a bootlegger. She sells booze to people on the weekends for a hefty price. On any Saturday or Sunday, there is an ample amount of visitors with requests for some Five Star whiskey or a two-four of beer. I know that this is illegal; I hear plenty of talk about hiding the stash in the back shed and paying off the cops who clue in. Some of the cops are her best customers. They nickname her Ma Barker.

There's another knock and my grandmother opens the side door. There is a loud bang and Nanny shrieks. The voice is loud and serious. "*Pull out the fucking wad in your tits, bitch,*" a man yells. We run out into the kitchen. Bea starts screaming as the masked man holds a handgun to my grandmother's head. The other masked man also has a gun, but holds it down at his side. They are dressed completely in black and I feel like I'm going to crap in my pants. There is complete chaos. All of the children, including me, run behind the kitchen table, crying and screaming. Aunt Bea quickly spirals into hysteria as she tries to gather all of us into her arms. The only calm one is my grandmother. She stands there, mildly frowning, as this dark monster holds the barrel of his gun to her temple.

"*If that's you, Jimmy, you cock-sucker, you're a dead man!*" she yells. The masked monster pushes the gun into her head and says, "*If you have half a brain, you old fat bitch, you'll pull that huge wad of money out of that hammock of a bra you wear!*"

"You don't have the balls to put a bullet in me, you little cock-sucker!"
Nanny screams.

"How would you like it if I put a bullet into one of those little snot-nosed kids?"
the mask blasts at her.

"You fucking prick," she says, almost in a whisper.

"Bea, take the kids upstairs," Nanny says quietly.

"Those kids aren't going anywhere, bitch," the mask tells her.

Nanny sighs heavily. "Let Beatrice take the kids upstairs and I'll give you
what you want," she says. Hearing her say my aunt's full name somehow increases
my terror.

The mask motions with the gun toward Bea. "GO!" he yells.

Sobbing, Aunt Bea gathers us and pushes us up the stairs to the bedrooms. My
sister Annie reaches a breaking point: "He's going to kill her, Aunt Bea! We have to
do something! We can't just leave her!"

"Don't worry, honey," Bea sobs. "Your Nan isn't stupid. She will give them what
they want."

In an instant, it is over. Nanny calls to us, "You can come down now."

We rush down the stairs, practically stumbling over each other, to find her
sitting, sedate, at the kitchen table. "Did they get the money?" Bea asks, still crying.

"Oh yeah," my grandmother replies. "I didn't have much choice in the matter.
The little fuckers also took two cases of whiskey. I think it was that cock-sucker,
Jimmy. Let me tell you, if I find out it was him, he's going to take a fucking snooze
under the soil at the Isle of Man."

The Isle of Man. This was the location of Grandmother Ida's cottage, right on
the weedy and sewage infested shores of the Rideau River. Sometimes, there were
logs of shit floating on the surface, or ones that were done their swim, resting
on the shallow, rocky bottom. The entire family spent many summer days and
nights driving down the Isle of Man Road toward the cottage after a stock up of
food and pop at Code's Corners on Hwy. 15. I don't know if Jimmy had to find his
eternal slumber under the soil out there, but I know that there were hushed talks
of bodies dumped on and in various areas of the Isle of Man, bodies of those who
dared cross my grandmother or the family. Some of my uncles talked about the
"fuckers" who found their rest at the bottom of the swamp down by the red barn.
I became petrified of this swamp. It was deep, pea green, and covered with a
healthy layer of scum. My brothers and I loved to search for frogs, but I wouldn't
let them near this particular swamp. I had nightmarish visions of fishing around
in the muck for leopard frogs only to latch onto a squishy bloated limb, or worse,
hair that was attached to a dimpled and disfigured severed head. The Isle of Man
would later become the setting for a much higher education.

V

CONSIDERING THE DISTANCE FROM NANNY IDA'S HOUSE AND the troubles in our neighbourhood on Montreal Street, my parents decided to relocate the family to what they said was "a better part of town" – Raglan Road, only a few blocks away. I thought that any place away from Joey Rowens had to be an improvement. We moved into 9 Raglan Road, another row house, right across the street from enormous oil tanks that gave me many sleepless nights considering that a single match could cause an explosion. Whenever I asked an adult about this possibility they would always reply, "Sure, that could happen." I figured that my parents saw Joey Rowens as a greater danger than exploding oil tanks.

Our family settled into Raglan Road and we children continued to attend St. John's Elementary School. My parents felt that Annie and I were old enough to walk home for lunch. Mom was still at home, taking care of Wally and Sean. Sometimes we had dimes in our pockets, gifted from Nanny and Grandpa Carron, and we would stop at the corner store, Ann's Confectionary, where Raglan Road met Montreal Street. Each time we ventured into the store, we ordered a bag of mixed-up candy from the male store clerk. It was amazing how much candy you could get for a single dime in 1972. As he filled my little paper bag with sugared spearmint candies and licorice pipes, I wondered: *Where the hell is Ann? It's called Ann's Confectionary, and we always have this old guy fingering our candy.*

After visiting Ann's, Annie and I always walked home slowly, savouring the sugar treats in our paper bags. We would save a few to torment our brother Wally. After dangling them in front of him, he didn't disappoint us as he cried and whined, until Mom put an end to it. Then each of us would give Wally a soft candy. He practically swallowed them whole without even tasting them.

Mother usually served us snot sandwiches and tomato soup for our home-made lunch. I hated tomato soup. I was so hungry that I gagged it down, but I always imagined I was eating a bowl of blood. I remember thinking: *snot and blood, what a lovely combination.* The bowl of blood made me appreciate the snot; I gobbled down the sandwiches. Years later, it took the art of Andy Warhol to show me that I could appreciate tomato soup in at least one way.

My father continued his work at Canadian Tire while we lived on Raglan Road; it was his income that supported the family. With his solitary support, providing for a family of six had to be arduous. I thought that was why he was always so miserable and took out his frustrations on his wife and children. When he came home, covered with oil and black grunge, I knew he had worked hard. I wanted to love him, like him even. He made that dreadfully difficult. He walked through the door on any evening, unpredictably drunk or sober. Either way, he blasted off and smacked my mother around the row house.

Dad came to surround himself with friends just like him. I will never forget Karen and Hank Antonio. They visited frequently and my mother seemed to forge a connection with Karen, who appeared so fragile. She had a tiny, thin body, dark hair, and all parts of her trembled, even her lips. I thought Hank was a gargantuan prick, just like my father. He looked like my father except that he had dark brown hair and his Adam's apple stuck out further, so pointy and sharp that it looked like a weapon. They had a son, Warren, who was about the same age as my brother, Wally. Warren was like his mother: tiny, fragile, and constantly shaking. They reminded me of Chihuahua dogs.

Karen and Hank are visiting with their son, Warren. Dad and Hank laugh and guzzle pints while Mom talks with Karen in the kitchen. Hank turns up the music. Cream is singing:

> *In a white room,*
> *With black curtains,*
> *Is the station.*

Hank and my father try singing along with Eric Clapton and sound like two assholes who just can't sing. I don't hear what they are talking about, because I am sitting with Mom and Karen at the kitchen table. Karen looks worried; she is twisting her hair with a trembling finger and rubbing her brow with her other hand. She looks like she wants to bolt out of the room. Mom senses her stress and keeps looking toward the living room where the singing assholes are.

Soon, all we hear is the music and two drunks trying to whisper. Karen becomes more agitated. Suddenly, Hank flies out to the kitchen and calls Karen a "dirty whore". Her shakes turn into twitches and she starts crying loudly. Hank grabs her up from the kitchen chair and punches her, full on, in the face. My mother and I scream. Dad looks on, calmly, from the doorway. Karen is on the floor. Hank yells, "Get up, bitch!" When Karen rises, she has blood spurting from her nose. I can't even tell where her nose is. He hits her again, sending her flying against the counter and then onto the floor.

Mother screams at him, "Hank, STOP, PLEASE!"

Hank shrieks, "Fuck you, you cunt, you're no better than she is!"

I look over at my father. He looks awfully pleased.

As Karen sits slumped on the kitchen floor, my mother runs to comfort her. Hank slaps Dad on the back and says, "Let's cork ourselves another, old boy!" That is exactly what they do while both wives sit crying on the floor.

Mom says, "Lynn, get some toilet paper." I run for it and hand it to her and she holds it gently against Karen's nose. As Karen continues to sob, Mom wipes her carefully and then asks me for a face cloth. Again, I run. I soak it quickly in warm water and take it to her. She places the cloth over Karen's face. When she draws it away, I see the faint image of her lower face in blood revealed on the terrycloth. It reminds me of Veronica wiping the face of Jesus; I had just learned about it at school. At that moment, I feel seething hatred for my father and Hank.

It seems that the rest of the kids are oblivious to the commotion downstairs. That is, until one of them screams. It is Warren. Karen scurries to her feet and we run upstairs. Wally tells us that the "toilet seat fell on Warren's pecker." We all look at Warren's penis; it's already swollen and purple. Karen stoops down and holds Warren. He sees her damaged face.

"What happened, Mommy?" he asks through his tears.

"Oh nothing, honey," she replies, now calm, "Are you okay?"

"It hurts really bad," he sobs. "That fucking seat landed right on it!"

"Please don't say that word, Warren. You know better," Karen tells him.

"I know that my pecker would really hurt if that happened to me," Wally says, concerned.

Warren laughs. Then we all laugh and Karen hugs Warren tighter.

Mom asks, "How about colouring books and crayons?"

"YES!" we scream. Warren's eyes grow large; he grins and stops shaking.

Karen, Mom, and the lot of us colour pictures in chosen books from the stack in my brother's room. My brother always picks the Christmas books with a gentle smile on his face. It could be June and he would pick a Christmas colouring book. We colour until the monsters downstairs fall asleep.

This was typical of a visit with Karen, Hank, and Warren. I felt protective of Karen and Warren and I wished Hank would die a grisly death. If anyone belonged in the pea green swamp at the Isle of Man, it was Hank Antonio. My father ran a close second.

The S & R bag holds only one photograph of life on Raglan Road, though we lived there for several years. Anyone looking at this picture would probably remark on the huge eyes and long lashes of the four children posing against the beige, ivy patterned wallpaper. The second remark would certainly be about the wide, almost genuine smiles displaying perfect sets of straight baby teeth. I remember that the photographer had to resort to silly tricks to get us to smile like that. He threw little rag toys into the air and let them fall onto the floor. Wally took the longest to smile. The photographer had to pull out all the stops. He flung one of the rag toys upward and hit the ceiling. The toy dropped down on top of picture taker's head. Wally burst into laughter and the shot was taken. He is beautiful in this picture. I look at this photograph often, just to see him smile.

We did eventually discover one thing that we could smile about on Raglan Road. There were other children on our street. We made friends with Kelly and Dennis Waters, who lived four houses away. Dennis was seven years old, a year younger than me, and Kelly was the same age as Wally. They both had heads of thick, white blond hair. I instantly nicknamed him "Dennis the Menace" after one of my favourite cartoon characters. Along with another boy named Tracey, who lived around the corner, we all kept each other occupied with mud pies, building forts out of wood scraps, and daring each other to eat bugs. Each of us stayed outside playing until dinner or dusk, whatever came first. It always took several shouts from our parents to get us to leave each other and head for home.

Initially, all the neighbourhood parents adored me. I ran a classroom out of our backyard. All the kids would gather near the wooden fence in our yard to play school. I was always the teacher. I made little notebooks for them out of scrap paper tied together with old string. They brought their own pencils. I conducted my lessons with mud and a stick on the surface of the wooden fence. I taught them spelling and math and thoroughly enjoyed giving them a quiz to see if they had learned anything. If they spoke while I was giving my lesson, they had to stay in for recess. After recess, I taught art class. Everyone was given paper and crayons and asked to draw an animal from their imagination or a picture of their favourite cartoon character. I never could resist showing off during art class, drawing far more elaborate creatures than any of the other kids. They would all stare in wonder at what I had drawn. They told me I was a good teacher. I sucked up every single word. My future was sealed at the age of eight.

I loved teaching the neighbourhood kids. When they learned something new, they smiled broadly and went home to tell their parents all about it. The parents started to provide new equipment and utensils for my classroom, like rulers and erasers. What I really wanted was a box of chalk. I shivered with envy as I watched my new teacher, Mrs. Tanner, write the date and lists of words in different colours on the blackboard in my classroom at St. John's. I begged my parents to buy me some chalk, to no avail. I didn't have the courage to ask anyone else, so I stole some. I didn't steal it from Mrs. Tanner. That was unthinkable.

While visiting Nanny and Grandpa Carron one afternoon, Mom took me over to Woolworth's with the intent to purchase her pantyhose. As she pondered the large egg- cups of Legg's Pantyhose, I expertly looked about the toy department and carefully placed a box of coloured chalk into my pocket. As we left the store, I felt clever and powerful. I had gotten away with it. I had my coloured chalk and nothing was going to be done about it. I could teach my backyard lessons with flair. The kids would be captivated and would turn into putty in my hands.

Back at Nanny and Grandpa's apartment, lunch was served on the shiny surface of the dining table. I couldn't concentrate. I didn't care about the beautiful sliced tomatoes topped with onion, the thick homemade bread, or the enormous slices of salted ham. I could only think of the brightly coloured chalk nestling in my jacket pocket. Frequently, I left the table to check my jacket and run my hand over the rectangular lump in its side.

Mother noticed. She asked me what I was doing and why I wasn't eating the wonderful lunch that my grandfather had prepared. My face grew hot. *Damn it to hell. Why did I always have to blush?*

Looking straight into my eyes, Mom pushed her hand into the pocket of my jacket and dramatically revealed the evidence of my crime. Nanny and Grandpa stared at me, obviously astonished and disappointed. I thought my neck would break as my chin dove into my chest.

"We are going back over to Woolworth's and you are going to tell them what you have done," my mother stated.

I begged, "Please don't make me do it, Mom! I will never do it again! I promise!"

"You're going to take it back;" she said, "you're not going to turn into a thief."

"We take stolen stuff from Nanny Ida. Your coat is stolen and so are my shoes," I said.

"Shut up!" Mom screamed. "I don't care what your Grandma Simmons does! That's not how I want you to behave!"

She took me and the beautiful box of coloured chalk back to Woolworth's. I was forced to go up to the cashier and tell her that I had stolen it. As I cried, she smiled at my mother and then kneeled down to me. She said, "I guess you've learned an important lesson today."

I continued sobbing.

"You must know that it's a sin to steal," she said.

"Yes," I replied.

"Well, I'm sure that you won't do it again." She finished with a smile.

"Never," I told her with complete conviction.

I continued my neighbourhood lessons with sticks and muck and was thrilled that my students still wanted to be there. Everything that I learned in my grade two class was taught to the kids who ventured into our backyard on Raglan Road, whether they wanted to learn it or not. If any of them insisted on disrupting my lessons, they were told to get out of my classroom. They could come back when they were ready to learn something.

But, like all classrooms, there can be enormous disruptions and complications. My first turned out to be a monkey. Literally. My father brought him home. I'm not sure what breed the monkey was; he didn't look like a chimpanzee. He had a blood red ass and was horribly violent to the point that he had to be caged in the back shed of our row house. Dad received him as payment for something or maybe as punishment because he lost a card game. Either way, the crazy, crimsoned-assed primate was a guest in our shed. Even though he was a violent creature, I felt sorry for him. It was his ass. It was so red and inflamed and I knew what it was like to have a sore bum. I wanted to pet him or put a nice warm cloth on his rump, but I knew he would rip my face off if I came near him.

My sister and I wanted to name him George, after Curious George, but we soon realized that he was far too nasty to be given such a prestigious name. We decided to call him Crusty because of his attitude and the raw, dry spots on his red ass. Crusty was good company for Ben, who was the huge rat that lived in the shed and scared the shit out of us almost every night. He was completely nocturnal and we named him Ben after Willard's killer pet rat in the movie. There was only one pro to Crusty and Ben's presence: our dog, Prince, was allowed to sleep in our rooms at night, far away from these dangerous creatures.

Crusty was so volatile that he was never allowed out of his cage or out of the back shed. He wasn't exposed to sunlight and it was awfully cold in that shed at night as autumn approached. Crusty was a prisoner and I ached to set him free, not just because he was stuck in our dingy shed, but because the neighbourhood kids couldn't come over once their parents heard that there was an aggressive monkey living at our house. Dennis and Kelly were forbidden to go near our yard. Only Tracey, from around the corner, caught a glimpse of Crusty. He rose to the challenge and went berserk in his cage. He grabbed a dried hunk of his shit and hurled it at Tracey, who was stricken with terror. I thought this was hilarious and decided to tell him about Ben. Tracey ran home and told his parents about the Hellers' House of Horrors. Word quickly spread around the neighbourhood and even Tracey was no longer permitted to visit as long as Crusty held residence in our back shed.

One cool morning, we awoke and headed down the stairs to the kitchen for breakfast. I immediately noticed that no rattling noise was coming from the shed, the noise that was Crusty's constant. I opened the shed door, hoping that Ben would not be there to greet me, and observed that Crusty and his cage were gone.

"Where is Crusty?" I asked Mom.

"Your father found another home for him," she replied.

"Where?"

"Look, Lynn, I don't know. Your father found that crazy monkey a different home and that's all that matters. I'm glad the dirty little bastard is gone. It was driving me nuts. Not only do I have to deal with rats, but a goddamned shit-eating monkey? Give me a break, Jesus Christ," she said.

I wasn't really upset to see that Crusty was gone. Now, some of the neighbourhood kids could come back to visit. I truly didn't think much of Crusty's absence until later that evening. When my family sat down to dinner, each of us was served a rather healthy portion of meat, far more than we were accustomed to. Meat was always scarce and treasured in our house. We would suck the finest threads of protein from the bones and if we could chew the bones, we would shred them, soften them with saliva, and swallow them.

On this particular evening, there was plenty of meat to go around and enough for seconds. This wasn't the only unusual feature of the meal; the flavour of the meat was also odd. Suddenly I knew. *Oh God, we're eating Crusty!* I felt my stomach flip and asked to be excused from the table.

"What's the matter with you?" Mom asked.

"I don't like this meat," I replied.

"What's wrong with it? It's steak. You're just not used to having good steak," my father said.

I'm not that stupid! You cooked Crusty! I thought.

"It tastes funny. I don't like it."

My sister and brothers continued to gobble it down without listening to me. My parents seemed to sense that I was about to mention Crusty, and dismissed me from the dinner table. I went upstairs to my room and flopped on my bed trying to control the heaving in my stomach. *What if I had chewed and swallowed part of Crusty's scabby red ass?* I wasn't able to eat meat for weeks.

With Crusty out of the picture, the neighbourhood kids were allowed back to our house and I resumed my early teaching career in my backyard classroom. Everyone returned with notebooks, pencils, and erasers. I was delighted. This personal Garden of Eden would not last for long. The demise of my neighbourhood classroom came one sunny September day during a backyard recess.

I thought that I would make a seesaw for everyone to enjoy. I found a thick wooden plank in our back shed and propped its center on top of an old tricycle. Wally and I tried it first. Though it was unstable and slid around a little, it worked! As soon as all the kids saw Wally and me teetering back and forth, they all wanted to try it out. Kelly Waters was the youngest and jumped out of her skin in anticipation; it was decided that she should be the next one to ride the plank.

I was the one to seesaw with Kelly. I thought that this was the safest thing to do since my sister and brother wanted the seesaw to fly up and down as fast as possible. With Kelly at the low end, I positioned myself carefully at the high end. I pushed my bum down gently and Kelly rose up off the ground. She laughed with glee. We continued a gentle teeter and totter as Kelly giggled loudly. Suddenly, the wooden plank shifted on the metal seat of the tricycle. Kelly Waters, who was on the high side at the time, lost her balance and fell head first onto the gravel of the driveway. Everyone gasped. I jumped off the plank and ran to her. To my horror, she started to scream. As she lifted herself up from the dusty gravel, I could see the large spot of red in her white blond hair. It glistened sickly in the autumn sunlight and grew quickly. As a bead of dark red blood fell onto Kelly's pale cheek, I picked her up and started to carry her toward her house. I couldn't take her into our house; my father was half snapped as usual. She continued to scream as all of the kids followed us up to her doorstep. Following a loud knock on the door, Mrs. Waters appeared and quickly sized up the situation. She screamed louder than Kelly did.

Mrs. Waters grabbed Kelly and slammed the screen door in my face. She yelled, "You goddamned crazy kids get out of here!" We scurried down the street toward my house. We stood behind some bushes and watched as Mr. and Mrs. Waters hustled Kelly and Dennis into their car. Kelly had a blood soaked rag wrapped around her tiny head. Tracey said, "They must be taking her to the hospital."

"Oh, you're one big friggin' genius," I said and regretted it immediately.

I paced up and down the sidewalk for what seemed like hours waiting for the Waters family to return home. I took a short break only to grab a sweater from my room, not wanting to miss a chance to apologize. As darkness approached, my mother called for me to come inside. I didn't change into my nightie and spent the night tossing and turning, wondering what was happening to Kelly. I wanted my clothes on so that I would be ready to say that I was sorry when they came home.

The next morning, my mother told us that Kelly was badly hurt and that she had to get many stitches in her head. She glared at me with disgust. Mom told me that Mrs. Waters was very upset by my behaviour. I went up to my room and cried myself to sleep. Losing the favour of any adult always crippled me and this time I deserved it, just like the last, when I had almost caused the death of another little girl.

That time it was my sister. My parents took Annie and me to Bennett's Grocery Store on Bagot Street for the bi-weekly grocery shop. Instead of taking us inside to stumble along as they pushed the grocery cart, they left us in the back seat of the car in Bennett's parking lot across the street from the store. I was six years old and Annie was five.

After a period, we wanted to make sure that Mom didn't forget to get us a lollipop if she had a few pennies left over. We knew that we were not supposed to leave the car. The thought of a spiral lollipop or a five pack of Bennett's suckers finally took its toll. I took Annie by the hand and opened the car door. We made our way across the parking lot to the sidewalk of Bagot Street. I looked both ways as I was always told to do and held onto Annie's hand.

I said, "Okay, let's run!" when I saw that the way was clear.

As we were running across the street, I let go of Annie's hand, thinking that we had made it, that it was a done deal. In the next instant, there was the sound of a horn and screeching tires. Rooted to the spot, I closed my eyes tightly and braced myself to be hit. There was a loud dull thump and I turned to see my sister's little body fly through the air and land several feet away from me on the sidewalk. I fell to my knees. There was an instant flurry of people running about. Some of them surrounded Annie and others checked on me.

I screamed, "I'm okay! My sister has been hit! Help us!"

I pulled away from a stranger who grabbed my hand and I ran toward the crowd around Annie. Another person grabbed me by the waist, lifted me up, and rushed me into Bennett's. I was kicking and screaming. "Don't let my sister die! Please don't let her die!" Suddenly my parents were there with confused and horrified looks on their faces. A screeching woman walked slowly into the store holding what looked like a dead baby in her arms. Annie's eyes rolled back in her purple head. The hysterical woman, the one who had hit her, was told by another to put my sister down onto the cold tile floor of Bennett's. *Oh, don't let her die here.*

Sirens. Medics. Police. Ribbons of tape and chalk scribbles. Annie was taken to Kingston General Hospital. My parents took me home and shut me in my room. They took the light bulb and told me that I could not come out. With booze on his breath, my father said, "If your little sister dies, it's your fault." They didn't tell me that she was okay until later the next day. They let me believe I had killed Annie.

The episode with Kelly Waters left me feeling equally criminal. I scouted for her like a private eye, but didn't see her for several days. Finally, I saw her playing with one of her dolls in her small front yard. I walked over to her and asked her how she was doing. I could see the stitches and the beginnings of a healthy, dark scab through her hair. Looking at the ground, she said, "I'm okay. I've got a dozen stitches." She said "dozen" as if she really didn't know what the word meant.

"I'm sorry that this happened, Kelly," I told her.

She picked at her doll's clothing, saying nothing.

"Do you want to come over and play with your doll at my house?" I asked her.

"I'm not allowed to play with you anymore, Lynn. Neither is Dennis."

"What? Why not?" I implored.

"My mother said that we can't."

"But why? Is it just because you got hurt?"

"My mom says that you and your family are trash," she said without looking at me.

It was a devastating blow, an instant gaping wound.

Fuck your mother, that dumpy, uptight four-eyed bitch, I thought.

Instead, I vocalized a child's retort: "Well who needs you and Dennis anyway? Especially you. You're nothing but a pain in the ass."

Kelly bowed her head and cried. I turned my back and never had much to do with her after that.

I started to spend more time with Tracey as a result. Tracey was okay, but compared to Dennis and Kelly, he was rather boring. He could rarely do any of my math or spelling lessons and acted the fool on purpose so that I would make him stay in for recess. This got on my fragile nerves. Soon, I stopped trying to discipline him and sent him out for recess with my sister and brothers, even though he had misbehaved during my class. It turned out that my four-year-old brother, Sean, was smarter than Tracey Garrison. I quickly began to lose interest in him. That is, until he rode over to our house one day on a brand new, very shiny, red bicycle.

Annie and I looked at him with awe and admiration. He was the first kid in the neighbourhood to get a two-wheeler. We wanted a bicycle more than anything. We begged Mom and Dad for one on countless occasions but the reply was always the same: "Even a used bicycle is too expensive for us right now." Who could argue with that? We were eating blood soup and monkey meat.

During his next visit, I asked Tracey if I might have a short ride on his beautiful new bike. He clutched his treasure close to his body and looked at me with a broad smile and a tilt of his head. He loved this. I almost told him to forget it when he suddenly said, "Sure."

"Wow, really? Thanks so much, Tracey! I want a bike like this so bad!" I said. There was one catch.

Tracey said, "I'll let you take a ride on my bike if you kiss me on the cheek."

Oh, you've got to be kidding, I thought. *I'd rather kiss Crusty's dead red ass.*

Ah, screw it. It's worth it for a ride on a new bike.

"Okay. But only a quick one and only on the cheek," I told him, "And you better have washed your grimy face today."

Tracey held onto his bike and leaned his head toward me. Fighting the urge to puke, I stretched my neck, without moving my body, and quickly brushed my lips against his cheek. Satisfied, he directed the handlebars to me. The first touch was sheer ecstasy. I felt the energy of the metal fire through my arms and fill my body. I sat atop the blue and white seat and placed my foot on one of the pedals. I pushed myself forward and began a gloriously smooth ride on Tracey's red machine.

"Only to the Waters' house and back!" he screamed after me.

Screw you, little buddy. I had to put my mouth on your scummy, pasty face.

"Yep! No problem, Trace!" I yelled back at him.

I rode his bike all the way up to Ann's Confectionary and turned around to see him running up the sidewalk toward me, completely enraged. I grinned and started the bike back down the sidewalk as fast as I could. I was headed right for him. He stopped still and stared at me with confusion and fear. As I reached him, I quickly swerved the bicycle around him and kept riding to the other end of the block. The torture was sweet but short-lived. Tracey started to cry. I hated when kids cried. I turned around, got off the bike, and walked it back to him.

"I'm sorry, Tracey. I was just having so much fun," I said.

Clearly embarrassed that he was crying, Tracey quietly took his bike and walked it back home without saying another word. I felt like a big shit and instantly lost all joy of the experience of riding a brand new bicycle.

What this experience did was prompt me to put more pressure on my parents to get us a bicycle. I knew that my pleadings held no weight with my father, so I had Annie do the asking. Eventually, there was success. Father managed to buy an old, rusted, purple, two-wheeler from someone. He must have bought it because he had standards and certainly wouldn't steal anything in such shabby condition. One evening, just before dinner, Dad led Annie and me out to his car. He proudly opened his trunk to display the rusted, dismantled parts of this bicycle. We screamed and jumped with utter joy. Neither of us cared that it was used or rusted. We knew that our father could make something out of anything. It was going to be a matter of short time before we were racing circles around Tracey Garrison.

Nightly, we pleaded with Dad to rebuild the bicycle. The sad truth is that the cycle never left his trunk until he sold it to someone else. He wouldn't rebuild it, even for Annie. We thought that he probably traded it for a two-four of beer. That was his style. When he told us that the bicycle was gone, he said that it was a piece of shit anyway and he wouldn't want his kids riding it.

Yeah, right. This from a guy who could build a working motor out of cardboard. I hope you enjoyed the case of beer, Dad, I thought.

This was only one of a series of promises and resulting disappointments that year. At school, a boy named Jamie Bowden took a liking to me. He was a student in my grade two class, and he wasted no time telling the entire population of the primary grades that I was his chosen one. At first, I was flattered and felt like I could actually be pretty, since it was Annie who was usually centered out as the beautiful Hellers girl. Adults likened her to Marilyn Monroe. When it came to me, they remained silent mostly, with the exception of those who whispered that I looked like a boy, clearly believing that I couldn't hear them.

Jamie thought I was fabulous. He told me so to my face. He said, "Lynn, I think you're great. You are so smart and pretty and I'd like to give you anything you'd ever want." How many grown women long to hear those words? I thought Jamie was full of shit, but I liked what he said—at first. His attention soon became boring and annoying. He told any kid who would listen that I was a "vision" and that he'd like to marry me one day. I wondered where he learned the word "vision" and figured his father probably taught it to him. Jamie was always a sucker for dopey romance lines and I really can't remember all of them. I didn't pay much attention to Jamie until he told me that he was going to buy me an Easy-Bake Oven for Christmas. Now that got my attention. I immediately envisioned myself making the most wonderful cakes topped with layers of chocolate and vanilla frosting. I started to be nicer and more polite to Jamie.

At the same time, I was writing letters to Principal Burton. It was part of my "special" program. Every week, she would drop off a letter to me and I would respond the same day. I told her about my wish for an Easy-Bake Oven. I didn't tell her that Jamie wanted to buy one for me. Somehow, I knew she wouldn't approve. I was very careful about anything I wrote to Mrs. Burton. Anything beyond the realm of Christian goodness was grounds for the strap. Although she was never aware of it, Mrs. Burton taught me how to be a very good liar. *Dear Mrs. Burton, How are you today? I am fine. I got to ride on a new bike this weekend and it was fun. My father has been trying to find a used bike for me and my sister. He has been looking hard. He is a really good Dad and takes really good care of us. I am sure that he will find one soon. How is your husband? Do your kids have a bike or an Easy-Bake Oven?*

I told Mom about my desire for an Easy-Bake Oven. She said that one of those was a little extravagant for a family like ours. Translation: we can't afford it. I knew that there was no Santa Claus at that point and was chastised for trying to impose my beliefs on my siblings. Mom and Dad still wanted me to believe in Santa Claus, but I didn't. I knew better. Unlike my sister and brothers, I read the tags on the gifts under the tree on Christmas morning. *Merry Chrismas, Lynn, love Santa.* Can't Santa spell Christmas?

It was the same at Easter. I got a chocolate bunny with a tag that read, "*To Lynn, from Peter Cottonail.*" Not only was it spelled incorrectly, the words were written in my mother's careful handwriting. If they were going to try to pull this bunk on me, they needed to disguise a few things—like the fact that they couldn't spell when they were hammered. It's no wonder that my parents practically despised me. I rarely missed a thing when we were children. I think I got on their nerves more than words could ever express.

Even though Mom said that an Easy-Bake Oven was too extravagant for our family, I giggled inside at the thought that I was going to get one anyway from Jamie Bowden. I imagined myself walking into the house on the last day before Christmas holidays with a brand new Easy-Bake Oven, and I knew that neither Mom nor Dad would make me take back such a lovely gift that could make sweet treats for everyone. I even stopped asking Mom and Dad for it, being so sure that Jamie was going to present me with one. He talked about it every single day in the classroom and at recess. Each time Jamie told me about the oven he was going to gift me, I smiled and told him that it was awfully nice of him.

"You deserve the best," he said.

On the day before Christmas break, Jamie did not give me a present. In fact, he avoided me as if I had a case of anthrax or the bubonic plague. He didn't come near me during class or at recess. I knew why. I wasn't going to get the Easy-Bake Oven he had promised me and he was too chicken-shit to say so. After school, Jamie approached me as I was about to leave St. John's.

"Hi, Lynn. I hope you have a good holiday and I think you're the greatest girl in the class," he said. I turned to look right at him and punched him, with the full force of an eight-year-old, directly in the mouth. He fell to the snow-covered ground and glared back at me in shock; tears appeared.

"You're full of shit," I said as I turned and walked home.

Unbelievably, Jamie never told a teacher, a parent, or another soul what I had done.

I agonized over most of the Christmas break, cringing every time the phone rang, thinking that it was Jamie's parents, or worse, Mrs. Tanner, ready to inform my parents about my very first act of physical violence. My worst fear was disappointing Mrs. Tanner; I held all of my teachers in highest regard and placed them on the tallest pedestals I could imagine.

I was finally put out of this misery and realized that I was in the clear when we returned to St. John's after the Christmas holiday. Jamie pouted and avoided me. He said nothing, but more importantly, Mrs. Tanner said nothing and hugged me to welcome me back to school.

A year later, Annie and I received an Easy-Bake Oven from our parents for Christmas. We couldn't wait to fire it up. Mom helped us mix one of the chocolate powder pouches with water and milk and we got to pour the mixture into the little baking pans. Once the pans were in the little oven, we jumped around with excitement and anticipation, waiting for the tiny cakes to rise and go spongy. The wait was far too long for us. We kept opening the oven to check on the cakes prompting warnings from Mother that they wouldn't cook if we didn't leave the door shut. We finally decided, on our own, that the cakes had to be finished. Far too eager, we took them out and tried to frost them. Frosting the still goopy mixture proved difficult. Annie and I grabbed spoons and ate the runny, chocolaty contents of each pan, completely uncooked. It was like eating Pablum, that icky, mushy baby food, except with a hint of chocolate flavour. I immediately lost interest in the Easy-Bake Oven. How the hell could anyone cook a cake with a light bulb anyway? It just didn't make sense.

V I

THAT WAS ALSO THE YEAR THAT MY PARENTS DECIDED THAT Mom should go back to work. Before having children, Margaret Hellers worked as a teller at the Royal Bank of Canada. Raising a family with four children required more than my father's income could provide, even in the 1970s. My brother Sean had reached school age and we were told one evening at the dinner table that Mom was hired back at the Royal Bank.

"With your Mom working, we might be able to afford a real house in the future," Dad said. "A house with land that you kids can play on and maybe we could have a vegetable garden."

We thought it all sounded great until we heard that we couldn't come home from school for lunch anymore. We would have to eat our lunch at school in our classrooms with the other kids. Mom and Dad said that they already had to hire a sitter to watch us after school and that having a sitter at lunchtime was far too expensive.

Sean had the most difficult time with the transition. The first day that Mom left for her job at the bank, Sean shook and sobbed uncontrollably. He didn't want her to leave him at school. I understood his dismay. Kindergarten was a terror, a joke, and a big pain in the ass. Mom was quickly shooed out the door by the teacher as Sean stood in the middle of the classroom, screaming.

My main concern with spending the whole day at school was that I would have to eat my lunch in front of the other kids in my class. Firstly, my mother wrapped our food in tinfoil while all the other kids had little plastic sandwich bags or plastic wrap. Secondly, our tinfoil chunks were thrown into old bread bags whereas the other kids had their perfectly wrapped sandwiches placed in tidy brown lunch bags or Scooby Doo and Flintstones lunch boxes. I began to see that we were poorer than other families, that we were, indeed, trash. Kelly Waters and her mother were right. My shame grew intensely.

What was inside our makeshift lunch containers was equally embarrassing. While the other children had peanut butter and jam sandwiches, chocolate brownies, grapes and an orange, the Hellers children had snot sandwiches.

Sometimes, when we were fortunate, we had chocolate chip cookies or maybe an apple. I remember wishing that I didn't think this way; it wasn't my Mom's fault that she only had Sandwich Spread for our lunches. At least we were fed something, except that we were always hungry. I felt a certain amount of guilt about my mother because I knew that she was trying hard to keep us fed. I could always tell when my parents got paid and did the grocery shopping; the next day, we would have peanut butter sandwiches, a luxury to us. The small jar of peanut butter didn't last long in a family of six, so surfaced the Sandwich Spread.

It was these snot sandwiches that caused me the most humiliation. I was filled with extreme anxiety with the approach of the lunch hour in my classroom, knowing that my lunch bag would reveal the dreaded snot on bread wrapped in gobs of used tinfoil.

Sometimes, one of the kids would ask me what I was eating.

"Wow, what's that?"

"It's a sandwich," I said.

"Yeah, but what *kind* of sandwich? That looks like puke! Are you really going to eat that?"

I began to wrap my sandwich with both hands so that no part of it was visible while I ate. As added insurance, I took my lunch into a corner and hid.

One day, Mrs. Tanner asked all of us to bring in something to share for a grand picnic that we would carry out on a blanket laid out on the classroom floor. All the students cheered with excitement. I cheered with them until I realized that I, too, would have to bring some food for the class picnic. It was to take place on Friday of that week so that we could come up with an idea and prepare something to bring. I figured that if I explained the situation to Mom, she would have me help her prepare something special.

When she got home from work, I told her about the upcoming picnic in my class. She was hustling around the kitchen trying to prepare dinner and didn't respond to me. I asked her if she had heard me.

"Yes, Lynn, for Christ's sake I heard you! Can't you see that I'm trying to get dinner on the table before your father gets home?"

"I know, Mom. I'm sorry. I just thought that I would tell you now so that you would have some time to think about it before Friday," I said.

"Look. Whatever I pack for you on Friday is what you're taking. I don't have the time or the money to go to any extra effort and your teacher will just have to accept that."

"Okay." I could see that she was under a great deal of stress.

When Friday rolled around, I anxiously ran to the kitchen to see what she had prepared for the picnic. I quietly reminded her about it the night before so that she wouldn't forget. She handed me a bread bag with several chunks of tinfoil.

"I made some extras for the kids in your class. Have fun at your picnic," she said as she bustled about.

On my way to school, I stopped near Ann's Confectionary to check the contents of the foil wrap before carrying on to school. To my horror, each ratty foil cell held a snot sandwich. *Oh God, what am I going to do? How could she make friggin' snot sandwiches for a special picnic? I love you, Mom, but how could you do this to me?*

I felt like throwing the foil balls and the bread bag into the garbage but there was no way I could go to Mrs. Tanner's picnic empty handed. Upon arrival at school, I walked into my classroom and placed my bag of food on the shelves with all the others. I immediately noticed the neat tidy packages: pans of Rice Crispy squares covered in plastic wrap, ceramic plates of brownies with coloured sprinkles, trays of peanut butter and sliced banana sandwiches cut into triangles, a pie plate of ham and cheese sandwiches. I wanted to find a deep hole and crawl as far into it as possible. I wouldn't even give a shit about how dark it was.

I was making my way through another *Mr. Muggs* book when Mrs. Tanner said the words that turned my blood to ice and my gut into a knot: "Okay girls and boys, it's time for our picnic!" All of the kids jumped up and down and cheered, except one. I quietly took my *Mr. Muggs* book and placed it gently on the bookshelf.

Mrs. Tanner placed the large checked-patterned blanket neatly on the floor near the reading center and asked us all to sit in a circle. Each student was given a large napkin and a paper plate. She would serve the food. *Oh God, she's going to open the snot sandwiches herself and now it's too late for me to throw them out.* All of my nerves started to hum and twitch. I wanted to run out of the room but that would only draw more attention. Mrs. Tanner started with the clear packages of sandwiches. The tray of peanut butter and banana triangles were passed around first. She moved on to the other wonderful sandwiches of ham and cheese, bologna and mustard. Each time a tray was passed around, Mrs. Tanner asked whom we had to thank for such a delight. We clapped to thank each contributor to the picnic. Then she asked a question: "Are there any other sandwiches packaged here that I haven't served yet? No dessert before the sandwich course is finished, children."

I sat in silence as I slowly nibbled the ham and cheese. Once we had gorged on the wonderful sandwiches, Mrs. Tanner moved on to serve the plates and trays of treats as we thanked the students who brought them in. As the squares and cookies were being passed around, Mrs. Tanner noticed the last bread bag still on the shelf.

"Now what do we have here?" she asked.

Where's the hole I can dive into? Maybe I should run to the bathroom.

She pulled out one of the misshapen foil globs and opened it. She looked confused. As everyone waited for her to announce yet another sweet treat, she said, "They're sandwiches. Who brought these in?"

No answer. She looked directly at me. She knew that they were mine because I was the only student who had not been thanked for their picnic gift. I was grateful that she said nothing to bring attention to me. Some of the boys said that they were still hungry and asked what kind of sandwiches they were. Mrs. Tanner looked between the bread slices and, with a contorted face, replied, "I have no idea." As soon as the boys looked at the sandwiches, they made screwy faces and said "Yuck! We don't want those. Who brought that crap?"

Mrs. Tanner said, "That's enough! That remark is very impolite. We have to be thankful for all the gifts of food we have been given." Mrs. Tanner met my gaze. She smiled weakly and I could tell that she felt sorry for me. This was far worse than the boys scoffing at my snot sandwiches.

That evening, Mother asked about the picnic. I told her it was fine. "Did your classmates like the sandwiches?" she asked.

"Sure, Mom. They were all eaten," I lied. I figured that white lies to spare a person's feelings were okay and not a real sin. The truth was that Mrs. Tanner had to throw the whole bag into the garbage. No one wanted the snot sandwiches, not even me. I felt terrible for my mother, even though she wasn't aware of it. She had tried to make the best sandwiches that she could for me.

* * * * *

Our family went through a mob of after-school babysitters once Mom took her job at the Royal Bank. Some were quite good with children and others were downright dreadful. The worst was a woman named Rebecca. She was a young single woman who took the opportunity to invite her various boyfriends over to our row house for a little afternoon delight. When one of her suitors was there, we were not permitted to enter our own house after school. We were told to go and play in the yard or find the neighbour kids to enchant us. Rebecca wouldn't even let us into the house if we had to go to the washroom. She said, "Hold it, or find a place to pee outside!" Soon, my brothers resorted to squatting in our back-yard as they released healthy tubes of shit. I informed my parents about Rebecca's idea of babysitting and they ignored me. Who the hell else would watch four young kids for the pittance of a wage my parents were willing to pay?

On the days that my parents were late or went out after work, Rebecca had the chore of feeding us dinner. She usually fed us one of two things: tomato soup or Kraft Dinner. These were the two things that she was able to cook. As we sat down to dinner, she demanded complete silence. *Shit, you're worse than my father,* I thought. She always ate the meal with us. One evening she used a spoon that had an odd bend in it to scoop up her KD and ketchup. After our parents had returned and she had left, the four of us children got together and looked curiously at the spoon in the bottom of the kitchen sink. It was crusted with that familiar powdered cheese mixture and dried smears of ketchup.

"That's the one she used," I said, "the one with the bend in it."

"It's disgusting," Annie said.

"It makes me want to puke," Wally added.

"Yucky," Sean said.

"From this day on," I stated, "not one of us will ever use this disgusting Becky Spoon. If we use it, we will get her scummy germs and be just like her. Do any of you want her yellow pit stains on your t-shirts?"

"NO!" my siblings screamed in unison.

"Good. Now remember. This spoon is the Becky Spoon," I told them as I dramatically pointed at the bent spoon in the sink. I felt like Captain Kirk on the *Starship Enterprise*; I was protecting my crew.

"We won't touch it again," Annie said.

"No way, man," Wally continued.

"No way," Sean repeated emphatically.

From that evening forward, any spoon with a bend in it was called a Becky Spoon and would only be used on the pain of death. Sometimes we caught Mom using a Becky Spoon for her soup or cereal. Inevitably, one of us would scream, "Mom! You're eating with a Becky Spoon! Get a different one. You don't want Becky's germs!" She always laughed and told us that we were crazy.

In complete contrast to Rebecca was our sitter Linda Feltcher. When our parents brought Linda into our house, we immediately knew that she was charmingly different. The first time that she babysat us, she brought craft paper, glue, markers, and crayons. I wanted her to move in with us right away. She taught us how to make pinwheels and sculptural animals out of various papers. She coloured pictures with us and praised all of our drawings. The greatest gifts from Linda, however, were the daily excursions to a nearby park. On warm, sunny days, she would pack picnic snacks and take us there to enjoy the swings, monkey bars, and sandbox. Afterward, on the walk home, she would take us for an ice cream cone. Wally had a crush on her. He told her that she was the greatest. She really was.

Then Linda became pregnant. She continued to be our sitter for a short time longer until her pregnancy made her ill. When she could no longer look after us, we actually mourned her and felt like we had lost a member of our family. I thought that her baby was going to be the luckiest kid on the planet.

After the loving and nurturing experiences provided by Linda Feltcher, we were subjected to the "care" of various young uncles, my father's brothers. Like Rebecca, they made us stay outside while they had their friends over for a hot-box drug fest. Annie, Wally, and I would take turns stepping on each other's backs to peer into the windows to see how the party was unfolding. My uncles' friends would shoot up while one of my uncles created a makeshift bong out of a Coke can. Most times, they forgot to feed us, being so overwhelmed with their own case of the "munchies." Sometimes we would make mud pies in the backyard, away from the shit corner of course, and pretend to eat them with wooden sticks. One day Wally was so hungry that he scooped a mud blob into his mouth. He chewed twice before spitting up. We heard the dirt and sand grind between his tiny teeth. Annie screamed in horror. I thought Sean's huge eyes would pop out of his head. That was it for me. I marched up to our front door and rapped loudly. My uncle Teddy answered and said, "Hey there, Norma, what do you want?"

Earlier in the year, my uncles took to calling me "Norma" after a young girl who was profiled in the *Kingston Whig Standard* because she was dying of a mysterious aging disease. My uncles thought I looked just like her. When they showed me the picture from the newspaper, I cried for an entire afternoon while they laughed uproariously. They cruelly took it further as they composed a chant: "Norma! Oooo, Oooo, Oooo. Norma! Oooo, Oooo, Oooo."

"Stop calling me Norma," I told Teddy.

"Oh, come on now, Norma. You need to relax," he said slowly with a wide grin.

"Uncle Ted, we're really hungry and you haven't given us a snack yet," I told him.

"Ah fuck! I'm really sorry, Norma. How about some chips and pretzels?"

"Sure," I said, "anything would be great."

"Okay, Norma. You wait here and I'll get you some."

He returned with two small bowls filled with salt and vinegar chips and some pretzels. "Take that and eat it outside."

I took the bowls to my sister and brothers and we established an eating routine in which we took one item from each bowl and didn't take another until everyone had finished their one chip and one pretzel. This way, nobody would get more than their fair share. After we finished the salty snack, I went back to try my luck at garnering some pop from Uncle Teddy to soothe our parched throats. He told me to get lost and take a drink from the hose outside. This is exactly what we did as we eagerly awaited our mother's arrival home.

Our daily unpredictable routine with these various babysitters and my loss of favour with some of the neighbourhood parents soon prompted me to contemplate and search for a means of escape. I was equally inspired by my father's continuous violence and my mother's frequent emotional explosions over a woman named Rita. While my father was completing his mechanics papers at a trade school in Cornwall, he had an affair with a young woman he met there. My mother found a letter and her photograph in the pocket of one of my father's jackets. Mom searched for her phone number and called her. She screamed into the phone and told Rita that she was fucking a man who had a wife and four children. Rita had no idea that Wade Hellers was married or that he had children. Through tears, she told my mother that she had actually gone the distance of introducing my father to her parents over an elegant dinner and that my father never once wore a wedding ring. Rita vowed that she would never see him again and, to my knowledge, she kept her word. Even so, that did not prevent Rita from being an unwelcome intruder in our house. It was the photograph. Pictures always hold so much power.

During the first confrontation with my father, when Mother revealed her knowledge of the affair, she tore the photograph into small pieces and threw them in my father's face. He retaliated with his usual physical violence, slamming her body into the stair railing before storming out the front door and leaving it wide open. After several minutes, to my amazement, I watched my mother kneeling in the shaft of sunlight from the door as she gathered up every single piece of the torn photograph. Still sobbing, she sat on the couch and taped the photo back together. I thought she had gone completely insane.

"Mom, why don't you throw that into the trash?" I asked her.

"Because I don't want to forget this whore's face," she answered.

My God, she really has gone insane, I thought.

I soon realized the true force behind this photograph. My mother brandished it like a lethal weapon against Father during her periodic spurts of rage and bravery. At some point during their battle, Mom would inevitably take the opportunity to run upstairs to unsheathe her instrument of harm from its mysterious location. Rita's patched photo would surely make its appearance if Joey Rowens was mentioned during an argument. Tit for tat.

After one skirmish, the weapon was left on one of the end tables. When no one was in the living room, I took the opportunity to carefully examine it. She was pretty but not nearly as beautiful as my mother. Still, I could tell that Rita was attractive, even though the white, jagged rip lines made her face look like a sloppy mosaic. I wanted to take the Rita mosaic and bury it under the shit in the backyard, but I didn't dare. This was the only instrument of influence that my mother had to give her an edge in battle.

I longed for an escape, a rescue for me and my siblings. I was only eight and my options were unmistakably limited. I came up with a daring request. I decided to ask my mother if I could start going to Nanny and Grandpa Carron's after school every day and especially on Fridays so that I could spend the weekends. To my great surprise, she agreed as long as it was convenient for my grandparents. I wasted no time calling them on the telephone to explain my splendid idea. Though excited, I felt enormous guilt because it could not involve my sister and brothers. It was a terrible lesson in survival, leaving people you love behind.

Of course, my adoring grandparents agreed to my request as long as their schedule allowed it. They worried about me walking all the way from St. John's Elementary School to downtown Princess Street. I told them not to worry. "I'm definitely old enough to take care of myself," I said with confidence. As luck would have it, I was mugged within the first month. On my way to their apartment after school, three teenagers accosted me on Montreal Street near the military armouries. There were two males and one female. The girl was the worst. She pushed me down and threw my books onto the grass. She poked my bag of dill pickle chips out of my arms. I bought these chips with a quarter given to me by my grandfather. It was this fact that enraged me, not that I was losing my chips. One of the boys picked them up, opened the bag, and started eating them as he laughed loudly. The girl continued to rifle through my pockets and took what little change I had. She said, "Wow, a whole fucking ten cents."

I sat on the grass and said nothing as they all joined in a choir of laughter. I was so terrified of them that I didn't even think of anything rude or clever that I would want to say. It was rather humorous that I was this afraid of them, yet I was so close to telling my father to drop dead.

Once they had their kicks, the one boy threw the remainder of the bag of chips at me and the girl told me to have a nice day. The other boy actually picked up my books and handed them to me. The girl said, "What the fuck are you doing, you little pussy?" He did not reply and the trio walked away. I was just grateful that they hadn't beaten the shit out of me.

When I got to my grandparents' place, I told them what had happened. My grandfather went absolutely ballistic. He yelled, "Those bastards! What did they do to you? Were they fucking hippies?!"

My grandmother broke in, "Earl! Watch your language!"

I said, "It's okay, Nanny. I've heard those words lots of times."

"No doubt," she replied in a low, quiet voice.

"They weren't hippies, Grandpa," I told him, "they were teenagers. The hippies are nice. I really like them. They're really friendly."

"Oh good Christ, she likes hippies," Grandpa said, disgusted, throwing his arms in the air.

"Earl!" my grandmother yelled.

"I'm sorry, Aggie. Okay, Lynn, where did this happen?" he asked.

I told them the story of my mugging drama. My grandfather wanted me to take him to the exact spot of the crime so that he could hunt down the guilty culprits.

"They're not going to still be there, Grandpa."

"Well, I suppose not. Starting tomorrow, I'm walking you to school and meeting you after school," he told me. I was thrilled.

He was a man of his word. The following day, he handed me an enormous paper bag full of lunch items as he put on a short-sleeved dress shirt over his customary undershirt that he tucked into his black pants, and then escorted me to school. I held his hand the whole way and felt so proud to be with him.

The lunch he packed for me was always divine and I never felt embarrassed. This made me feel more guilt about my mother and her attempts to feed four children when my father was more concerned with cases of beer than loaves of bread. Grandpa packed ham and cheese sandwiches, jellyrolls, a banana, and chocolate pudding. Most times, he packed so much food that I had to bring some back home with me. At the end of the school day, there he would be waiting for me by the fence with a huge smile across his toothless mouth. I didn't bother with any of the kids; I ran to him and excitedly grabbed his hand to begin our walk. He always gave my sister and brothers a hug before we left the school. Annie was given the responsibility of escorting our two younger siblings home. I was constantly conflicted with guilt because I knew that they wanted to come with us.

During this period, on our walks to Princess Street, Grandpa couldn't resist the urge to scout the streets for the kids who had mugged me. He would point out every teenager and ask me if they were one of the offenders.

"No, Grandpa. That's not one of them," I told him each time.

The truth was that I never did see them again. "One of God's small mercies," Nanny explained one night, before hoisting me onto her window ledge and completing our nightly ritual recitation of "Twinkle, Twinkle, Little Star".

Grandpa lasted one more week walking me to and from school. He became far too exhausted to continue the pace. He asked me if I felt safe enough to continue on my own. "You bet," I replied. I was so grateful that I had had those two weeks of walks with him on my own.

"You make sure that you tell me if anything happens to you, honey, because if anyone hurts you again, I'll break their little fucking neck," Grandpa told me, well out of earshot of my grandmother. He meant it; I could tell. It never occurred to me to tell him about anything that ever happened on home turf where there was an expectation of safety and security beyond the teenagers and hippies of the streets.

V I I

IT WAS DURING MY GRADE THREE AFTER-SCHOOL AND WEEKEND visits to Nanny and Grandpa Carron that I learned about Watergate and that Nanny had terminal cancer. These two events became entwined and synonymous. Richard Nixon faced the brutal fire at the same time as my grandmother. For this reason, I felt sympathy for him, especially when I eventually saw snot running down his nose on national television.

When I first heard about Nixon and Watergate, I pictured a floodgate letting loose. I saw an enormous deluge that Nixon must have caused and apparently, his "plumbers" were being no help at all. I didn't really get it; why would the President of the United States unleash a tidal wave on his country? It would be years before I learned that Watergate was the name of a hotel where Nixon had his henchmen bug the Democratic headquarters. But in 1973 to 1974, I thought Nixon was being swallowed and beaten by a huge flood, just like my grandmother.

While various politicians discussed and debated the events of Watergate on my grandparents' small television, my grandmother got dressed for an appointment with her doctor. I listened to the newscast while my Nanny prepared herself so quietly. I watched her put on her clip-on pearl earrings and straighten her light green dress. My grandfather was equally quiet and tried to keep busy by polishing the dining table. I sensed the seriousness of both situations. As Walter Cronkite took his solemn tone about the Watergate involvement of John Ehrlichman, Howard Hunt, and G. Gordon Liddy, my grandparents surprisingly said nothing, when usually Watergate was a hot topic in the apartment.

We arrived at the hospital by taxi and Grandpa and I watched Nanny greet the reception staff as a nurse led her down a short hall and out of sight. We silently leafed through magazines in the waiting room. I could tell that Grandpa was worried. He hadn't smiled all day.

"Nanny's okay, isn't she?" I asked him.

"Of course she is, honey," he replied, "she's just having a check-up."

The check-up took a very long time, at least from a young child's point of view. Nanny came down the hall from her appointment with a straight mouth. She looked stunned. She said nothing as my grandfather put his arm around her waist and I took her by the hand. The fault line had shifted and the tidal wave began, but I didn't know it yet.

"How would you like to go for an ice cream cone, Lynn?" Nanny asked with a wide smile.

"Oh, I would love it, Nan!" I replied, grateful that the tone of the moment had lightened.

"Let's go get some ice cream, Earl," she said.

"Anything," he replied, as he held her close.

* * * * *

Nanny was admitted to the Hotel Dieu Hospital in the cancer ward. My mother took me aside after breakfast one morning to tell me. She said the word. Cancer. I knew what it was. It had spread to her liver. I started crying immediately, before she had even finished telling me about Nanny's situation. She hugged me and cried too. It was one of the most tender and gentle moments that I have ever shared with my mother.

I went to school. I couldn't stop crying, but kept trying to hide it. My grade three teacher, the wonderful Mrs. Blair, noticed and initiated a prayer circle. She asked if anyone wanted to devote a prayer to someone. My hand went up first and that was extremely rare. Mrs. Blair addressed me:

"Lynn, do you have someone or something that you want us to pray for?" she asked.

"Yes." I kept crying.

"My Grandma Carron has cancer," I blurted out. "My mother says that she might die."

I gasped and cried harder.

Mrs. Blair was rendered speechless. My classmates beside me tried to comfort and talk to me, but I asked them, kindly, to please leave me alone. My teacher began the Our Father prayer and everyone participated with complete reverence. I did my best to follow along.

Mrs. Blair phoned my mother. Mom left work to pick me up from school. On the way home, we both sobbed together. She took me to Ann's Confectionary and bought me some chocolate milk to soothe my stomach. It always seemed to work.

I told my mother that I wanted to see my Nanny as much as possible. Mom took me to the Hotel Dieu Hospital and helped me learn the route to my grandmother's room. The nurses and doctors came to know me very well and we always shared the peace sign. I told my mother that I wanted to visit Nanny every day after school. Because she worked downtown at the Royal Bank, she said that was okay. I could go home with her afterward or spend the night with Grandpa. Either way, I needed to see Nanny.

I returned to school a couple of days after the prayer circle. Beautiful Mrs. Blair had the class write letters to one of two people. Earlier in the week that I told my class about Nanny, we had a visitor who brought us fresh clams in the spirit of exploratory cuisine. I don't remember the woman's name, but she was the other letter recipient. Most of my classmates chose to write to Nanny, as did Mrs. Blair, though I know that she wrote to the other lady too. She was always fair. She gave me a large envelope of letters to present to my Grandma. I thought that this was the nicest thing that anyone had ever done for my family; I smiled at all of my classmates. Many of them came to me to put their arm around me or give me a hug. Jamie Bowden approached me carefully and told me that he was so sad to hear about my grandmother. At that point, all was forgiven with Jamie Bowden.

After school that day, I excitedly ran most of the way to the Hotel Dieu Hospital. I couldn't wait to present Nanny with the envelope of letters. When I arrived at her room, my mother and grandfather were already there. Patting the bed, Nanny said, "Climb up here beside me, dear."

As Grandpa helped me position myself beside her, I noticed small purple bruises on the thin, almost transparent skin of the tops of her hands.

"Why are there bruises on your hands, Nan?" I asked her.

"Oh, they're from needles," she replied.

I shivered. That had to hurt. I couldn't even bear to have the thick pad of my finger pricked for a tiny spot of blood.

"I have a surprise for you," I told her as I revealed the large envelope.

"Well, what do we have here?" she asked with a lovely smile.

Mom and Grandpa chimed in with "Oh and ah."

We watched Nanny open the envelope with shaking hands. I fought back tears as I watched those trembling hands, clear signs of her weakened state. She carefully removed all of the neatly folded letters and began reading them.

"What a nice thing for your friends to do," she said with an unsteady voice.

She read each one of them aloud for all of us to hear. Among the well wishes, the sentiments of "get better soon," and descriptions of my tearful day in class, one letter stood out:

Dear Mrs. Carron,

Thank you for visitting our clas. I sur did like those clams. I hope that you come agian.

From Mark

I looked at the words on the page as she read. *Oh, you friggin' idiot, Mark,* I thought, *can't you get anything right?* In my head, it sounded like my father's voice.

"I don't understand this one," Nanny said.

"That letter is for another lady who visited my class, Nanny," I explained with exasperation. "She brought us some clams and Mark must have mixed her name up with yours. He's such a goof. He never pays attention to anything important. And look, the dope can't even spell," I told her.

Everyone started laughing. Nanny laughed until her belly hurt. Suddenly, the mistake that Mark had made wasn't such a bad thing. Even though I thought he was a dumb turd, he had made my Nanny laugh. She later entertained all her visitors with Mark's "clam" letter.

Each day after school, I went to the hospital to spend time with her. We did countless crossword puzzles and read stories to each other. We shared her gifts of sweet, sugar slices of limes, oranges, and lemons arranged beautifully in a light brown box with blue tissue paper. We took turns trying the endless different chocolates, always taking a small bite so that we could display the surprise centers of toffee, cherries, or hazelnuts. I did drawings of daffodils, tulips, and sunflowers. My grandfather taped the paper garden to the wall so Nanny could see it.

Inevitably, my grandfather would arrive with magazines, a small bundle of flowers, and more treats. He routinely gave Nanny a kiss on the mouth before placing the flowers carefully in a mason jar. My mother would make her entrance soon after, once her workday was done. We engaged in lively chats about Nanny's favourite nurses, Mom's annoying manager at the bank, and President Nixon's looming impeachment. I could never keep up with the impeachment talk, so I leafed through Nan's new magazines and continued munching on her chocolates. Mom always had to leave first; she had dinner to prepare at home. Each time, she asked me if I was coming with her and each time I told her that I wanted to stay with Nanny and Grandpa. The routine rarely varied.

"Well, you'll have to ask Grandpa if that's okay," Mom told me, as she smiled slyly at her father.

"Is it okay if I come home with you, Grandpa?" I asked politely.

As he patted me on the leg, he said, "Of course you can come with me! I'll make you a delicious dinner and then we'll have a checkers tournament. What do you think about that?"

"Yeah!" I squealed, "Thank you so much, Grandpa!"

Once Mother had left, Grandpa and I waited with Nanny until she finished her dinner and received her medication. Most of the meals didn't appeal to her and she would only pick at them, really just moving it all around instead of eating it. Grandpa always encouraged her to eat something and she would force bits of it down just to please him. She was served segmented plates of runny corn, mushy meat that reminded me of Prince's canned Zip dog food, and mashed potatoes that looked like the thick, pasty glue I used at school. I eventually tasted both the hospital potatoes and my classroom glue and found that the latter was far more appetizing.

After my grandmother had her evening medication, Grandpa and I would kiss her and begin the short walk back to Princess Street, telling her that we would see her again the following day. Back at their apartment, my grandfather started his promised delicious meal.

"What are you going to make for us tonight?"

"How about some chicken legs, green beans, and mashed potatoes, and when I say mashed potatoes, I mean the GOOD kind," he said.

"I can't wait," I told him as I jumped up and down. "Is there anything you want me to do to help?"

"Nothing at all, dear. You go on in and watch television," he said as he snapped fresh green beans into a silver pot. To this day, I smile every time I hear those green bean sounds, *snap, plunk*.

As I went into the living room, I took my place on the couch, leaving my Nanny's spot clear in case she suddenly came home. It would be wrong to sit in her place anyway. I wouldn't even let my teacher or the queen of England sit in her place. No way.

Instead of the evening news, which seemed to be on every channel, I took my tablet of paper and began sketching. I drew a picture of Grandpa, Nanny, and me getting ice cream cones down by Confederation Park in Kingston. It was one of my fondest memories. I worked on this drawing using meticulous detail; in it, Nanny had a vanilla cone, Grandpa had maple walnut, and mine is chocolate. *I will give this to Nanny as a present.*

While working on the picture, I heard the tinkling of ice on glass in the kitchen and the "glug, glug" of liquid pouring into it, making the tinkling sound of the ice even more pleasant. I decided to investigate. After all, Grandpa might be pouring some ginger ale for me, as I was consistently concerned with the state of my own guts. Upon entry into the small kitchen, I watched Grandpa as he finished pouring himself a large glass of white Bacardi rum, no mix. I knew that he drank it as often as he could, working hard to keep it hidden from Nanny. She did not approve and scolded him like a child whenever she caught him, but she wasn't there.

"You're having a nice glass of rum, Grandpa," I said, smiling.

Caught by surprise, he jumped, causing some of the rum to spill on the counter.

"Um, yes I am, dear," he replied, "and please don't tell your grand-mother, okay?"

"I won't. I know that she doesn't like it and I wouldn't want her to be mad at you."

"Thank you, dear. Your Nanny doesn't understand that I need it to steady my nerves."

"It's okay," I told him. *At least you're not mean like my dad.*

No he was never mean, in fact, he was quite entertaining. As we sat eating at the coffee table and despite my declarations to the contrary, he became convinced that I needed more food, took my plate, and staggered into the kitchen, piling it with a heap of seconds as he giggled like a boy. I ate and ate until my tummy popped out.

He told me, as he gulped his rum, "I lived through the Great Depression, sweetheart, and I can't bear the thought of anyone being hungry. Hunger is a terrible thing."

After dinner, we played a game of checkers that Grandpa lost miserably. He slurred, "You're priddy good at dis game." I laughed. He was never much of a challenge when he was taking his rum.

"Well, I should be good, Grandpa, because you are the one who taught me to play."

The drink didn't only affect Grandpa's performance at checkers. He seemed to cough and hack much less than usual and his spit can didn't see as much action. I was undeniably grateful for this. To say that my grandfather was a heavy smoker is an understatement of the highest order. I rarely saw his right hand without a homemade butt hanging between his yellow-brown index and middle fingers, the latter bent into a dramatic hook after being slammed in the door of a car when he was a boy.

Between his incessant smoking and his early work in the deep, black, Nova Scotia coalmines, his lungs were a mess. His constant companion was an old tobacco can stuffed with Kleenex. He emptied his lungs and throat of the thick, gray oysters of mucous and expertly dropped the gobs into the tissue-lined can, which he called his "spit can". Every time he smoked a cigarette, the gobs would fly. If he had a few drinks, he could count on a reprieve. It was the thick, indefinable chunks floating within the soupy contents of my grandfather's spit can that made me vow that I would never smoke.

That evening after checkers, Grandpa poured himself another rum and we watched *M*A*S*H*, a show we both loved. We watched Hawkeye and Trapper expertly flirt with the pretty nurses as Radar alerted the unit to the incoming wounded. I was profoundly affected by *M*A*S*H*, its playful humour always cut short by the horrors of war.

Regardless of how much he drank, Grandpa consistently and expertly prepared my bed with pristine white sheets and soft blankets on the pull-out couch. Before going to sleep, he never failed to ask me to say a special prayer for Nanny, which I never failed to do:

Dear God and Jesus,

Please watch over Nanny and take good care of her so that she can get better. Please don't let her have any more pain. She has had enough. Watch over Grandpa too. He's worried and lonely without her. Oh, and look out for my mom, my sister and brothers. Thank You God and Jesus,

Our Father, who art in Heaven...

The words I spoke to God rarely changed and I always ended with a heartfelt Our Father prayer. There were certain occasions that I felt compelled to add one further request: *Dear God and Jesus, if there is any way that you could make my father go away and never come back, I would really appreciate it.* This was long before I started praying to God to kindly remove my father from the Earth in a terrible fiery car crash.

While Nanny was in the hospital, Grandpa and I prepared the apartment for her return. We waxed and polished the wood floors, did all the laundry with the old white wringer washer hooked up to the kitchen sink, scoured the tub, and planted Grandpa's prized tomato plants in pots on the back deck of the apartment building. This was the time I discovered what an incredible artist he was. I watched intently as he lovingly planted each tomato stalk and staked them with a careful, steady hand. As I watched him arrange the leaves and the blossoms, tying them gently with attractive knots to the stakes, I thought of my own drawings. He, too, was mindful of detail, placement of lines, and balance. His work was beautiful. When his plants finally bore fruit, they reminded me of tiny Christmas trees with full, shiny red globes of colour.

While Grandpa planted his tomatoes, he sipped on a glass of rum. He had to take advantage of the moment, since Nanny would be home soon. Once the last plant was tucked into the soil, he took me aside for a chat. We sat on the old wooden chairs on the back deck and, as he finished his glass of rum, he explained that he had some hiding places for his drink.

He said, "I'm going to show you all my new hiding places, and when your grandmother gets home, I want you to distract her with something to get her away from my secret spots. Your Nanny is an excellent sleuth. She's better than Sherlock Holmes, for Christ's sake. She always finds my stuff and pours it down the sink, but if you give her a distraction, she might forget about what she's looking for. Maybe you could show her a drawing or something, aye?"

"Sure, Grandpa," I replied with a grin. I didn't relish lying to my grandmother, but I thought she would, indeed, be happier if she didn't know the booze was there. It didn't really occur to me that she would surely know when he was drinking anyway and be upset whether she could find the bottle or not.

Grandpa showed me his secret hiding places one by one. He hid a "mickey" of Bacardi in the toe of one of his huge rubber boots sitting upright among the countless pairs on the mat; another behind a large silver potato pot at the very back of a low kitchen cupboard; and my personal favourite for its ingenuity, the bottle that was hidden in a pinned sleeve of an overcoat inside the curtained closet by the bathroom.

The day that Nanny finally returned home, the apartment was spotless and Grandpa had put fresh flowers in a vase on the gleaming dining table. Uncle Harland, Grandpa, and I excitedly jumped into Harland's car to bring her out of the Hotel Dieu. When we picked her up, she smiled broadly, but I could see that she was very weak. Uncle Harland and Grandpa had to hold her up by her arms and seat her into a wheelchair. I was horrified.

I asked, "Do you have to use a wheelchair now, Nanny?"

"No dear," she replied smiling, "it's just to help me get to the car."

I looked at her very closely. She was much thinner. I could see cords of sickly purple veins sticking out of her needle marked arms; her neck appeared to miraculously hold her head on with wiry tendons. Her hair was dull, gray, and thinning. She was no longer smiling and her brown eyes were glazed over and looked like mud. Though I had visited her every single day in the hospital, I had not noticed the transformation until that moment, when she was no longer lying down in the hospital bed. All parts of her seemed to be slowly disappearing, except for her stomach. It seemed to be swollen and didn't fit with the rest of her body. She looked like she wasn't going to give two shits about Grandpa's Bacardi rum stash.

Back at home, Grandpa, Harland, and I worked diligently to make sure that Nanny was comfortable and cared for. She was delighted with all the extra work we had done with the apartment. We helped her out onto the back deck so that she could watch the sun dance all over Grandpa's tomato plants.

She smiled and said, "Earl, these plants are wonderful and I need to get my hair done."

The dramatically odd juxtaposition of her thoughts made us all laugh until tears appeared.

The following day, my mother came over and dyed Nanny's hair. She styled it for her with rollers and bobby pins followed by a little Dippity Do on the bangs. Mother had fine hair herself and had a unique and effective way of making hair look thicker than it was. Nanny looked renewed and was thrilled with my mother's handiwork. This became a weekly routine, my mother going over to her parents' home to style her mother's hair. I always went with her and loved to watch her add more colour and volume to my Nanny's life.

VIII

I BECAME DETERMINED TO SPEND THAT SUMMER WITH NANNY and Grandpa Carron, the summer of 1974. Before school one day in late June, I phoned them and asked if they would have me for the whole summer. I had already asked Mom, and she said that it was okay as long as my grandparents agreed. They did. I couldn't wait for school to be finished.

I had also made a new friend at school. Her name was Charlotte Clark. I liked her immediately because of her name. I had just finished reading *Charlotte's Web* with Mrs. Blair. Charlotte Clark wore leg braces periodically after having suffered with polio. She was very kind and intelligent and I loved making her laugh. If I could stay with my grandparents, I would be able to see more of her as well. I decided to introduce Charlotte to them.

On the day of the visit, Charlotte's parents gave us money to take a taxi to 187A Princess Street. On the way up the long staircase of the apartment building, I realized that I had told Charlotte nothing about my Nanny's illness. All I told her was how spectacular my grandparents were. As we entered the apartment, I nervously looked at Charlotte and then at my Nanny who was sitting in her usual spot on the couch. Nanny looked terrible. She was still wearing her nightgown and slippers; her hair was a mess and her stomach protruded grossly, pushing at the buttons of her gown. She knew I was embarrassed as soon as I didn't introduce her. She looked away and stared at the television.

I took Charlotte into the kitchen and introduced her to Grandpa. He chatted with us good-naturedly and offered us some juice and a jellyroll. We said no thanks because we were headed to the park near Charlotte's house.

"Well, it was very nice to meet you, Charlotte," Grandpa said.

"It was nice meeting you too, sir."

As Charlotte and I left my grandparents' home, we walked silently past Nanny. I looked at her and saw that she was still staring at the television, saying nothing. As we left the apartment, I felt like I was going to puke. I had ignored my beloved grandmother. I was ashamed of her because illness had altered her appearance to an astonishing degree. *Lynn Hellers, you are a selfish piece of shit.* How could I deny knowing her, of all people?

"What's wrong with your grandmother, Lynn?" Charlotte asked, "It looks like she's pregnant."

"She has cancer," I told her, almost in a whisper.

"Oh, God! I'm so sorry. Now I remember. She's the one we wrote letters to."

"Yes," I replied.

"Wow, that's really sad," Charlotte said.

"Yes it is. Um, Charlotte, I don't really feel like going to the park anymore. Would you mind if I just walked you home? I need to go spend time with my Nanny."

"But I thought we were going to play for a while," she replied, disappointed.

"I'll see you at school tomorrow, okay? I don't think that my grandmother is feeling very well and I should talk to her."

"Okay. Maybe we can go to the park next week, then."

"Sure."

I practically pushed poor Charlotte home, taxing her aching back and legs. After saying hello to her mother and goodbye to her, I ran my hardest back to Princess Street. When I walked into my grandparents' apartment, I was extraordinarily winded. I bent over because my side ached and had to sit down on the floor of the entryway to remove my sneakers. Nanny was still staring at the television watching *The Edge of Night*, one of her favourite soap operas.

Slowly, I approached Nanny and sat gently beside her on the couch. Still breathing heavily from my run, I leaned into her. Without shifting her gaze from the television, she asked me how my visit was with Charlotte.

"It was okay," I told her, "but I really felt like coming back home."

Nanny smiled and patted me on the leg. I wanted to cry.

"Would you like to do the Whiz Word with me?" she asked.

"I would love it," I replied, gulping and fighting tears.

As Nanny and I worked our way through the word find puzzle, Grandpa made us tea and brought us a plate of Peak Freans. All seemed right with the world.

Until Canada Day, 1974. With school finished, I had been staying happily with my grandparents. When July 1 rolled around, Grandpa took me to the Smoke Shop and bought me some small fireworks and sparklers so that we could celebrate our nation's birthday on the back porch of the apartment building. We weren't supposed to shoot fireworks from there, but Grandpa said we could break the rules because he was the superintendent of the building. This was true. He always had to clean the apartments before a new tenant took over and rid the place of the layers of crud and dirt along with the array of the used syringes taped to the tops of the door frames. He cursed the "hippies and freaks" every time he had to do it.

When we brought the fireworks home, Nanny was delighted that we were going to have a little Canada Day party. She even asked Grandpa to pour her a gin and tonic, which he did with a skip in his step. It was license for him to hit the Bacardi. We planned to make a full night of it. I squirmed with anticipation and couldn't wait to set off one of the fireballs. Even before nightfall, Grandpa took us onto the deck and shot off one of the small rockets. I squealed with excitement at the wonder of the light and colour, green fireballs, red fireballs, and bursts of white sparks. Grandpa lit a sparkler for me and I made pictures in the air.

Grandpa said, "It'll be even more spectacular, honey, when it's actually dark outside. Let's go have some dinner and then we'll fire off the rest of 'em, aye?"

"Okay, Grandpa. I can't wait! Happy Canada Day!"

As he prepared our dinner, my parents showed up. They said that they were picking me up to go out to Nanny Ida's cottage to shoot off fireworks. Everyone was going, my family, my aunts and uncles, their kids, my grandmother Ida, some of her friends, and my uncles' friends. There was a mound of fireworks to set off and the plan was to follow up with a huge bonfire. I really didn't want to go and leave Nanny and Grandpa Carron, but my parents said the magic words: "Your sister and brothers miss you."

"Can you come with us Nan and Grandpa?" I asked.

"Oh, no dear," Nanny said with a smile, "that would be far too much activity for me."

I was torn. I missed my sister and brothers and was excited about the prospect of watching almost endless fireworks.

It was as if my grandparents were reading my mind. Grandpa said, "Here, dear, you take this bag of fireworks with you and then you can enjoy them with Annie, Wally, and Sean."

"But you bought these for our own party, Grandpa. Then you and Nanny won't get to see them," I told him with deep concern and a measure of guilt.

"We got them for you, honey, so you take them with you and enjoy them, okay?" Nanny added.

"Really?"

"Yes, sweetie. Here, take the bag and have a good time," Grandpa said as he hooked my arm through the bag.

"There you go," my father said, "we'll shoot them off at the cottage with all the others."

I walked over to both Nanny and Grandpa, hugged and kissed them, and thanked them for the fireworks.

As we left my grandparents' home, I had mixed feelings. I wanted to see the kids and all the fireworks, but I felt guilty about leaving Nanny and Grandpa's Canada Day party. Once I entered the car, my mind eased. There sat my sister and brothers with huge, excited smiles.

"W-w-we are g-g-going to w-w-watch f-fire w-works, L-L-Lynn," Sean said, grinning. He had already started to stutter. I don't remember exactly when it began, but it took many years for him to shake it. Sometimes we cruelly made fun of him.

"I know," I replied, "it's going to be fun. Nanny and Grandpa Carron gave us some fireworks too."

We arrived on the Isle of Man just before dark. The party was well underway. All I had to do was look at all the cars randomly parked in the driveway, on the grass, or halfway in the woods; one Buick practically on top of the other. There were two old rusty, yet functional, refrigerators outside the cottage door. They were clearly full of booze, judging by the full cases of beer stacked beside them, always plenty of adult drink to go around. Music blasted from the stereo set up outside. It was the unmistakable raspy voice of Janis:

> Busted flat in Baton Rouge,
> Waitin' for a train,
> I's feelin' nearly as faded as my jeans.

Janis Joplin, *Me and Bobby McGee*

Before we even reached the side yard of the cottage, cousins ran to greet us, as did several drunken uncles. The only sober uncle was my Uncle Jimmy. Though he was one of my father's eight brothers, he was only seven and a half years old, my grandmother's tenth child. Behind him, I saw the enormous heap of wood and brush that was to be later ignited for one of the infamous Isle of Man bonfires. With each greeting we were told about the unending supply of fireworks that we were about to enjoy.

Just then, one of my aunts said in a slurred voice, "Lynnie, it's your responsibility to look out for all the kids and make sure the little ones don't go near the water." Suddenly I realized why my parents had made a special trip to pick me up at my grandparents' apartment. This was not uncommon. Whenever there was a large family gathering, I was consistently told that I was in charge of all of the younger children. Did they forget that when kids were in my care that they ended up with their heads cracked open and got hit by cars? I immediately realized that this July 1 event was not going to be near as enjoyable as I had hoped. How right I was.

Because most other adults there were irretrievably drunk and because he had just arrived, my father set up the sand bucket near the shoreline for the fireworks. Everyone squealed with excitement with each colourful burst of light and the loud pop, pop, whistle, pop, from the paper cones and tubes. As per tradition, we finished with the explosion and burning of the little schoolhouse. We all cheered as loud as we could. I kept my responsibility by ensuring that none of the children got too close to the sand bucket.

After the fireworks, all the adults took a break to get another beverage, while my Uncle Garrett started the bonfire. I, too, went into the cottage to find myself a glass of pop. The place was a colossal trashcan. There were empty bottles and gobs of macaroni salad all over the counters, table, and floor. There was dirt grimed into the lines of the linoleum. Ashtrays overflowed, keeping good company with the spilled garbage bag, and there were half-eaten hotdogs on the table and one on the arm of the dingy couch. A used baby diaper was rolled into a ball and placed on the stove. Every light bulb had a swarm of night bugs dancing around it. Thick-bodied spiders hung and nestled in their webs all over the ceiling and in the corners. The only place that had more big, juicy spiders was the outhouse. Enduring the unbearable stench was one thing, but this tiny chipboard structure was an arachnophobic's worst nightmare. I preferred to piss in the long grass and shit in the woods.

In the kitchen, I found my Nanny Ida mixing herself a large Five Star whiskey cut with cola. Nanny's eyes clicked. Her hair was separated into gobs of bleached curls. There were red lipstick smudges all around the rim of her glass. Even plastered beyond belief, she still managed to reapply her lipstick but she couldn't swipe a brush through her hair. I asked her if I could please have a glass of soda.

"Sure, Lollipop," she slurred. She closed one eye while she looked at me and rocked against the counter. She staggered to the indoor refrigerator and pulled out a huge bottle of orange pop.

"Here you go, hon," she said, "and be sure to share it with the other kids."

"Thanks, Nan," I replied with a smile.

I hated orange pop, but when she opened the fridge, I could see that it was the only option. I took the bottle outside and we all passed it around as we watched the bonfire throw its flames into the air. As the fire wore down, my uncles discovered that we were short of wood. They skulked quietly through the dark, explored several cottages down the river, and returned with someone's picnic table that they promptly tossed onto the fire. No one thought anything of it.

My parents and all the other adults continued to get pleasantly polluted, making jokes about prior crimes and incarcerations or vividly discussing their boldest bodily functions. The most creative of them would grace the group with a story that combined the two: "The last time the cops dragged me in, they thought that I had swallowed a bag of my stash. To prove them wrong, I shit right there on the floor in the police station," someone said. Howls of laughter echoed through the night air.

My cousin Darren remembered that my grandmother had brought several bags of marshmallows that were just begging to be roasted. All of the children spun into an intense frenzy and bombarded her for the bags of sugar pillows.

"You each need to get yourselves a good stick," Nanny Ida said slowly.

"Okay!" we all screamed in unison.

I took my sister and brothers to get a good pointy stick for marshmallow roasting. There was no shortage in the thick brush out back of the cottage. We endured the mosquitoes with the rest of the kids, and broke solid green twigs for the fire. My brother Sean was having trouble with his and panicked as the other children raced toward the bonfire with their roasting skewers in hand.

He yelled, "L-L-Lynn, I c-c-can't g-get th-th-th-this stick!"

I almost made fun of him until I saw his huge terrified eyes in the semi-darkness.

"It's okay," I told him, "I'll help you. Here, let me try."

I managed to break off a good length of stick and I stripped it of leaves for him. He smiled widely and said, " Th-thanks! L-Let's go!"

After the marshmallow roast, all of the kids started to drop like flies. I was tired too, but didn't dare shirk my responsibility, especially when it came to my sister and brothers. Some of the children would be sleeping in Nanny Ida's cottage and others would sleep in Aunt Judy and Uncle Steve's cottage. One was right beside the other, but the big party was usually at Nanny Ida's. I wondered, with all the people there, where everyone was going to find a place to lay their heads.

My Aunt Bonnie orchestrated the initial sleeping arrangements. My siblings and I would sleep in the room full of bunk beds in Nanny Ida's cottage. My cousin Darren and my young uncle Jimmy would sleep together on a top bunk. Annie and I would take a lower bed, while my younger brothers had a single of their own.

After a short chat with Darren about going fishing the next day, everyone started to fall asleep. Sleep was always difficult at the cottage because of the noise. On this occasion, Johnny Cash and the *Folsom Prison Blues* took over where Janis and the others left off, always turned up to the max, while most of the drunken adults were screaming to be heard.

At some point in the middle of the night, I woke up to the smell of musty blankets and a hand rubbing my chest. It was a large hand. My tiny breasts had just begun to grow, resulting in a painful, itching sensation. I didn't move and hoped that the hand would just stop and go away. It didn't. I wanted to scream, but I couldn't. No sound would come out of my open mouth. I think that I stopped breathing. Suddenly all of my nerve endings fired. I sat bolt upright and quickly scrambled over the body beside me. Then he spoke:

"Relax, okay," he said in a whisper. I knew the voice. It was one of my Uncle Garrett's friends; I caught him staring at me during the bonfire. At the time, I just thought that he was rudely curious, wondering, as so many had before him, whether I was a boy or a girl.

I leapt out of the bed and noticed that my sister was gone. Despite my worry about her, I stumbled my way through the darkness, tripping over one passed out drunk after another, all lying haphazardly over the hard, dirty floor. I fell heavily on one body that released a barely audible groan. I made it through the maze of bodies to the cottage door and escaped into the cool night air. As I left the steps and rounded the corner, I slipped and fell into a large puddle. Once the stink hit my nostrils, I realized I was sitting in a huge pool of vomit. Someone had emptied their stomach right outside the door on the path to the river.

Again, I wanted to scream, but I couldn't make a sound. *This has to be a nightmare.* But it wasn't. There were smelly chunks of puke on my hands and the ass of my shorts. This was far too real.

I ran. I ran fast. I ran as fast as I could over to my Aunt Judy's dock. I slid off the end and tried to scrub my body as best I could. Soaking wet and sitting on the dock, I braved the mosquitoes and marvelled over the beautiful night sky. I prayed to God, out loud, to have Nanny and Grandpa Carron come get me. Then I screamed.

I X

NOT UNLIKE NANNY CARRON, MY PHYSICAL SHELL BEGAN TO transform. I became a character from a Kafka novel, a bug lying on its back; I became Wilde's picture of Dorian Gray as its beauty altered into sheer ugliness, a reflection of what laid inside. I stopped bathing. Stopped washing my hair. Stopped giving a shit about what I smelled like.

It is this photograph of me in my Grade 4 class, wrinkled in the plastic S&R bag, that best reflects my metamorphosis. If I asked anyone who didn't know me to find me in this picture, they would have a difficult time, because they would probably be looking for a girl. Even the photographer who took the picture that day at St. Patrick's Elementary School was confused. He placed me in the middle row complete with smiling young boys. The girls stood on a bench behind us or sat, upright and proper with hands folded, on a bench in front. Charlotte is sitting there, up front, with her checked pants and a beautiful small-toothed smile that joins the rosy full cheeks of her cute baby face. When the photographer placed me in the middle row, I was too embarrassed to make him aware of his error. I was grateful that none of the other kids seemed to notice. Maybe they all thought I was a boy named Lynn.

This was understandable. I stood there smiling with hideously crooked teeth, a gap between the two front ones that was as spacious as any doorway. My head looked as if it might drip grease at any moment, the cords of fine hair saturated with body oil and separated into rows, revealing spaces of bare scalp. I wore a brown suit trimmed with orange, a perfect match to the one my sister Annie wore that day, only she looked like a girl and made a pretty picture. My Nanny Ida insisted on stealing matching clothes for us even though we weren't twins, a habit that really got on my nerves. *Can't you steal me a different outfit, Nan? I don't want to look like my prissy sister.* Of course, I never had the guts to voice my fashion angst to Ma Barker.

It didn't take long before other people started to notice my poor hygiene. At every visit, Nanny Carron, with a great, excited smile, would ask me if I would like to enjoy a warm bath.

"Nope. I'm fine," I replied each time.

She went so far as to find an encyclopedia entry that explained the importance of good hygiene and how there were millions of germs all over our bodies that we couldn't even see. After I read it, she asked again if I might like to have a bath.

"Nope. I'm fine, Nan."

Soon, most adults I encountered were trying to get me to bathe. I visited my Aunt Sheila and my cousin Patty for a week that summer. We swam in the lake near their home in Verona, walked the railroad tracks, and picked wild grapes and raspberries. We had fresh tomatoes topped with minced onion as a side dish for dinner. It was a glorious visit except that there was no way that the lake water was going to cut through the grease covering my little head. Nightly, Aunt Sheila suggested that I have a bath after Patty was finished her cleansing ritual.

"Nope. I'm fine, Aunt Sheila," I told her each time.

"Well, would you like me to wash your hair for you at least, honey?" Aunt Sheila asked.

"No. That's fine. I think I'll just go outside and play."

"It really wouldn't be any trouble, Lynn, and we have this nice smelling Breck shampoo," she told me.

"No. I'm fine. Can Pat come outside with me?"

"Sure," she said in a low, defeated voice.

When Aunt Sheila dropped me off at home after the visit, I overheard her tell my mother that she couldn't get me to have a bath or wash my hair. She said that I wouldn't even use shampoo or soap when I was swimming in the lake.

I heard my mother reply, "Yeah, I know. It's like pulling teeth to get her to wash herself. She must be going through something."

"You might have to force her," Aunt Sheila said.

Later that day, my mother approached me in the kitchen. "You need to wash your hair and have a bath."

"But I'm not dirty."

"Christ, Lynn, you're filthy!" she screamed. "Look at your goddamned hair. It's an oil pit."

"I don't feel like having a bath right now. I'll have one later," I told her, hoping to ease her rising tension.

"Well, you had better have one because it's getting embarrassing. And look at your clothes! They're a mess and they're what a boy wears. You're so *masculine*," she hissed.

What the hell does that mean? I wondered. I knew that it couldn't be good, considering the disgusted look on her face and the way that she said it, like she had suddenly discovered that she had stepped in fresh dog shit.

I left her seething in the kitchen and found a dictionary. I needed to know the meaning of *masculine*. I went to my room and quickly found the word.

Oh God, she thinks I'm like a MAN.

I was mortified. I read the definition over and over. My tears buckled the page of the dictionary. *Mom, how could you say something so mean to me? Dad's right, you are a bitch.*

Then I considered it. Maybe *she* was right. It became commonplace for me to be confused for a boy. Once, a store clerk at Woolworth's asked me the dreaded question. When I told her that I was a girl, she said, "Well, you never can tell these days."

I knew that I didn't want to be a boy, but I wasn't sure that I wanted to be a girl either. There was no way that I wished to have a penis; my cousin Darren showed me his during one of our "I'll show you mine if you show me yours" sessions and I thought that the little, wrinkly, droopy tube of flesh was perhaps the ugliest thing I had ever seen. But I did want to cut off my budding tits. I figured that when I was old enough I would save the money to have them surgically removed. I wore baggy shirts and sweaters to hide them, even though they weren't very big at all; Cousin Darren called them my "mosquito bites". They certainly itched and pained like mosquito bites.

One fact became increasingly clear: the more I looked like a boy, the greasier I let my hair become, and the more I stank, the less people wanted to touch me. This was quite okay with me.

Out of respect for Nanny and Grandpa Carron, I bathed during the lengthier visits with them. After all, I needed to nestle beside them on the couch and I knew that being clean made my dying Nanny very happy. She always pulled me closer and told me how good I smelled after my bath. I knew that it was her way of encouraging me to wash myself more often. It worked; at least it did with Nanny and Grandpa Carron.

I did everything I could to make my grandmother happy as she got sicker and weaker. I knew that she was dying but I could not imagine her actually being dead. I was not prepared. I was not prepared for any of it.

Nanny's physical body altered rapidly. She became rail thin as if a strong breeze could be dangerous enough to snap a limb. Her stomach became so distended that she found it difficult even to walk to the washroom. Grandpa had to hold her up and guide her across the smallest spaces. She could no longer leave the apartment. What upset her the most about this was that she couldn't attend Mass at St. Mary's Cathedral. Nanny resorted to watching the *Mass for Shut-Ins* on television and reading her prayer book almost constantly. Her hair now grew in patches behind her sunken temples and styling it was out of the question; she kept it combed back behind her ears. She wore only light nightgowns and housecoats. My mother bought her so many pretty ones, mint green, pink, and yellow.

Grandpa never took his eyes off Nanny. He gave her everything she asked for and then some. If she wanted a magazine or a pack of cigarettes, he handed me the money and I ran for them while he watched over her. If she wanted a glass of water, he made sure that it was poured into the most beautiful glass with plenty of ice. By this time, Nanny's hands shook so badly sometimes that she had to drink with a straw.

Most of that year was a blur. I couldn't concentrate on much of anything other than Nanny Agnes. School was pissing me off. I didn't want to interact with any of the kids; I preferred to spend recesses alone as I locked and unlocked a miniature padlock on the school chain link fence. The lock was my dime gift from a bubble gum machine. I knew in my ten-year-old mind that I must have looked like what my classmates commonly called a "retard," an indicator of unusual behaviour, but I didn't care. There was something comforting about the lock's clicking sound. Often I fantasized that unlocking it would bring me into some new and wonderful world where I could just be with my grandparents and Nanny was no longer sick. Sometimes I would secure it to the fence before the bell rang so that I could go out and unlock it again at lunch or the next recess. It was my very own secret and I felt exhilaration when I discovered the lock still attached to the fence. Every day after school, I put the miniscule key into the padlock and made my way to Nanny and Grandpa's apartment.

I had lost interest in being friends with Charlotte. She made friends with a girl named Christine who hated my guts because her boyfriend said that I was nice. It was amazing to me that I could be hated for that. I learned much about love and hate that year. My grandparents taught me about love, but hate was fairly new to me. Sometimes I hated my father and I certainly hated his friend Hank Antonio.

On the schoolyard, I learned that I was supposed to hate Americans. The Americans came in the form of a new student named Lisa Madison. Lisa was tall, blonde, and blue-eyed, and I thought that she was pretty. Our teacher explained that she and her family had come from one of the United States. I soon discovered that was nothing to be proud of. During recess, when the teachers weren't around, some of the kids started calling her "yank" and "baby killer". I decided not to be friends with Lisa by proxy.

I asked Grandpa why the kids at school would call this new American girl such names. He said, "It's probably because of Vietnam. A lot of people are upset that Americans are still fighting over there. These kids at school don't know anything about it, honey. They hear this shit from their parents. Just ignore them."

Ignoring them might work for me, but what about Lisa Madison? Lisa took a great deal of verbal abuse and some pushing around. I did nothing to help her. In fact, I watched. One day the violence escalated. Someone pushed her from behind while she was eating a crescent of an orange. She started to choke and gag. Then she went silent and turned blue. A girl ran for a teacher, who pounded Lisa's back. The stringy, mushy chunk flew out of her mouth. She barfed and then started to cry.

I felt terrible. I suddenly realized what brutes we all were. How could a ten-year-old girl who eats oranges at recess be a baby killer? The following day, I approached her with a bag of mixed candy and asked her if she wanted one. She had a look of extreme shock and fear; she hesitatingly moved her hand toward the bag. Maybe she thought that I was going to gift her with cyanide tablets sprinkled with arsenic or some other equally deadly concoction. Lisa lifted a candy from the top, no fishing around in the bag, and popped it into her mouth. I swear that she waited to see if she would die. When she realized that she was still breathing, she smiled and said, "Thank you very much."

"You're welcome," I replied genuinely while alleviating some of my guilt. At the same time, I knew that we would never be friends.

∗ ∗ ∗ ∗ ∗

When school finally and gratefully let out for the summer, I took my little padlock and left without saying goodbye or making plans with anyone. I went directly to stay with Nanny and Grandpa Carron. Nanny was in a very bad state. The VON nurse made daily visits to assist Grandpa with Nanny's needs. I did not become aware of the immediacy of her dire condition until I overheard the nurse talking to Grandpa in the early hours of the morning on that day in June:

"Earl, you need to know that she will probably not last through the week," she told him. I was lying in bed, on the pullout couch, and I heard him gasp painfully. My weeping was instant and silent.

"Oh God, no, please," he said. I could tell he was crying too.

"I will try to make her as comfortable as possible," the nurse said in her soft voice.

I cried myself back to sleep. When I awoke, I found my grandfather sitting in a chair in the doorway of the room where Nanny laid, staring at her with his elbows on his knees and his hands on his chin.

"Good morning, Grandpa," I said quietly.

"Hello, dear," he replied without taking his eyes off of her. "Why don't you go get yourself some cereal for breakfast?"

I asked, "How is Nanny doing?"

"She's sleeping right now, dear. Go get some cereal." His voice was flat.

I went into the kitchen and chose one of the ten little boxes of Kellogg's cereals from the variety pack that Grandpa bought for me because I loved them. I carefully cut the box with a butter-knife and poured the milk. After two or three spoonfuls of Raisin Bran, I felt like vomiting. Nanny was going to die and I was trying to eat Raisin Bran like nothing was wrong. I poured the remainder into the toilet and flushed.

"Can I get anything for you or Nanny?" I asked Grandpa. Just then, my grandmother started jerking and heaving while lying in her bed. Grandpa ran to her and helped her hold her head over a large plastic bucket. She spewed a deluge of dark brown gunk from her mouth, both into the bucket and missing it, hitting the floor and Grandpa's hands. I started crying again. If death had a smell, this was it.

Nanny didn't even complain. Not once did she voice her pain or any fear. The closest she ever came was a small wince.

After he had cleaned her, Grandpa handed me some money and told me to go shopping for a while on Princess Street. He had given me several dollars to add to the pot of change I had been saving and told me to go get the "thing" that I wanted at S & R. The thing that I wanted, and had been saving for, was a small, yellow Barbie bicycle. I didn't even have a Barbie, nor did I want one. I just wanted the striped, bright yellow bicycle. If I couldn't have a bike of my own, I could at least save for this one that cost only seven dollars. Grandpa gave me more than enough money to finally get it.

As I walked slowly down the great flight of stairs of the apartment building, I felt numb until I opened the door and the beautiful sunlight and the heat hit my body. It was one of those perfect summer days full of brightness and smiling faces, laughter and ice cream cones, music and colour. The outside did not reflect what was happening inside. It all seemed so very wrong. I turned in the opposite direction of S & R Department Store that housed my treasure and reached the corner where a poster in the door of The Book Merchant caught my eye. I gaped and was mesmerized. In front of me was the huge head of a shark pointing up toward an ocean's surface where a minuscule, female body swam without care. It was an advertisement for Peter Benchley's *JAWS*; it had been made into a movie and had just been released into theatres. Now this was something I had to see. For that moment, my mind left the cancer that was eating my grandmother from the inside and it entered an underwater world where unsuspecting swimmers were hunted and chewed up by sharks. I imagined the enormous triangular teeth ripping into human flesh—my flesh. The rush of fear that I felt was exhilarating; my scalp tingled and my entire body broke out in goosebumps. I knew that I would have to see this movie. I had an intense desire to see people being torn limb from limb.

I finally made my way to S&R. Venturing up to the third floor toy department was always one of my favourite pastimes. I slowly roamed the aisles of boxed dolls, tea sets, and bagged marbles until my eyes rested on the coveted "thing", the yellow, plastic Barbie bicycle. There it was. Only $7.59 and I had more than ten dollars in saved coins. I could actually buy it this time. I no longer had to leave the Barbie aisle disappointed. Holding onto the box, I examined the picture on the front. The bicycle looked just like a real one, complete with sprockets and chain. There were colourful stickers that could be applied to all of the bars. I stood there staring at it for a long time. I played with the coins in my pocket. I can't really explain why I did it, but I put the box back on the shelf and left the store. I don't recall what my thoughts were; maybe I figured it was wrong to purchase this toy for my pleasure when Nanny was lying in bed at home, dreadfully ill.

I walked slowly, trancelike, back to the apartment making tinkling sounds with the change in my pocket. Before I even entered Nanny and Grandpa's home, I could hear several voices behind their door. I walked in to find my mother and Aunt Sheila there. They looked terribly worried and talked in hushed tones. Their eyes were watery and their noses were red. They didn't pay any attention to me and I wondered if they realized that I was even there until Grandpa asked me what I had purchased.

"I didn't buy anything, Grandpa," I replied.

"Why not?" he asked, "I thought you wanted some little plastic bike."

"I'll get it some other time," I told him as I poured water into a glass.

"How is Nanny?" I asked.

He told me the truth in a choked voice, "She has slipped into a coma, honey."

Slipped into a coma? "What's a coma?" I asked worriedly. She couldn't walk; how could she slip into anything?

"Well, Nanny is in a deep rest. Her eyes are open but she might not know that you are there," Aunt Sheila finished, as my mother and Grandpa wept.

"Can I please see her?" I asked, beginning to cry.

"I'll take you in to see her, dear." Grandpa took my hand in one of his and carried a box of Kleenex in the other.

As soon as I looked at her eyes, I knew what *coma* meant. I will never forget those eyes as they stared straight at something I could not see. Her mouth hung open slightly as a line of brown fluid poured from its corner and down onto the sheets. Grandpa handed me a Kleenex.

He said, "I have to make some phone calls, dear. Will you make sure that you wipe Nanny's mouth for her whenever that stuff starts coming out?"

"Of course, Grandpa," I replied, terrified of this responsibility.

As my grandfather left the room, I seated myself on the bed beside Nanny. The stream of dark brown from her mouth was almost constant. I wiped her as she stared into space.

"I'm here, Nanny," I told her. "Can you hear me?"

Not even a flinch.

I started to weep while I continued to clean her face.

My grandfather re-entered the room and told me to take a break and visit with my mother and the other family that had arrived. I leaned down to her and whispered, "Twinkle, twinkle, little star, how I wonder what you are. Up above the world so high, like a diamond in the sky. I love you, Nanny."

I left her bedside and entered the living room to join the rest of the family. I don't think that it was one or maybe two minutes later that my courageous and beautiful Nanny died. It was that sunny afternoon, June 26, 1975, one day before her sixty-sixth birthday.

Grief was absolute and all consuming. No one knew what to do. Grandpa wept loudly as he stood in the doorway to the room where Nanny laid being held by my Aunt Mary. My mother and the others sobbed together and paced the apartment. I sat on the couch, my usual spot beside Nanny's seat, and held onto her Catholic prayer book. I needed to have something of hers to hold. My hands became steel clamps that held this book, unmoving, against my chest. I knew that I would lose my mind if anyone tried to take it away from me.

Just then, there was a knock at the door. It was my mother's other sister, Aunt Gayle. She knew as soon as the door opened and the pandemonium spilled into the hallway. "Oh God, she's gone, isn't she?" Gayle screamed. My mother and Sheila rushed to hug her.

Someone took control. I don't know whom exactly. We were ushered into Harland's bedroom and the door was closed so that Nanny's body could be removed without us having to watch. Before I knew it, I was being pushed out of the apartment in the care of my young Aunt Tanya. My father had called her to come and remove me from the difficult situation. I took Nanny's prayer book and went with her. I could not be consoled. I wept profusely and constantly. Tanya tried everything. She offered to get me chocolate milk, candy, chips, anything. No, no, no, no. I wanted to be with my Grandpa, and if I couldn't be with him, then I wanted to be alone.

She took me to 16 James Street of all the places. Of course, this was Tanya's home. For me, it was like being tossed into a lion's den or a witch's cauldron. She didn't know what to do with me, so she left me there watching television. I couldn't blame her; she was still only a teenager and I was bawling and blubbering snot all over the place. Thankfully, I had the dumpy living room to myself. I mindlessly stared at the TV and watched the commercials that bombarded the room: *Cherry, Cherry Blossom, with its thick chocolate on the outside, Mmmm, Mmmm, Mmmm... and its creamy on the inside, Mmmm, Mmmm, Mmmm.*

While the television continued to drone on, I turned up the radio. I wanted the entire room filled with loud sound, no quiet spaces. Paul McCartney and Wings asked me to *Listen to What the Man Said*, Olivia Newton John begged *Please, Mister, Please* and America prompted more tears with *Sister Golden Hair:*

> And I keep on thinkin' about you,
> Sister Golden Hair surprise,
> And I just can't live without you,
> Can't you see it in my eyes?

I sat on the couch with Nanny's *Catholic Press Prayer Book* on my lap. It opened easily on page 138, a sign of its frequent use, the section titled *Prayers Concerning Death:*

> O most merciful Jesus, lover of souls, I beseech Thee, by
> The agony of Thy Most Sacred Heart and by the sorrows of
> Thine Immaculate Mother, wash clean in Thy Blood the sinners
> Of the whole world who are now in their agony and who
> Are to die this day.

> Amen.

There were also numerous prayer cards sandwiched between its pages along with invitations to my grandmother to share in various prayer Novenas at Easter and on Mother's Day. Nanny obviously found some comfort within the covers of this book and for that I was grateful and would hold it in reverence always for this reason. But to say that I understood it would be a lie. Nanny prayed several times every day. She prayed both silently and out loud. She went to Mass and when she couldn't get there, she watched it on TV. She visited priests and they came to the apartment and the hospital to visit her. Not one of her crosses or medals escaped blessings from the Church. She even bought me a little silver cross and a St. Christopher medal and had them blessed by her parish priest before clasping them around my neck. Her faith was unshakable and as solid as a perfect diamond.

In this way, I could not be like her, as much as I tried. I was pissed off. Pissed off at God and Jesus. She asked for comfort and instead she got a cavernous hole in her side, a grossly bloated stomach and floods of brown puke all over the place. I know that my Nanny did not want to die so soon, but God and Jesus did not listen. I asked them myself and she died horribly anyway. No matter what I asked, my prayers never seemed to be answered. I started to think that the whole God and Jesus thing was one big lie, one big crock of shit. Still, I continued to pray and to hang onto the weight of my religion from a long delicate thread and it was only out of respect for Nanny.

On the day of her funeral, my parents took my siblings and me to 16 James Street. No matter how much I begged, I was not permitted to attend her funeral. I had not stopped weeping and it was decided by all of the adults that I might be further traumatized by the experience. *You have to pick this time to give a shit about my feelings.* I thought I was going to lose my mind. I wasn't going to be able to say goodbye to her properly. I punched my uncle Jimmy in the head for no reason and everything turned black.

X

"I THINK THAT MAYBE I SHOULD TAKE HER TO A SHRINK." IT was my mother talking to my Aunt Bea as she exhaled a cloud of smoke from her cigarette.

"Oh God, do you think it's that bad?" Bea asked, genuinely concerned.

"All I know," my mother replied, "is that she seems to be turning into a basket case."

I began to overhear several serious talks about ushering me to a psychiatrist. I cried often without explanation. I cried while I waited in the car for my parents as they shopped at Canadian Tire. I cried as I sat in the wooden fort we built in a tree at our new house in rural Inverary. I cried as I watched over my sister and brothers while shut in the car at the parking lot of the Legion 560, waiting until my father had filled himself with booze. It was as if I was trying to rid my body of all of its water. No water on my body and no water in it. I could dry up and blow away.

Nothing could make me happy until Aunt Tanya told me that she would take me to see the movie *JAWS*. I was beyond excited. She took Annie and me to the Capitol Theatre on a sunny afternoon. From the onset of the underwater footage and the compelling musical score, I was captivated. I don't think I blinked once during the entire movie, determined not to miss even one second. I was gleefully terrified. My desire to see people torn apart and rendered bloodless was finally satisfied. At the same time, I cheered along with everyone else when Brody's bullet hit the air tank that blew the killer shark to pieces. Now I had something utterly visceral to occupy my mind, visual images to match how I felt. I didn't need a shrink. I needed *JAWS*.

After Nanny's death, my grandfather became consumed with grief. He was passed around from one house to another of his grown children and drank rum almost constantly. He still had the apartment, but everyone knew that was only temporary. It became clear that he should not be left alone and wasn't taking very good care of himself. I managed to see him on one visit to my Aunt Gayle's in Amherstview that summer. Most of my aunts, uncles, and their children were there. Grandpa had shut himself up in one of the bedrooms and we were told not to disturb him. Some of my younger cousins disobeyed and entered his room. My grandfather's voice boomed through the house,

"Get the fuck out of here! I just want to be left the fuck alone!" he hollered.

I could hear the children crying as they came running down the stairs.

I remember. *I slowly walk up to my Grandpa's room disobeying the general order to leave him be. The door is still open and the room is dully lit by one lamp on the night table. He is sitting on the edge of the single bed with his face in his hands, his spit can positioned on the floor between his legs. He is sobbing and I know that my heart is going to break. I walk over to him and carefully sit down beside him. He takes his hands away from his face and sees me. He gasps and sobs loudly taking my hand in his. We sit and share our tears undisturbed. What is going to happen to us?*

* * * * *

Life became surreal without my regular reprieve at Nanny and Grandpa Carron's home. It was like entering a Salvador Dali painting, the one where his lover, Gaia, invites the viewer into a world of rot and decay with her sinister smile and a handful of lush grapes. My family had now relocated to a house in Inverary on the outskirts of Kingston. The house was small but new and my parents got a "sweet deal" because the man who was building it dropped dead in its center from a massive heart attack. My father had to finish laying the carpet and painting the walls. Outside of this house, the world was sublime. There were large spaces, fields of hay and corn, forested areas, ponds, and farms. Inside this house, even though it was brand new and freshly painted, the world verged on the grotesque.

My parents drew their battle lines and both got mindlessly drunk while doing it. There was never a shortage of alcohol in the house but one would be hard pressed to find anything to sandwich between two slices of bread. My mother was the one who did the grocery shopping once every two weeks and as she unpacked the bags from Bennett's Grocery Store, she never failed to exclaim:

"Everybody better take it easy with the groceries, because once they're gone, they're goddamned GONE. I don't have any more money for food. Are you listening to me, you little pigs? This is it. So slow the fuck down."

It didn't escape my notice that my parents claimed that they were out of money for food, but they could certainly scrape together the thirty dollars that it cost at the time to buy a case of beer from the bootleggers on the weekend. They seemed to always be able to manage that.

Weekends were rarely pleasant in the Hellers house. Starting on Friday evening, my father would take his customary spot at the kitchen table beside the patio door. He began with his audible gulping of the first bottle of beer, followed by another, and another, and another until he had to finish late Sunday night. His skin and his sweat consistently stank of beer. He managed several outdoor chores like mowing the lawn, tilling the garden, or working on his car while he got blistered with booze. When he actually put his mind to something, it seemed like he could accomplish and build anything. Though he was a drunk, he was a hard worker; he just couldn't manage to hang onto a job for very long. He worked for a string of garages like Canadian Tire or Firestone. He either quit or got fired and often blamed both circumstances on his "prick of a boss". He even had his own business once, a joint effort with my Uncle Darren, senior. They called it Hellers' Automotive and I think it was the best financial success my family ever enjoyed, but like everything else, it didn't last. Every time he lost a job, my mother's tears would flow as she worried about losing the house and affording groceries.

"Why don't you go fuck yourself," my father says as she weeps. "You don't understand at all. You would sit and watch me bust my knuckles for that lousy prick for the rest of my life, making a shit wage."

"At least it's a wage!" she screams back, "Now what the fuck are we supposed to do?"

"You fucking cunt," he hisses between clenched teeth. "Are you looking for a swat?" he asks as he heads out the door.

Mom goes into their bedroom crying and chain-smokes her Player's cigarettes for what seems like hours. She knows that tough times are ahead yet again.

During one particularly rough spell, we lived for over a month on potatoes harvested from the garden and the odd package of hamburger. My mother tried to devise as many creative ways to prepare potatoes as possible. We had them mashed, boiled, and fried. When she could afford a package of ground beef, we had shepherd's pie or hamburger gravy over boiled potatoes. The prospect of another month of potatoes made me cry too.

We also resorted to fishing for smelts in the cold streams near our home. My father took us out at night with nets to scoop the little fish into buckets of icy water. Now we could have smelts and potatoes for a couple of weeks. It was a nice change.

When my father was out of work, he drank even more, almost every day. He stopped occasionally to take a nap on the couch where he pissed himself more times than I can count. Our couch and living room always smelled like human urine, cigarettes, and stale beer. Every time I sat on the couch to watch television, I wanted to puke from the stench. There were so many stains that its surface looked like the map of some other bizarre world where countries and islands overlapped each other. Eventually it came to the point where my sister, brothers, and I sat on the carpet to watch TV. Mom stopped sitting on it too. The couch came to be used only by my father. I don't know how he managed to stand the odours of his own waste. Sometimes he made it to his bedroom during a drunken stupor and pissed up my mother's back, staining her nightgown. At night, he pissed everywhere but the toilet.

As he sat his intoxicated carcass in his usual spot at the kitchen table one night, Mom asked him how much money was collected for Nanny Carrons's headstone. She had been buried in the cemetery on Division Street and there was no marker for her grave. The entire family was asked to contribute whatever they could.

My father said, "Well it's slow fucking work with your cheap family. The stone costs $500 and we've got half that collected. Do you think I can work fucking miracles? Tell your fucking sisters and their husbands to dig a little deeper into their pockets."

I now knew why I didn't buy the Barbie bicycle that day; I was meant to give that money toward my Nanny's grave marker.

"Mom, I have some money that I want to give for Nanny's grave stone. I've been saving this money for a long time and I know that there is at least twelve dollars. That should help a little bit," I said.

"Oh Lynn, that is so generous. Are you sure? You've been saving for that toy for a very long time," my mother said, smiling.

I immediately left the table and went to my room to collect the coins I had saved. I had them in a tin dish and brought it out to my mother. I handed it to her. I saw tears in her eyes.

"Well aren't you just the little show-off?" my father said, staring at me.

"Right," I replied, "I'm trying to impress you." Sarcasm dripped from every word.

In an instant, he reached across the table and slapped my face.

Why don't you go fuck yourself with a greasy socket wrench, you son of a bitch. I knew that if I had said it out loud, he would probably have knocked me unconscious. This was just the start of willing my father to fuck a variety of his Snap-On tools.

My mother gasped and asked, "Why did you do that, Wade?"

Her empathy prompted my tears.

He slurred, "Because she's a little show-off. She thinks she's hot fucking shit. She needs to be taken down a notch or two."

"Are you crazy?" she cried. "She just gave her only money for her grandmother's headstone!"

"Yeah, because she wants to make us look like a couple of assholes," he said.

"Oh, fuck this shit!" she screamed. "I'm going to bed." She grabbed her purse and quickly tucked it under her arm as she stomped toward their bedroom, leaving me there with the monster.

As I wept, he glared at me. "See what you've caused?"

"Dad, I'm tired. I'm just going to go to bed too," I told him in a shaky, low voice.

"Good! Get the fuck out of my face, you fucking show-off!" he screamed.

I didn't wait around to see if he had anything else to add. I leapt from the kitchen chair, hustled to my room, and threw myself down on the bed, weeping.

Are you there, God and Jesus?

If you are listening, I need your help. Please, please help me find a way to get out of this loony bin. Take care of Nanny and Grandpa, Mom, Annie, Wally and Sean. Why can't you make my father go away? He's so mean. I'm sorry that I thought of those swear words.

Are you listening to me? Amen.

X I

"WHEN I LEAVE, I'M TAKING TWO OF THOSE FUCKING KIDS with me!" It was my father's booming voice. We were at the cottage on the Isle of Man, and their argument woke me as usual. Their arguments could wake the dead. *Can you hear them, Nanny?*

"What the hell are you talking about?" my mother screamed.

"Are you deaf, bitch? When I leave this fucking outfit of a family, I'm taking two of the kids," he screamed back at her.

"How in Christ's name can you pick between your kids?" she asked. With my mother, everything was always "in Christ's name".

"It's easy," he told her. "I want the two that are going to amount to something. I want Annie and Wally."

"You sick bastard," Mom said. "How can you say that?"

He replied, "Well, I certainly don't want the other two losers. They aren't going to amount to a goddamned thing."

How lucky for Sean and me, I thought. *I'd hang myself from the willow tree outside before I would go with you.*

This event incited my mother to question each of us every time they had a blowout. "If your father and I separate," she asked, "which one of us would you want to go with?"

"YOU, Mom! You!" we all said. She already knew the answer. Not one of us could imagine being separated from her and ending up with my father, not even his chosen ones.

His chosen ones. Annie and Wally. Not even they were exempt from his humiliation and abuse. My father wasn't overly particular about where he directed his anger. He berated Annie in front of guests, hosts, and at dinner tables about stuffing her "bloody rags" down the toilet and blocking up the septic system. She had started her period early, at the age of eleven, and he felt he had to announce this to the entire world. We waited for him to put out a news flash. Upon hearing the menstrual news, people did not know how to respond. They smiled uncomfortably or looked at Annie with sympathy, while my father guffawed to no end. Either way, Annie ended up in tears as my father graced the room with his favourite joke: "I don't know how you can trust something that bleeds for a whole week and doesn't die!" Ha, ha, yuk, yuk.

Wally was even less fortunate. His humiliation came with incredible violence. My parents got him involved in hockey because my Uncle Darren had signed up his son, Darren Jr. Darren showed an early talent for the sport; and therefore, my father thought that Wally should do the same. In fact, my brother did have a gift for hockey. He was very athletic and took to the game like a fish in water. My uncle provided him with some of my cousin's old hockey equipment and my father bought him a helmet and elbow pads. Wally was fast and very skilled and it wasn't long before he was playing center position for the LaSalle Tire Flyers. Then the team made him captain. For once, my father actually *was* proud and my brother glowed with the approval.

Little did my brother know of the pressures of his new position. My father thought that his son was going to be the next Bobby Orr. Wally skated and scored, skated and scored and most of it to please his father. Everything was fine, until Wally made mistakes.

"What the fuck was that stupid move at the blue line?" father screams at him from the driver's seat of the car. "You just stood there while the other team took the goddamned puck."

"Dad, I scored two goals," Wally says weakly.

"I don't give a shit about your two goals! Big fucking deal! It's not a hat trick. What do you want, a fucking medal? You keep playing hockey like that and you're not going to get very fucking far."

In tears, my brother screams, "I'm doing the best that I can, Dad! Could you do any better?"

His father leans over the seat and gives him a solid swat in the head. "You watch your fucking mouth you little prick," he says as he turns the key in the ignition. Wally cries all the way home. Not one of us, including Mom, says a word, knowing that he would not hesitate to pull the car over to belt any one of us.

My brother's plight is visible in this picture stacked among the other hockey photos in my bag. It is a 5 x 7 colour shot of him skating to a stop in the direction of the photographer, ice dust spraying into the foreground. He is wearing his red and white LaSalle Tire shirt with the big white "C" on its shoulder and black hockey pants. The hair on his head is fine and wispy and flies back with the force of his movement. But it is his eyes and mouth that tell the story. His eyes are large, brown, and obviously worried, as if he is concerned about whether this photo will be correct; I know he is wondering if it will please his father. His mouth is straight, a tense line, not even a hint of a smile. He is not having fun.

Wally's hockey career lasted only a few years. Between the pressures of All-Star and my father's incessant violent criticism, my brother took up smoking cigarettes and sometimes pot. It took a while to figure out that Wally was into something; he was skating slower and hacking up a lung on and after the ice. He stopped caring about the game and his performance. When my father chastised him after his very last game, he said only: "Yeah, I know."

"You know what?" his father asked, sternly.

"I know that I did a crappy job. You don't have to tell me." *Cough, hack.*

"What kind of answer is that? So, you're just giving up, is that it?"

"I guess so," Wally answered matter-of-factly.

"Well then I'm not putting any more of my fucking money into you, if this is how you're going to repay me. You're an ungrateful little bastard," his father added.

My brother said, "Yeah. That's fine with me."

That day, after we arrived back at home, our father's anger climbed several levels. As Mother screamed and wept, he hit Wally and threw him around the kitchen, knocking over chairs and spilling Prince's dog dish. Wally tried to fight back, which made our father's anger even more feverish. He struck my brother in the mouth. Wally's head snapped back and blood pooled on his lips and smeared across his big white teeth. Here it ended, with the sight of blood.

"Go clean yourself up, you little pussy," his father said as Wally ran crying to his room. "That'll teach you about lipping back at me." His hockey dream of having sired his own Bobby Orr was over.

Father made loathing him extraordinarily easy. I wish that I could say that life with him was peppered with some good days, but that would not be true. He rarely had a kind word for any of us. At times, there was a kind word for my mother when he was grinding his groin against her ass as she prepared his breakfast at the kitchen counter.

"Aahh, that feels good. You have a nice ass," he said as she blushed and tensed her body.

For good measure, he followed up by sliding his oil-stained hands between her legs.

"Wade, stop it," Mom hissed.

"Oh, don't be such a frigid bitch," he replied.

"The kids can see," she said.

"So what? The boys will learn a move or two while they have their breakfast," he told her, smiling slyly.

I fought the urge to puke up my Shredded Wheat right there on the kitchen table. Wally and Sean looked equally disgusted and embarrassed and stared straight into their cereal bowls. I had to say something.

"You're a pig," I said, as I looked right at him.

"What did you say?" he asked with a furrowed brow.

"I said that you are a pig. What you're doing is gross and makes me feel kinda sick."

He broke out in laughter. "Well, I guess you're going to end up even more frigid than your mother," he told me, still laughing.

I knew that I would eventually pay for my comment somehow. That night, he watched me throughout dinner and plunged a fork into my arm for putting my elbow on the table. He had his rules about etiquette.

XII

WITH LIFE AT HOME BEING WHAT IT WAS, THE FOUR OF US increasingly looked forward to going to school every day. At least we were safe there, and didn't have to listen to our parents slur curses at each other. We were all very obedient children and had great respect for our teachers. Each of us loved learning and tried to excel at school. I loved teaching my sister and brothers anything: the fractions that they were struggling with, spelling tricks, or how to draw an accurate map from our house to the school. They always gave me their attention so that playing school was still a weekly activity in our house.

We attended more Catholic schools like Holy Family in the Rideau Heights and Holy Name on Hwy. 15. At Catholic schools, everything is "holy"–holy Jesus. We went to Holy Family School for only a year; thank holy Jesus, Joseph, and Mary. I was still in a deep state of mourning for Nanny Carron and I walked around the grounds of that school in a daze for the entire year. For a Catholic school, it had to be the roughest elementary school we ever attended. When I wasn't getting my ass kicked at recess, I was getting it kicked behind bookshelves in the math enrichment program because everyone who wasn't one of my classmates thought that I was a boy. Not only did I look like a boy, I was very scrawny, making me an easy target. One kid head butted me on the schoolyard and nearly knocked me unconscious. Another boy rounded a corner and slammed his fist into my gut, sending me breathless to the ground. No matter, I still wanted to be at school, because it was at Holy Family that I met my favourite teacher, Mrs. McCain. She nurtured me like a mother and sealed my desire to become a teacher just like her. The year that she taught me, she lost a baby. I thought that this was another of God's cruel displays of power. If anyone deserved to be a mother, it was Mrs. McCain.

But it was at the second holy school, Holy Name, where I met the person who made me want to bathe again and shampoo my hair. Her name was Dana Richards. She and her family lived in a tiny subdivision near the school. She had long sandy-coloured hair held back with butterfly barrettes. She wore flared jeans and stylish tops and was the person who saved my life during the first week of school.

Upon my arrival at Holy Name, I tried to integrate myself with the other kids by joining their games of "keep away," in which two teams attempt to keep a ball away from each other by passing it back and forth without letting it touch the ground. I was quite athletic and figured that I would be an asset to either team. Without asking if I could play, I grabbed the ball and ran, showing them how fast I could go, and then I expertly passed the ball to another girl. They all stopped and stared at me. A girl named Kelly said, "You can't play with us. We already have enough people."

Another girl said, "Kelly, that's really mean."

"Oh, okay. I'm sorry," I replied as I began to walk away through the center of the group.

I could see that some of them were looking at me with complete contempt and that "how dare you try to mix with us" look.

As I passed, they started darting their eyes and exchanging grins. Suddenly one of them yelled, "Get her!" Two girls threw me to the ground while the rest of the group piled on top of me, one by one. The weight and pressure on my body increased rapidly to the point that I couldn't breathe. At the beginning, I was screaming for them to stop but soon no sounds were coming out of my mouth. The world started to turn spotty and then black. I knew that I was losing consciousness and that they were going to make me die.

It was then that the girl named Dana screamed, "Get off her! She's turning blue!" One by one, the girls rolled off me and scrambled to their feet to view their handiwork. I could hear some of them laughing as I gasped for air. I raised myself onto my hands and knees and spewed my lunch all over the ground. I sat on the grass and cried. All of the girls went silent and stared at me. Minutes later, the angel named Dana brought me pieces of paper towel to clean my face. I pulled myself to my feet and walked away to lean against the outside wall of the school. Dana and some of the others followed me. They stood there with me as I continued to weep.

"We are so sorry," Dana said.

"Yeah, we really are," chimed the others.

"It won't happen again," Dana added.

And it didn't. In fact, I was welcomed into the group with open arms after that. I think that initially it was my reward for not ratting them out. Eventually I had a solid circle of friends and, for me, Dana was at its center.

The closer I became to Dana, the more I wanted to be pretty, just like her. I mistakenly thought that it was enough to merely comb my greasy hair every morning. Still, I was being confused for a boy. I didn't get it. I tried to make sure that my green stretchy pants and t-shirts didn't stink too much and I really was working on my hair. What more could I do? The answer came one day during a playful wrestling match with Dana.

During an in-class recess, Dana and I began to banter with each other over who was stronger. An arm wrestle turned into a full-fledged body wrestle in which Dana pushed my head under her arm and held it. When I finally escaped her hold, I saw her look at her hand with a disgusted face and then she rubbed her fingers against her jeans, as if removing some dangerous substance that she had touched. She was trying to rub away the oil from my hair. Out, damned spot!

I was thoroughly mortified. Dana was the object of my greatest affection and she was clearly repulsed by my filthy mane of hair that looked like the underside of a duckling caught in an oil spill, a true natural disaster. I didn't mind being touched by Dana; in fact, I enjoyed her physical contact. I didn't want her to find me repulsive. I wanted her to think that I was beautiful, just like her. It was obvious that if I continued to ignore my personal hygiene, she was never going to think that I was pretty and would probably never touch me again.

That night, I told my mother that I wanted to have a bubble bath. She nearly fainted. Mom was so excited that she ran the tub for me and let me use some of her special floral bath oil. For once, I didn't have to use someone else's bath water or share the bath with my sister or brothers. I had refused to bathe with them long ago anyway, after my brother Sean shit in the tub and his poop bumped against my arm. I scrubbed my skin until it was red and washed my hair so vigorously that I built a mountain of soap from the suds on my head.

"Doesn't that feel good?" Mom asked as she peeked at me from the bathroom door.

"Yeah," I replied, "it really does. This soap smells really nice too. Can I use it again sometime?"

"Of course you can!" My mother was elated.

When I was finished and joined my sister and brothers in the living room, they stared at me, astonished.

"Wow. You finally washed the buckets of grease out of your hair," Wally said.

"Why don't you shut your face, liver lips? At least I brush my teeth," I said.

"I brush my teeth, you dink," my brother retaliated, blushing.

"Yeah, only when they're yellow because they're caked with scummy plaque!" I yelled.

Annie said, "You should try curling it a little with my curling iron." My sister was the one who usually diffused the arguments and fights I had with my brothers.

"Would you show me what to do?" I asked her.

"Sure," she replied. "I'll show you before school in the morning."

"I'm really tired of people thinking that I'm a boy," I said.

"Well, I'm really tired of people thinking I'm a girl." It was Sean.

Recently, friends of mine at school starting confusing Sean for a little girl. So did our bus driver. One day while I was talking to him on the schoolyard, some kids came up to me and said, "This must be your other sister. She's so cute!" Sean blushed so intensely that his head looked like a giant tomato.

"He's a boy," I told them.

"Oh, sorry," one of them said. "It's just that you have such pretty long blond hair."

He did have pretty long blond hair. Haircuts were few and far between in our household. The odd time, Mom would take a pair of scissors to one of us, giving us crooked bangs or a nip in the ear. Sean did look like a girl and I did look like a boy. Another of God's cruel jokes, I guessed.

"Let's cut your hair!" I screamed excitedly that night in the living room.

"Yeah!" Annie said. "We'll make you look like a boy again."

Sean sat still and thought for a moment before saying, "Okay, but don't cut my ear!"

"Oh, this is gonna be good," Wally said, laughing.

I went to my mother and asked for the scissors that were huge metal shears designed more for cutting wire than hair.

"What do you want those for?" she asked.

"I'm going to cut Sean's hair," I replied. "Because some kids at school think that he's a girl."

"Oh. Good. It needs cutting anyway," Mom said as she went to her drawer to find the scissors.

"You mean you'll let me do it?" I asked completely surprised by her reaction.

"Sure. Why not? He won't let me do it because I cut his ear last time."

I raced into the living room with the scissors and yelled, "Let's do it!" Sean sat himself on one of the kitchen chairs as I prepared a glass of water and a comb to start the deed. Annie and Wally propped themselves up at the table, watching and giggling with anticipation. I wet his hair by repeatedly dipping the comb into the glass of water. Then the cutting began. I picked up chunks of hair and clipped. Sean was fine until I came near his ears; hearing the shears so close caused him to wriggle and whine in fear that I might snip off a lobe. Annie and Wally gasped as I took inches off the back.

"Holy crap, Sean," Wally said. "Wait until you see this."

In the end, the result wasn't half bad, with the exception of some chunky spots near the tops of those precious ears.

"H-Hey, that l-looks pretty good, Lynn," Sean said as he peered at himself in the hall mirror. Even though anything would have been an improvement, I had to admit that it did look a lot better.

Minutes later, Wally was begging for the same coiffure. It was the beginning of many haircuts that I would give my brothers. My mother thought I had a future as a hair stylist. *Are you kidding? I'd rather serve coffee and pie to fat truckers like Alice and Flo on TV.* I couldn't imagine having to stick my hands into the unpredictable hair of strangers on a daily basis. Way too close and personal for me.

Every now and then, one of my parents had to take my brothers for a real haircut. Because I didn't know how to thin out their thick hair, they both ended up with a wedge cut in which the bottom of their hair stood out from their neck by several inches. Annie told them both that she could park a good-sized Buick in the shadow of their hair. Sadly, this wasn't much of an exaggeration.

The day following our alteration, Sean, Wally, and I went to school feeling like completely new people. Annie had shown me how to use the curling iron that our grandmother Ida stole for her on one of their "shopping" sprees. My sister was always good cover for my grandmother when she hit the stores. Annie held onto a bag that my grandmother stuffed with various items such as bobby pins, pantyhose, and even facecloths. If Annie wanted anything, like a doll or some candy, that went into the bag as well. My sister truly enjoyed these outings. She always came home with a multitude of treasures that made us all jealous.

My brothers and I received several compliments toward our individual transformations. Some of the girls compared my new fine hairdo to that of Toni Tennille of the Captain and Tennille. Love *will* keep us together. There were so many positive remarks that I knew the days of swimming in my own filth were over. The fear of anyone touching me without my permission was replaced with a sureness that I would react like my Grandpa Carron told me to: "Kick 'em in the balls."

XIII

"THIS GUY IS ONE FUCKING PSYCHO," MY FATHER SAID. HE WAS reading the newspaper as he sat in a lawn chair sucking on a beer bottle by the shore of the river at my Nanny Ida's cottage, slurping on the brown bottle like a puppy nursing its mother's tit. I peered over his shoulder to read the huge, bold print: "*The Son of Sam Strikes Again.*" It was the summer of 1977 when the notorious .44 calibre killer stalked the streets of New York City, stealing all of the headlines from the big-toothed peanut farmer who was President of the United States and from the hook-nosed Prime Minister, Pierre Trudeau, who was running Canada. This was basically all I knew of our North American political leaders at the time; they were both funny looking. I knew more about the Son of Sam and his victims than anything about our world leaders.

"Can I read that after you?" I asked him.

"Why don't you piss off somewhere and leave me alone," he said. "I'm trying to enjoy a moment of peace."

"I'm sorry," I replied. "I was just asking if I could see it after you."

"What the fuck would you know about any of it anyway?" he shouted.

"Probably more than you do."

That did it. I knew I had crossed another line. If he got a hold of me, I would be bruised meat. He lunged at me, screaming, "You mouthy little bitch!" He missed me and fell back into the chair. I ran away from him, laughing. "Try to get me now, you dink." I couldn't believe that I had said it. Now I knew I was dead. He jumped back out of his lawn chair and chased me around the yard. I was too fast for him. I ran to the enormous willow tree by the water and began climbing rapidly. In his pissed state, I knew he would never be able to climb the tree. I positioned myself on the highest branch that I could reach. I sat and watched him.

What he did next propelled me into a state of terror. He positioned his lawn chair under the tree and removed a long, thin branch. He carefully peeled off all of the leaves to make a switch. He opened another bottle of beer from his cooler and sat calmly in the chair looking up at me, waiting.

"I'm not coming down," I said.

He serenely replied, "We'll see about that." He was too sedate. I knew I was in for one hell of a thrashing. He had me trapped like a bug in a jar.

The only thing to do was to wait him out, and that's what I did. Visitors arrived at the cottage with their children ready for festivities and a barbeque. My father garbled his hellos to every one of them. Each asked him what the hell he was doing just sitting there, holding a stick under a tree.

He said, "Look up there," as he pointed his unsteady finger at me.

My Uncle Darren laughed and asked, "What, are you kidding me? You're sitting here waiting to spank her?"

"She needs to learn to respect me," my father replied.

"How long have you been sittin' here, man?"

"I'll sit here for as long as it takes."

"Fuck brother, relax and give it up," Darren said, still laughing.

Father replied, "Don't worry. I'll be with you soon."

My uncle shrugged and walked away giggling. Several people, including my mother, came out to tell my father to let it go and enjoy himself. He wouldn't have any part of it. I sat on the limb of that willow tree for hours while he poured an endless stream of beer down his throat. When he had to have a piss, he merely got out of the chair, turned his back to me, and emptied his bladder onto the grass.

Eventually, he passed out. I knew he would. He sat there, sprawled in the chair, with beer bottles surrounding him on the grass. I quietly slid myself down, landing softly on the ground. I stealthily walked over to him and fought the urge to bludgeon his sleeping head with a Molson Export bottle. I walked into the cottage and everyone said, "Finally, it's done!"

"Did he finally let you come down?" my mother asked as Darren headed out the door to talk to his brother.

"Uh, not exactly. He passed out cold. Uncle Darren is about to wake him so I'm getting out of here!" I told her.

"Yeah. You better make yourself scarce," she said. This was always the extent of her motherly protection.

I took my red transistor radio that was shaped like a car battery, a gift from Uncle Harland, and headed down to Judy and Steve's dock. I sat on the end of it, listening to music, as I kicked my legs into the water. Stevie Nicks and Fleetwood Mac were singing:

> *Thunder only happens when it's raining,*
> *Players only love you when they're playing.*

It was one of my favourite songs, but Fleetwood Mac got one thing wrong. Thunder didn't only happen when it rained. Storms could happen on a bright sunny day with a clear blue sky, and the most frightening thunder could happen even on a warm and cloudless starry night in New York City.

* * * * *

After a while, my two brothers joined me on the dock. They had their fishing rods and were ready for their evening score. We were all avid anglers, with the exception of Annie, who couldn't stand to touch anything dirty or slimy. Sean was the most intrepid fisherman. Wally and I stood in awe of him and how many fish he could catch. It was his determination. He would endure any conditions, rain or shine. Sean knew the right lures to use and modified some of them to create his own special variations. He had an uncanny knack of knowing what lure to use for any climate condition at any time of day. Wally and I comforted each other with the fact that we were more athletic and could draw better than our baby brother could. We all found endless ways to compete with each other in an attempt to alleviate our crippling insecurity.

"You should put on your shirt, Sean," I told him as he cast his rod off the end of the dock. My maternal suggestion came as the result of his previous injury. Sean's determination and passion for fishing left him scarred, literally. A couple of years before, he had gone fishing by himself in my grandmother's silver rowboat on a clear, hot, sunny day. As usual, he fished for hours. He wasn't wearing a shirt. When my parents checked on him, their only concern was that he was still sitting in the boat off the shore. As Sean walked up to the cottage with his string of healthy but dying bass, my mother and I noticed his unusual appearance at the same time.

"What's that on his chest?" I asked.

"Oh shit," Mom said. "Oh fuck, he's burned."

She ran to him and screamed, "Jesus Christ!"

He wasn't even aware of the problem until he looked down at the sacs of yellowish fluid hanging all over his chest. His face was swollen beyond recognition. My parents wrapped him in a sheet and the entire family rushed into Kingston General Hospital Emergency. On the way, Sean began to react to his burns, shaking violently with his teeth chattering. My mother tried to comfort him as best she could. By the time we reached the hospital, my baby brother was screaming and then went strangely quiet. Annie started crying. "Mom, is he going to be okay?"

"Of course. He just needs to see a doctor," she replied worriedly.

Sean was in the hospital for two days to undergo treatment for third degree burns on most of his upper body. When the whole family went to pick him up, he looked like a little mummy, wrapped in layers of white bandages. He must have been given some serious painkillers because his head lolled to the side and he was barely conscious.

He was left with visible scars all over his chest and shoulders. These were large, irregularly shaped white splotches that reduced in size toward his stomach. He would be forever sensitive to the sun and was told to keep himself covered in the summer. He hated wearing a shirt in the sun and needed constant reminders to protect himself.

Once Wally and Sean had finished their evening fish off the dock, the three of us headed back over to the cottage in hopes of gobbling a hotdog or hamburger for dinner. We could smell the lit barbeque, prompting us to drool like Pavlov's dogs, and could hear the voices of everyone gathering outside.

"Do you think Dad is going to kick my ass?" I asked my brothers as we walked the path.

"Only if he remembers," Wally replied.

This was the truth. In his boozy haze, our father often forgot about events prior to his passing out. Occasionally he awoke to find that he had given one of us a black eye or had split our lips. "Oh, did I do that?" he always asked. "Good thing you're tough like your old man and can take it."

"What if he does remember and comes after me? He'll kill me. I called him a dink. I don't know if he's going to forget that."

"J-just run," Sean said. "Y-y-you're faster than he is, es-esp-especially when he's d-drunk."

"Yeah, but I'm hungry. I won't get any dinner if I have to take off."

"Don't worry. I'll bring you something," Wally said. "If he goes after you, just run up to the old bus and I'll meet you there with some food."

The old bus was just that. It was an old, rusted orange school bus that had long ago delivered its last student. It was permanently parked at the edge of a wooded area and we played in it almost every day, having apple fights and carving obscenities into the seats.

On one of the seats, someone had used a penknife and wrote: *Annie sucks cock.* Below it: *But Darren sucks bigger cock.*

The old bus was well known to all of us children and the language used within its walls was always colourful. My brother's idea to meet there was perfect. None of the adults ever ventured to the old school bus unless someone went missing for more than five hours. Five hours seemed to be the magic number; that meant that a meal was missed. Something had to be dreadfully wrong if one of us missed a meal, even if it was snot sandwiches. I once went missing on a summer day on the Isle of Man. I didn't show up for lunch and hours passed. My mother was hysterical and called my father away from work, and then called the police. Law enforcement and island cottage residents spent the entire afternoon scouring the woods and shorelines; some of them went out in boats with long poles to fish through the weeds. I was later discovered sound asleep on one of the bunks inside the cottage. I was so thin that there was no visible body lump under the blankets. My mother had to have been awfully embarrassed when confronted with the fact that she wasn't even aware when one of her kids took a self-imposed nap right under her nose.

As my brothers and I approached the cottage, we saw our mother and Aunt Bonnie placing condiment jars and paper plates on the picnic table. Uncle Darren flipped burgers and dogs on the barbeque with one hand while holding a beer in the other. Beside him stood my father. He was weaving back and forth on his feet as he took a long drag off his beer bottle. His eyes were tiny slits. Wally and Sean separated from me to check out what was cooking. I walked over to the picnic table and asked if I could help with anything. Mom looked at me with a worried face and said, "Sure. Could you get the plastic forks and knives out of the cupboard for me?"

"No problem," I replied.

I walked past my father and Uncle Darren at the barbeque. My uncle asked, "Hey, how's it going, Lollipop?"

"Really good," I replied with a smile. "I'm just going in to get the forks and knives."

My father looked at me with confusion and then looked down at the ground, cocking his head. He was trying to remember. *Better speed up your step*, I told myself. I quickly skipped into the cottage and filled both of my hands with plastic cutlery. On my way to the picnic table, my father came up behind me and smacked me with tremendous force on the back of the head. I flew to the ground, dropping all of the plastic utensils.

"Wade, what the hell are you doing?!" screamed my aunt.

"She did something disrespectful and now it's over, right you little bitch?" he said as he turned to look at me. My mother just shook her head.

I quietly picked up the cutlery and placed it on the picnic table.

"Are you okay?" Aunt Bonnie asked. "Yep," I replied. There was no way that I was going to give my father the satisfaction of my tears.

When everyone sat down to dinner, I took the red-handled jackknife that my grandfather gave me, along with my hotdog, up to the old school bus. I sat in one of the back seats and ate my dog with mustard. Then I took the knife and began carving: *It is my father, Wade S. Hellers, who sucks the biggest cock.* I sat there for a long time, reading it over and over again, laughing with enormous pleasure and exhilaration.

XIV

"GUESS WHO'S COMING TO LIVE WITH US," MOM SAID ONE morning over breakfast.

"Who?" we asked in frightened unison.

"Your Grandpa Carron," she replied with a gentle smile.

"Yeah!" my brothers yelled.

"Oh really, Mom?" I asked. "Are you trying to joke with us?"

"It's no joke," she said. "He's coming the day after tomorrow to live here with us."

"Oh this is the greatest!" I yelped. "I can't wait! I'm going in to clean my room before he gets here."

"Well, we need to talk about rooms," Mom said. "Lynn, you will have to share a room with Annie. Wally and Sean will share the room that your father is building in the basement."

Annie and I stared at each other. "Oh, it's worth it to have Grandpa come live here," I said. "It sure is," Annie conceded. We arranged our "new" room with an imaginary line down its middle that we actually measured with a measuring tape. The same was done with the closet; she got the left side and I got the right. I told her to keep her prissy shit on her side of the room and she told me to bite her ass.

When Grandpa Carron arrived, we barrelled him over with hugs and kisses. He seemed genuinely pleased to be in his new living arrangement. The four of us kids took him to his new bedroom and watched him unpack his things. Mom told us to leave him alone and give him some breathing room.

"Oh, it's okay, Margaret," he said, laughing. "I really don't mind at all. After I'm finished here, how would you guys like me to make you some home-made donuts?"

"Yahoo!" Wally hollered.

"Oh boy, that would be great, Grandpa," Annie said, grinning widely.

My grandfather made the best tasting donuts on the planet. He always made three different kinds: plain, sugared, and chocolate covered. He had brought all the ingredients and his baking equipment with him.

Grandpa made his spectacular donuts at least once a week. As we walked down the steps of the school bus at the end of the day, we could smell the familiar spicy dough cooking in hot oil before we even entered the house. We ran directly up the stairs and into the kitchen every time and were greeted with a huge platter of sweet delights to choose from. Whenever Grandpa wanted to make something special or interesting, he gave my mother a small grocery list and the money to buy the items. While my grandfather lived with us, we ate more and better than we ever had. He made his own fish cakes with cod, haddock, and onion; he made his special "pottie", a meat pie derived from his Acadian roots made with beef, pork, and rabbit. He roasted chickens and made pot roast that tasted like it could be served in a fine dining restaurant. To us, he was a master chef.

Along with a list of groceries, my grandfather often asked my parents to stop at the liquor store for some Bacardi rum. If they picked him up a bottle, he would buy them a case of beer. This situation worked fine for all of them until Mom became worried about Grandpa's increasing requests for alcohol. It didn't take long before he started to fall down. He walked out of the patio door, forgetting that there were no stairs there yet, and landed face first into the rocky fill at the back of the house. He lost several layers of skin off his forehead and the bridge of his large nose. Both eyes went black. My grandfather laughed about it but my mother didn't see the humour at all. She pleaded with him to slow down on his drinking.

"Jesus, you're just like your mother," Grandpa said, laughing. "She always had a fit if I had more than a couple of drinks."

"It's just that I worry, Dad. I don't want you to really hurt yourself. You were lucky this time."

"Okay, dear. I promise that I won't have so much and I'll be careful about what I'm doing, aye," he said.

I knew that Grandpa was just trying to placate her. I had heard him say these very words to Nanny when she was alive. I knew that if he couldn't keep this promise to Nanny then he certainly wouldn't be able to honour it with my mother; he would just resort to sneakier measures.

This is exactly what he did. He went to my father, behind my mother's back, and asked him to pick up the rum and not to tell; in return, he would pay for any beer that my father wanted. My father, of course, had no problem with this ruse. Soon there was a steady river of firewater running through the Hellers house. Mom eventually became aware that Dad was picking up twenty-six ounce bottles of rum for Grandpa and that Grandpa was helping to finance their addiction in return. She succumbed and surrendered her worry in an alcoholic fog.

The three of them spent every weekend, from start to finish, completely intoxicated. Sometimes my mother would spend the entire weekend in the same nightgown while my father sat around in his underwear, farting, unconcerned that his "jewels", as he called them, were almost visible and the crack of his ass was a dark line down the back of his Hanes wear. He eventually donned some pants but usually ended up pissing in them. Thankfully, Grandpa always managed to put on his pants, but often went shirtless, exposing his large, wiry haired chest.

With this much booze mixed in with my father's horrific temper, there was bound to be trouble. There was at least one violent episode per weekend and soon Father was throwing his fists even midweek after work. Friday evenings were the worst. My parents fought about everything and anything, from finances to the amount of salt that was put into the spaghetti sauce. It was always clear when my father was going to go off about something. With his lips perpetually wrapped around his brown bottle, his face would start to change. His eyes became bulging, skittish orbs, his brow wrinkled with deep furrows, and the muscles in his jaw tensed. Then he would throw out the bait.

"Who was that you were talking to when I picked you up at the bank?" he asks Mom as she slices cucumbers for dinner.

"Debbie Gunther," she answers. "She's a teller."

He doesn't waste any time. "She looks like a cheap fucking whore to me," he says.

"You don't even know her, for Christ's sake. You think every woman's a whore," she retorts.

"Well, it's true. I haven't met one woman who hasn't been a cock-sucking slut at least once in their life," he adds, raising his voice.

"Now don't start that stuff, Wade," my grandfather cuts in as he hacks and spits into his tobacco can.

"If I wanted your goddamned opinion, Earl, I would ask for it, aye."

"Don't talk to Grandpa like that," I say. There is a short pause.

"Why don't you fuck off, you nosy little cunt," Father says to me. "This doesn't concern you so screw off!"

"Oh that's nice, Wade," Grandpa says. "I can't listen to this anymore." With tears in his eyes, he picks up his spit can and heads toward his bedroom.

Seeing her father upset sends my mother over the edge.

"Now look what you've done," she screams. "You're such a fucking asshole!"

He flies at her and grabs her face in one hand. "I'm an asshole, am I?" he asks, squeezing her face until it puckers grossly. "Whores make friends with other whores," *he tells her through clenched teeth. She swats and pushes at him and he grabs her around her neck, never letting go of her face with his other hand.*

"Stop it, Dad!" I scream at him as I grab onto his arm. He uses this arm to easily toss me to the floor.

He lets go of my mother. "This house is full of cunts and whores!" he yells as he snatches another beer out of the fridge and busts out the door, almost ripping it from its hinges.

My mother starts weeping and I can see the red stripes on her face where his fingers were. She stops making dinner, picks up her purse, and goes to their bedroom.

I quietly walk down the hallway of our house and I hear my beloved grandfather whimpering in one room while my mother sobs loudly in another. Suddenly the thought strikes me: I don't want my father to just go away. I want my father to die.

I began to pray for it, though it meant breaking one of the most important Commandments. Whenever he was off getting drunk, as long as he didn't have my mother or siblings with him, I asked God and Jesus to make his gold Buick Riviera connect with a giant oak tree at sixty mph or careen off of a ravine and burst into flames. After all, he was accustomed to driving drunk, day or night, with or without passengers. Completely intoxicated, he got behind the wheel of his car on countless occasions with my equally polluted mother in the front passenger seat and we four children in the back. This happened mostly late at night after a host's booze supply had run out and he invariably drove with one eye closed in an obvious attempt to make the center line turn into one instead of two or three. Annie and I nervously took turns leaning over the front seat to correct the wheel whenever he crossed the line or veered onto the gravelly shoulder of the road, while Wally and Sean lay asleep in contorted positions on the backseat or the car floor. My parents could not let these special family moments pass without having a violent argument, which often ended with my mother leaping from the moving vehicle or my father stopping suddenly and telling her to "get the fuck out!"

During one particularly volatile drive home, my mother leapt from the car, causing injuries that required medical attention. I always wondered at her lunacy, diving from a moving vehicle, skinning her body and tearing her clothes from head to foot. Of course, she generally mustered enough sense to wait until my father was approaching one of the infrequently noticed stop signs or red lights before she would grace us with her artful swan dive. Eventually, my father caught on and when he stopped at any light or sign, he would ask in slurred words:

"Isn't it about time you jumped out, you crazy bitch?"

"Ah, fuck you," was the frequent reply.

"No, seriously. It might save you from getting a hole in those fucking pants," he would bark as he sped on.

"Just watch the road, you one-eyed motherfucker," she always spat back.

There were never more of my passionate and violent requests for Father's demise than when he went hunting for duck or deer. As always, when he was away hunting for a few days, my mother made it seem like we lived in true family bliss, a familial utopia. Her face temporarily lost all of its tightness and her smile grew wide. She brought home bags of marshmallow treats stuffed in small waffle cones, chips, dip, and popcorn. Mom didn't dare treat us in a special way when he was there; any attention or treats were to be showered upon him. Her extra coins had to be spent on alcohol or bags of chocolate cookies meant to be enjoyed only by him and were completely off limits to us. Wally and I took the odd belt in the head for sneaking some of my father's Chips Ahoy in the middle of the night. But when Dad was away, all was different; my mother joyfully helped my grandfather prepare dinner, laughing and joking with all of us. As they prepared delicacies like homemade pizzas, Grandpa drank his rum while Mom had some beers, but they didn't get drunk like they did when my father was around. We all played Monopoly and Clue until Annie won or we were too tired to finish. As the date of my father's return inevitably approached, our shoulders started to slump and my mother lost her smile and became silent.

There was only one occasion when I thought that my prayers were finally answered. I prayed for a mysterious hunting accident, a pool of quicksand, or a bear mauling. To this day, I have guilt for praying for such things, but I must continue to tell the truth.

My father went missing during one of his duck hunting expeditions. God and Jesus *were* listening. That is what I thought.

He and my Uncle Darren did not return at the end of the day following one of their hunts. Aunt Bonnie and my mother received the news, prompting them to load up all of their kids and head toward the farmhouse and hunting camp to help search. After three days of no appearance, helicopters were brought in. My mother and aunt took us to tie pieces of their clothing around barbed wire and nail bits of it to fence posts in hopes that my father's hunting dog might pick up the scent and lead them to safety. I thought that I had truly developed an evil nature when I considered backtracking and removing the bits of cloth and burying them at the farmhouse. I felt sorry for my Uncle Darren, but I did not want my father to be found. I fantasized that my uncle would walk out of the woods unscathed with a horror story that my father had met his end in the jaws of a bear or became dinner for a pack of wolves. As each minute passed without their return, I became more and more convinced that my prayers had been answered.

They walked out of the woods after five days. Both were big eyed, thirsty, thin, and smelled like swamp, but were otherwise fine and healthy. They were greeted with hugs, kisses, and tearful happiness from their wives at their safe return and then quickly launched into the story of their ordeal. Everyone was rapt with attention, except me, the evil one. I loved survival stories but I did not want to hear this one. No sir. Like a small inaudible breath of air, I blew out the back door unnoticed.

Once outside, I could not contain myself. "No, no, no!" I said, shaking my head. "You've got to be kidding me!" I yelped aloud. I looked up at the steel gray sky. I asked, "How can you let Nanny suffer and die like that and then let someone awful like him live after five days in the cold woods? This is impossible. You don't even listen to me when I ask for nice things to happen to people. He beats the crap out of us and you watch it happen. What kind of a God are you?! I don't know why I bother talking to you at all!" That night, I said no prayers.

X V

"I'VE GOT TO GET DIS BIRD INTO DA OVEN FOR THANKSGIVIN' dinner," Grandpa said as he staggered slightly, a glass of rum in his hand. He had prepared the stuffing the day before with his famous potato, savory, and sage recipe. As I peeled carrots, I watched his large hands do their work; one buttery hand held the leg of the large turkey while the other took the stuffing from a pot and awkwardly filled the cavity of the bird, dropping gobs of it onto the counter and the floor.

"Oopsy daisy," he said with his toothless smile.

"It's okay. I'll clean it up, Grandpa," I told him.

"Thanks, dear. I need to have dis friggin' turkey in before yer parents get back."

My parents had gone into Kingston to get more bootleg booze. They had run out and could not foresee Thanksgiving without a little spirit to accompany dinner. Turkey preparations were left in the charge of Grandpa Carron, who had been hitting the Bacardi sauce since the early morning. He tossed the white bird into the black roasting pan, slid it into the oven, and topped up his glass before peeling the potatoes.

I joined Annie, Wally, and Sean in the living room for a game of Crazy Eights. Grandpa stayed in the kitchen making the final preparations and drinking rum. By the time my parents arrived home, the dinner was ready and Grandpa, who was intoxicated into oblivion, was trying to keep it warm. Mom and Dad stumbled in with their open bottles and another full case of beer. They had apparently enjoyed some of the spirit elsewhere before returning home.

"Well, let's get this prize turkey on the table, aye," Mom said.

"Yahoo!" Wally and Sean yelled. "We're starving!"

As he took a haul off his brown bottle, my father said, "I'll take it out and carve it."

We seated ourselves around the table and waited for the bowls of peas, carrots, and potatoes to be followed by the coveted platter of turkey meat. As

Father removed the lid from the roasting pan, the room seemed to explode with sound:

"What the fuck is this?!" he bellowed fiercely.

"What's the matter?" Mom asked.

"Take a look at this fucking turkey," he replied angrily. "It's in the goddamned pan upside down, for fuck's sake. Your father is supposed to be a cook and he puts the fucking bird in the pan upside down. What idiot does that? Earl, you put the fucking turkey in the wrong way! You've ruined the goddamned dinner."

"Whaddya mean?" Grandpa asked, very concerned.

"Look at this, Earl," Father said as he probed inside the bird's neck area. "It's not only upside down, but all of the top skin has stuck to the bottom of the pan! There's no moisture. How the hell are we supposed to make gravy? It's ruined! Holy fuck! Look at this! You left the giblets and neck inside it in the fucking bag!"

"Oh, Jesus," Grandpa replied quietly. "I'm so sorry, Wade."

"You're sorry? You better be sorry, you goddamned drunk! What the fuck are we supposed to eat now? Not to mention that we paid a lot of money for that piece of shit in a pan!"

Grandpa Carron began to weep. "I'm sorry," he said again.

"It's okay, Dad," Mom said. "We can still eat it. Wade, it's not that big of a deal. The thing is still cooked, for Christ's sake."

"Not a big deal? Who's going to eat that piece of garbage? The meat is burnt and the fucking bag of guts is still inside it! I wouldn't touch that fucker with a ten foot pole!"

I took a look for myself and indeed it was stuck to the bottom of the pan and lay upside down, dry and crispy, looking like a huge scab. I looked over at Grandpa, who continued weeping as my father ranted and raged.

"We can still eat it, Dad," I said loudly, "Leave Grandpa alone! It's not his fault that you guys took forever to get home."

"You shut the fuck up!" he screamed at me. "I didn't ask for your two cents!"

Then he dramatically loaded the entire contents of the roasting pan into a green garbage bag. My brothers gasped.

"Don't throw it out, Dad," Annie pleaded. "We'll eat it."

"I wouldn't feed that fucking thing to Prince!" Dad yelled back at her.

"Oh Wade, what did you have to do that for?" Mom asked, beginning to cry.

Grandpa, still sobbing, rose out of his chair, picked up his spit can, and staggered down the hall to his bedroom. In her usual fashion, my mother picked up her purse and followed the same path to her own room, leaving the four of her children standing in the kitchen with bulging eyes and gaping mouths. The four of us listened to our father spew more obscenities as he flung the bag of turkey out the door and onto the ground. He took his beer and headed down the stairs into the basement. The four of us stood there looking at each other until my sister broke the silence:

"Well, isn't this a pleasant Thanksgiving?"

"Why should it be any different than any other holiday?" I whispered. "He's such a dick. Just because he's miserable, he has to ruin things for everybody. He made Grandpa cry again. I hate him."

"I'm starving," Wally said. "I was really looking forward to that turkey."

"M-me too," Sean added.

Annie had an idea. "Maybe it's still okay. He did put it into a fresh garbage bag."

We quietly opened the door just in time to see Prince dragging the large turkey scab across the back yard. "At least Prince is going to have a good dinner," Wally said.

The four of us started laughing in unison, trying to do it as quietly as possible so that our father wouldn't hear. We laughed until our bellies hurt.

It was a typical holiday in our house, though this incident had been rather tame. Easter, Thanksgiving, Christmas. All of them were excuses for that special kind of Hellers party with free flowing alcohol, drugs, hurled insults, random punches, black eyes, and a little blood spatter.

Christmas was generally the most eventful and soul damaging. As children, we were torn over the festive season; we looked forward to the two weeks off school and the gifts nestled under the tree, but knew that none of this came without paying a tremendous psychological price. Considering their meagre income, my parents did quite well providing gifts for four children, but did an even better job at fucking us up in the head. Every year we hoped that it would be a different story, a Hallmark card version of the holiday that might make Norman Rockwell puke. Every year we were disappointed. We had to be content with the illusion of the warmly lit windows of the snow-covered cabin with the red and green wreath attached to its door that graced so many Christmas cards sent to our house.

The season always began with so much excitement and hope. The four of us brought the wooden ladder out of the basement to fish the decorations out of the attic. We were so careful with each string of garland and each glass ball because we had so few of them. One thing we had plenty of was the shiny ceiling streamers that, when stretched out, formed glittering rows of cut out snowflakes, candles, or indefinable webs. Every year Mom bought a new one to add to the collection. We made sure that every single one adorned the living room ceiling. The centerpiece was a silver tube that hung down lower than the rest and appeared to spill out a fountain of colourful icicles. The result was a garish, tacky arrangement of glossy foil that Liberace would have adored. We thought it was absolutely beautiful.

The Christmas photos are few and far between and are the most difficult to look at. Each one holds its own horror story underneath the evergreen and glitter. The S&R bag that loosely holds my family's history yields only six holiday pictures and all of them contain hints to the violent secrets and the inescapable true trash existence that we lived every day.

In this photograph, my mother is sitting on the lap of my handsome and smiling Uncle Darren, who was still alive in the late seventies. She has her arm around his neck as she laughs into the yellow telephone attached to her ear. She is still dressed in her quilted night robe that she has been wearing for the whole day on Christmas Eve. Her hair is a shadow of what it was the day before when she washed and curled it. Uncle Darren and my mother are hammered. He is wearing a red and black hunting shirt and leans into her with his eyes closed and a half consumed cigarette in one hand. Behind my mother's head, on the window revealing the blackness of the night, is a Christmas fireplace with stockings sprayed on with fake snow. There is another man in a chair whose head is cut off by the photographer; Mom leans against his body as she sits on Uncle Darren's lap.

"You just can't help yourself, can you?" Dad asks Mom after the guests have left.

"Help what?" she asks.

"Flirting with my brother and our friends. You're a fucking slut and they know it too," he tells her as he puffs on his cigarette.

"Oh would you fuck off with that shit! I wasn't flirting with anybody."

"Could have fooled me, you whore," he said. "Who was that who was wiggling around on my brother's fucking lap?"

"Give it up. I don't want your brother. Why in God's name would I want to get involved with another goddamned Hellers? Do you think I'm a sucker for punishment?"

Grandpa Carron is at my aunt's house for Christmas Eve and Annie, Wally, Sean, and I are sitting in the living room trying to make it through the black and white version of A Christmas Carol *with Alistair Sim. Sean is fading fast until the fireworks start. I can see them from where I'm sitting.*

"You cunt! Don't you dare insult me or my family," he yells as he rises and moves toward her.

She slaps him in the face.

Oh, God. *Good one, I think, but now you're dead.*

He goes at her and shoves her into the fridge. He smacks her in the face and asks her how it feels. She begins crying and strikes back at him. He grabs her by the throat. Annie and I run out to the kitchen and scream for him to stop. Mother's red face is covered with black trails of days old mascara that has run from her eyes to her cheeks. She gasps for breath as he holds her head against the fridge.

"Please, Daddy, stop it!" Annie shouts hysterically.

"Leave her alone!" I scream.

"Fuck off!" Dad yells as he continues to choke her. Her face changes from red to an ugly shade of violet against the yellow refrigerator.

Wally runs into the room. He jumps my father from behind, locking one arm around the monster's neck. "Let go of her, you asshole!" he screams at his father, strengthening his chokehold.

After swatting Mom in the head, Dad turns on Wally. He flings my brother easily against the cupboards and backhands him solidly in the face. Blood flies from my young brother's lips and nose, spraying the wooden cupboards and the floor. Mother lay there in her quilted night robe, wearing bracelets that make a tinkling sound on her shaking wrist as she fights to bring air into her lungs.

"You're crazy!" I screech at Father as I grab him around the waist. He pulls me in front of him and calls me a "disgusting, dirty, whore" before belting me in the mouth and knocking me to the kitchen floor. There is the familiar metallic taste of blood in my mouth. Annie cries loudly and Sean tearfully pleads, "P-p-please, st-stop, Da-da-daddy."

"Oh, fuck all of you fucking losers!" my father shouts. "Merry fucking Christmas! Go to bed, you little bastards." My mother had already retreated to their bedroom. We walk drearily to our rooms, all of us crying as Wally and I dab at the blood on our faces.

"I d-don't th-th-think S-S-Santa is coming t-to th-this house tonight," Sean says, whimpering. I refrain from going into my snotty speech about there being no Santa Claus. We have all had enough.

"Don't worry about that," I tell him before leaving him at his room. "Santa doesn't really hold your life against you."

Somehow during the night, my parents had come to enough senses to put the gifts under the tree, each with a tag and a bow. Not only that; there were stockings left at our bedposts with tangerines, hard candies, and small puzzle games. One or both of our parents had managed to pull it together despite the tragedy of the eve. I always knew that Santa was really my mother. After all, the packages were perfectly wrapped, the tags displayed her tidy printing, and the stockings were always equal, each with the same amount of candies and small, plastic toys, neatly hung from the bedposts. There is no way that my father would have bothered with such fine details for his children. Even if he wanted to, he was perpetually far too drunk.

On Christmas morning, all was forgotten, or so it seemed. This was how it always played itself out. We woke up thrilled that we had a stocking to occupy us until Mom and Dad crawled out of bed. Once they were up, everyone excitedly surrounded the Christmas tree and took turns opening gifts. No one dared say anything about the events of the night before, not after Santa had showered us with games, puzzles, and The Six Million Dollar Man. I knew that all of the clothes we received were purchased at a huge discount price from my Nanny Ida and her den of thieves. I had seen the sweaters, shirts, and pants among the mountain of stolen goods, piled to the ceiling, on her queen size bed down at 16 James Street. My mother sat there all smiles with bruises around her neck as my father handed her a tiny silver package that held yet another piece of jewellery, always her favourite gift. I never understood it. She had bruises on her neck and Wally had dried blood crusted in one nostril, but you would think that you had suddenly entered some twisted episode of the Cleaver family Christmas.

As soon as all presents were opened, my mother began preparations for Christmas dinner while the four of us played happily with our new Operation game and Dad snapped the cap off a bottle of beer after lighting a cigarette. Sean found it difficult playing Operation because his hands would not stop shaking; he went after a rib and the forceps hit the metal making that horrible buzzing sound as the patient's nose lit up red.

"Th-th-this is a h-hard game," he said.

He became so frustrated that I tried to steady his hand with my own so that he could have the pleasure of removing at least one body part. It was no use. As hard as I tried, I could not prevent the vibrations of his hand and he inevitably got the "Buzzzt!" sound that caused him to shake even more.

Even more annoying was the voice of Elvis singing his Christmas songs on our top loader wooden stereo. The King had already died and my father couldn't get enough of his music:

> *I'll have a blue Christmas without you,*
> *I'll be so blue just thinking about you*
> *I'm going to have a blue, blue, blue Christmas.*

I wanted to smash that record into a thousand bits just like I had done with his John Denver *Thank God I'm a Country Boy* LP. I told him I had accidentally stepped on it while dusting the stereo. It was years later that I confessed I had deliberately snapped it over my knee. Father had a penchant for overplaying good music until it sounded like fingernails running down a chalkboard.

It was during the Christmas feast, however, that the tone of the day began to change. We kids gobbled down the special meal that Mom had prepared, while my father only picked at it, his eyes beginning to narrow and his brow starting to sink.

"You should have more to eat, Wade," Mom told him. She knew that he was trying to avoid ruining his beer buzz. We all were aware that there was going to be more trouble. With the meal finished, the four of us went to our bedrooms and played with our new toys just in time to escape the hurricane that ran through our kitchen as our parents fought the night away.

X V I

"OH PLEASE DON'T GO, DAD!" IT WAS MY MOTHER. WEEPING, she held onto the arm of Grandpa Carron. "Please don't make this any harder for me than it already is, dear," he said in a shaky voice.

"We can work this all out," Mom told him as she gasped for air.

Annie and I walked in on the scene. "What's going on?" Annie asked worriedly.

No answer, just weeping. "Mom, what's wrong?" I asked, my heart sinking.

"Grandpa, please talk to us," I begged.

Just then, there was a knock at the door. It was my Uncle Harland, Grandpa's only surviving son. I saw the serious look on his face and I still did not clue in. My mother cried harder and put her head down on the kitchen counter.

"Grandpa, please tell me what's going on! You're all scaring me," I said. Uncle Harland walked past us and headed to Grandpa's room. He returned carrying two suitcases.

"I have to leave, honey," he said in his choked voice.

"What are you talking about?" Annie asked with tears in her eyes.

"I'm going to live with your Uncle Harland." Mom ran from the kitchen to her bedroom sobbing loudly.

"No, Grandpa." I barely got the words out and knew that I was going to lose it.

"I want you kids to know that this is not your fault and I'm going to miss you terribly," Grandpa said. "I just can't stay here anymore." Then he left. Just like that. That fast.

Annie and I ran to our mother. "What happened? Why is Grandpa leaving us?" I screamed with hysteria rising. Mother was crying so hard that she had a difficult time speaking.

"Please tell us, Mom," Annie pleaded.

Finally, she found the words. "Your Grandpa is leaving because he says he can't live in the same house as your father anymore. He can't stand the way that he treats me."

"Does Dad know about this?" I asked.

"Yes. He thinks that it's a good idea," Mom replied softly with her eyes lowered.

Oh you big fucking bastard, I thought. *Now you drove my Grandpa away. I hate you. I hate you. I HATE YOU.*

"Why do you put up with his crap?" I screamed at her. "Why can't we all just get the hell out of here and move as far away from him as possible?"

She blubbered, "Your grandmother Carron always told me that your father would be the death of me." The man smacked her kids around almost daily; her father had just walked out of our house deflated and sobbing and she could still only think of herself.

Later that day, my father walked into the house, drunk as usual, and began frying hamburger in a pan. I did not hesitate; I went right at him:

"Grandpa left," I said disgustedly.

"Yeah, I know," was his short reply. He didn't even lift his eyes from the ugly pink meat in the cast iron pan.

"You made him leave," I added with venom dripping from every word.

"Well, it was for the best," he garbled. "Your grandfather was going to burn this house down eventually. Have you seen the cigarette burns on the carpet in his room? And he's been so drunk lately, that he can't hit his fucking spit can. There's huge fucking gobs of phlegm on the rug and the walls."

My blood boiled.

"You must feel like a big strong guy, getting rid of an old man like that. Do you think you're so perfect? You can't even get through one night without pissing your pants."

"You disrespectful little bitch!"

In a flash, he picked up the hot pan of hamburger and flung it at me. Just as quickly, I ducked as the pan hammered against the wall spilling its contents all over the floor and a kitchen chair.

I bolted for the front door. I ran down Latimer Road and into the nearby woods. I ran until I was exhausted and flopped down under a group of lilac trees knowing that I would never respect my father and that our war would be eternal.

X V I I

I have always been scared of you,
With your Luftwaffe, your gobbledygoo
And your neat mustache
And your Aryan eye, bright blue.
Panzer-man, panzer-man, O You-

Sylvia Plath, *Daddy*

ANNIE AND I BEGAN OUR SECONDARY SCHOOL YEARS AT
Regiopolis-Notre Dame Catholic High School in Kingston during the fall of
1979. During these years my father's rage, brutality, and general neglect grew to
heights that I had never imagined. He came to be diagnosed with rheumatoid
arthritis, a crippling and debilitating disease that one would only wish upon their
worst enemy. At first, the doctors thought that he had muscular dystrophy and
that he would certainly end up in a wheelchair. *Shit, he's going to regret making
all those jokes about Jerry's kids,* I thought. To him, everyone who had an unusual
quality, a disability, a different race or religion, or a different sexual orientation
was either a joke or an "enormous boil on the ass of humanity." He complained
incessantly about the "packies", "carpet flyers", "gimps", "niggers", "chinks", "fags",
"wops", "spics", and "Shylocks". The man's hate knew no boundaries. He often
went on tirades while having his gas pumped at a service station by a "packie",
with his window rolled down and well within earshot of the attendant.

"Jesus H. Christ, you can't stop for gas anywhere without being served by
some fucking carpet flyer. I wish they would stick to their own country like the
brown shit that they are. Hey kids, do you know what that red spot is on their
foreheads? Well, it's a fucking target! Ha, ha, yuk, yuk."

114

While we sat in the back seat on one particular occasion, Annie sensed my tension, shook her head at me and whispered, "no."

But I could not help myself.

"I don't see what the problem is, Dad," I told him. "At least they can hold a job."

"You mouthy cunt! You shut the fuck up or I'll turn around and stuff my fist down your throat! What the fuck do you know about it? These brown fuckers and the slant eyed nine-irons saunter into our country and take all the goddamned jobs!"

"All they're doing is working hard to provide for their families. They're pumping gas, Dad. Is that a job that you actually want? If it is, I'm sure you could get one," I said.

"You fucking smart ass," he harped. "What are you, a packie lover? A nigger lover?"

"I respect what they do. They're only trying to survive like the rest of us."

"Listen, dumb bitch! They don't belong here! We were here first! This is our country!" he screamed at me. Annie grabbed my arm, a signal that I should stop right there. No such luck with the mouth I was developing.

"What do you mean, 'We were here first'?" I asked him, "You're Dutch-German, like you've always said. That means that part of your family came from Europe. Your family wasn't here first either," I added snidely.

He leaned over the seat and gave me a swat on the side of the head. "That's enough of your fucking mouth."

I cried silently all the way home. When we got there, Annie and I went to our bedroom. I dropped onto the bed and put my face into my pillow.

Annie sat on the bed beside me. "If you would just stay quiet, Lynn, he wouldn't hit you like that. You keep going on and on and then he gets so friggin' mad that he belts you. Why? Why can't you just stay silent?"

I lifted my face away from the pillow, snot pulling in a thin string, and looked straight at her. "Because he's wrong," I told her.

* * * * *

Annie and I developed a game, a ritual that followed Father's brutal attacks, an exercise that allowed for some ventilation. It began after one of Dad's particularly vicious blitzes upon my head. After escaping the monster, I ran to my bedroom closet and shut the door. My closet became my safe haven. I sat in there, in the dark, sobbing as I banged my head repeatedly against the wall. While doing this,

I felt exhilaration; I controlled my own pain. I thought that I was turning into some kind of psycho until my sister rescued me.

She walked into my bedroom and knocked on the closet door. "Go away," I said tearfully, even before I knew who it was.

"It's me, Lynnie," Annie said calmly.

I wiped the snot from my nose with my bare forearm and opened the door. She slid right in beside me, holding a reel-to-reel tape recorder and microphone. This recorder and microphone came to us as the result of a grander tragedy. My Nanny Ida's boyfriend, Bill MacIntosh, had been killed in a car accident while under the influence of alcohol and drugs; everyone knew he had been shooting up. Nanny had long been divorced from Walter Simmons. Her new love's entire body was crushed. My father had to identify the remains for his grieving mother and he told us, in tears, how Bill's head was swollen to at least three times its size. Both his forehead and chest cavity were mush. My grandmother told my father to take the contents of what was left of the vehicle and do with it as he wished. Dad brought home the reel-to-reel and an eight-track tape collection in a brown and beige case and presented both to Annie and me. Often, I ran my fingers over the slices and gashes on the surface of the tape case: *This happened when Bill's head got smashed in.* At the time, eight-track tapes were quickly becoming obsolete but the tape recorder held our interest. It was this reel-to-reel that Annie brought to the closet.

"We're going to make a tape," she said.

I was in no mood for recording our favourite renditions of Juice Newton's "Just Call Me Angel of the Morning" or Debbie Boone's "You Light Up My Life."

"I don't want to sing, Annie," I told her.

"Oh, we're not going to sing anything," she said. "We're going to make our own newscast."

"What?" I was completely confused and could not stop my nose from running.

"A newscast," she replied, "I'll be Barbara Walters and I'm going to interview you about what just happened." We both loved Barbara Walters.

"Are you out of your friggin' mind?" I asked her, yet I was more than mildly intrigued.

"It'll be fun. I'll be Barbara and I'll ask you about what happened. You tell me all about it and then we'll listen to it."

I had to laugh. My sister always made me laugh.

"Okay then," I said. "You start." My tears had already stopped.

Annie pressed the play and record buttons and held the microphone to her face. "Good afternoon. This is Barbara Walters reporting from the closet of Lynn

Marie Hellers. The events of today have been disturbing to say the least. Lynn, can you provide any details for our listeners?"

"Yeah, sure. I got my ass kicked, Barbara," I replied.

"Who kicked your ass, Miss Hellers?"

"My prick of a father, that's who."

"And how do you feel about your father at this moment?" Barbara asked.

"He's a fucking bastard, Babs, and I hate him. Is that clear enough? Basically, one of us is going to die. It's either him or me. One way or another, I've got to escape this hellhole." I answered. "Or should I call it the Hellers-hole."

"You would actually kill your own father?" Barbara questioned.

"Why not? We're just lucky that he hasn't killed one of us."

As she carefully placed the microphone to my mouth, Annie inquired, "If you were going to kill your father, Miss Hellers, exactly how would you do it?"

"I'd put poison in his fucking dinner, Babs."

"You might want to seek some help, Miss Hellers. This is Barbara Walters reporting from a dark, scary closet."

None of my answers were intelligent or articulate. They all came from the deepest, yet safest, anger and rage that I could muster within the four tiny walls of my wardrobe.

The only cease-fire that occurred between my father and me happened when I went to school. I came to look forward to boarding the bus that stopped outside of our house every day at 7:10 am, sharp. The four of us took the same bus; Wally and Sean were dropped off at Holy Name Elementary School and Annie and I switched buses there and continued the lengthy ride into Kingston until we reached Regiopolis-Notre Dame High School. Though I was happy to get out of our house, I did not want to go to Regi. All of my elementary school friends, including my precious Dana, went to LaSalle Secondary School on Hwy. 15. It was our mother who insisted that we attend Regiopolis; she had gone to Notre Dame as a teenager in the early sixties when the boys' school of Regiopolis was separated from the girls' school of Notre Dame. She wanted us to continue our Catholic education and to spare us the drug culture for which LaSalle was so renowned. I thought that this was hilarious in light of the fact that our parents drank alcohol incessantly, smoked hash from a bong, and our uncles popped pills and shot up in front of us every time they got the chance.

Though it was an improvement over my home environment, my introduction to Regiopolis-Notre Dame was lonely, lacked lustre, and made me want to overdose on my mother's nerve pills. I sat among the hundreds of students in the gymnasium on the first day, completely anonymous, staring at the floor, shaking nervously, and wanting to die. I wore a new pinstriped shirt that I bought with some babysitting money and a pair of faded beige pants that were too short, too tight, and irritated my crotch. It was the only day that month that I would be able to wear regular clothes; the girls were to be imprisoned in Dress Gordon Tartan kilts and white blouses for the next five years, the boys in suits and ties. We all eagerly waited for the two non-uniform days at the end of each month, during which we were supposed to have our kilts and suits dry-cleaned. Not once did my sister and I do this. Our family could not afford such luxury. Instead, we sporadically washed our kilt by hand in the kitchen sink or took our chances with the washing machine. Most times, my kilt smelled like a drawer of dirty socks. I started to coat my kilt with a layer of my mother's FDS crotch spray just to cover the odour of dirt. Every now and then as we prepared for school in the morning, Annie and I would catch each other sniffing our own kilts, look at each other, and bust out laughing.

Academically, I entered a deep, thick cloud of gray in grade nine. My head felt like it was filled with heavy wet gauze. I went from special and enriched programs–including grade eight math and language in grade five, placement in grade eight when I was in grade seven, grade ten spelling and math in grade eight–and then achieved mediocre results in the grade nine advanced level program. I didn't give a shit. I cared more about being excused to the washroom where I would compulsively wash my hands until they looked like white bloated fish fillets. If I couldn't get to the washroom, I licked and sucked the ends of my fingers to make them feel wet and clean. I spent many of my grade nine school hours engaging in this ritual. That is, until my father hurled insults in my direction, calling me an idiot and asking if I was brain dead for getting 70% in Canadian history.

"What would you know about it?" I told him. "You didn't even finish grade nine."

"You mouthy little fuck!" he howled back. "You better start showing me some respect!"

"I hate to break it to you, *Dad*," I said sarcastically, "but respect isn't just automatically given; it's earned."

I have absolutely no idea where I picked up the balls or the stupidity to talk to him this way. He hit me so hard on the side of my head that I saw an explosion of little white spots on a background of black.

"Thanks, Herr Commandant," I choked out. I *had* learned something in history class. I quickly retreated to our little tree house that was really an old doghouse that we had hauled up into the branches. I wrapped my arms around my legs, put my chin on my knees, and cursed the very ground my father walked on. I begged God, who never seemed to listen to me, to help my family or to make me strong enough to kick his sorry ass like he kicked ours. I needed to find a way out. I needed to escape the prison walls of our house, walls that were far more confining and suffocating than the spider-covered ones of the three-foot by four-foot doghouse in the tree.

XVIII

"DO YOU THINK WE'RE EVER GONNA GET OUT OF HERE?" I asked Annie as we lay on our beds one late evening.

"Sure we are," she replied. "We aren't going to be here forever. We'll finish school and move on with our own lives. We'll eventually get married and have our own families and live in our own houses."

"I'm *never* getting married," I told her.

"Oh, you say that now," Annie replied, "but someday you'll do it. What if you meet some really hot guy? You liked that Mike guy at our grade eight party. What about him? He was cute and seemed to like you."

"Yeah, sure, until he met Claire Mills. Then I became a houseplant sitting in the corner. Guys are assholes. All they care about is looks and rubbing their dick against you when dancing to the slow songs. They're a bunch of pigs. They think you're smart and funny until some twit with huge tits walks by them."

Annie laughed. "Yeah, you're not wrong about that one."

"What do you know about it?" I asked. "All the guys like you. You've got blond hair and you're pretty. They actually *look* at you. They're always asking me if you're going out with anyone. They tell me that I look like a lion. What the hell is that supposed to mean anyway? A lion. It's because of my thin hair and my crooked teeth. I need to get these teeth fixed." I poked my index finger into my mouth.

"You don't look like a friggin' lion, Lynn."

"That's what John keeps saying," I explained. "That fucking asshole on our bus. He keeps calling me 'lion' in front of his dopey friends. They all laugh their guts out and tell me how hideously ugly I am. One of them told me that he wouldn't give me a screw even if it was one of the little silver kind in a hardware box. They're nasty bastards and I hate them."

"You have to ignore them," Annie said with a serious look.

"Oh, that's easy for you to say, beauty queen. They all like you. It doesn't matter anyway. I don't care. If getting married means living like Mom and Dad,

120

then I'd rather be burned at the stake, and only after they pulled out all of my fingernails before lighting the match."

We laughed ourselves to sleep.

My sister had long been the beautiful one. Boys became suddenly dumb and goony around her and men complimented her. Our father proudly showed her school pictures to his friends and they speculated that she had a promising future in modeling. She had shiny blond hair, striking hazel eyes, and a perfect complexion–ideal for a Noxema commercial.

I, on the other hand, had a promising future haunting houses. I was considered the smart one, as if a girl couldn't possibly have both looks and brains. Thin, spider web, cotton-candy hair crowned my freckled face that showcased those dreadfully crooked teeth. Even though hygiene and personal care were no longer issues for me, I was still considered a "dog face". Kids who didn't know me wasted no time in pointing this out. The casual cruelty of children toward other children is unbelievable and soul damaging. But it was the cruelty of adults that solidified my complete discouraging perception of myself.

Party time at 16 James Street. My parents take all four of us to Nanny Ida's house and we are the only children there. The kitchen table is crowded with scruffy men and I make a game out of counting their tattoos. A couple of these men are my uncles and some of them are Nanny's Joyceville Institute buddies or members of Hell's Angels. They talk about stabbings, slitting throats, and catching muskellunge in the lakes of Ontario. Nanny and my mother are the only women there, but my mother sits outside of the circle near the door. With a beer in hand, she looks very nervous and I think that she is sitting there to make a quick escape if need be. I mentally will her to make sure she takes us with her.

My grandmother, as always, commands the room. She holds a cigarette in one hand, elbow on the table, and swings the other around in the air calling the group a crew of "cock-suckers". There is a good deal of laughter and smoke pollutes the air as all seem to exhale in unison. Nanny Ida is plastered. Her eyes blink and click and mascara leaves dark crescents below her eyes. She hasn't been as careful with her lipstick this time; there are only smudged and cracked remnants at the corners of her mouth. Still, she is aware of everything and everyone. She is always a formidable presence. No matter who enters her house or sits at her table, they must show her respect.

I look at her in awe. She both frightens and intrigues me. I admire her—her strength and her unwillingness to take shit from anybody. Anybody except family; she takes a good deal of shit from them. I have always revered both grandmothers, Nanny Carron and Nanny Ida, but for very different reasons. Nanny Ida looks at me and I freeze.

"Hey, how ya doin' there, Lollipop?" she asks.

I blush at her attention. "I'm okay, Nanny. How are you?" I ask, smiling.

"Fucking fantastic, my dear." She looks at me, hard.

After a gulp of whiskey and cola, she turns to my father. "Why don't you take that kid to get her hair cut? It's like a fucking sparrow's nest." The room erupts in laughter. Even if it isn't funny, it's considered funny just because Nanny Ida says it.

"C'mon Ma, what am I supposed to do with that?" Father says with a giggle, pointing to me, while looking around the group. More laughter.

"I could maybe do something with that."

It's my uncle, Randy. He has just begun his career as a hairstylist, cutting women's hair and trying to make his way in the business. His creative ventures involve drawing a portrait of the sitter adorned with a hairstyle of choice, beautiful drawings in pencil and charcoal. Randy is an artist with an incredible ability to render, and always does the right thing for his sitter.

"Well, buddy, there's some kinda challenge for ya, right there," Father says.

Everyone in the room stares at me. "I don't want my hair cut," I say plainly, looking around the room. They laugh.

"Don't ya want to be a pretty girl like your sister?" It's one of the Hell's Angels, smiling through the substantial hair on his face, with large gaps between his teeth. I stare at the floor and feel the heat of my face intensify. I look to my mother. The crevasses on her forehead are deep; her cigarette goes to her mouth and she twists a ring on her finger. She avoids my eyes. I realize that this is going to be bad.

"You are getting that fucking rat's nest cut," my father says. "You're a fucking embarrassment. Do something with that mess, brother." He nudges Randy, gulping long and hard on the brown bottle.

"C'mon here, Lollipop, and I'll give you a cut," Randy says, patting a chair and smiling. He's trying to be nice about it.

Flatly, I say, "No." I move and stand beside my mother.

"She doesn't want to do it, brother," Randy says to my father with a shrug.

The Hell's Angel lets out a loud snort.

My father sets his bottle firmly on the table and looks around the room at all the faces. He grins. I know that grin. I am definitely in for it.

"Get your scrawny ass in that chair, Lynn, and get that hair cut." His eyes bore into me. All my muscles and bones go suddenly flaccid. I might pee my pants.

"C'mon, Lollipop," Nanny Ida adds. "You'll feel so much better."

I tell her the truth. "No. I don't want to, Nanny. I feel fine. I don't need to feel any better." Father looks at me as if I have just told the queen of England to go fuck herself.

"You dare say no to your grandmother? My mother?" His eyes wobble and vibrate, a crazed look one might have just before committing mass murder from a watchtower.

Nanny Ida laughs and says in her deep raspy voice, "It's alright, Wade. Lolly doesn't want to do it. It's okay." The Joyceville cons laugh along with her. It's expected.

Father glares at me. "It most certainly is not okay, Ma. She needs to learn some fucking manners and I'm a little sick of looking at that ugly scruffy head. She's a fucking disgrace. I'm embarrassed."

There is more nervous laughter; no one wants to participate anymore, yet no one changes the subject. My grandmother's eyes tick and flicker; she looks at the ceiling as a puff of smoke shoots from her mouth. Something has to happen because she is getting bored. My father makes his move. He awkwardly rises from his chair and staggers toward me. I am ready. I have known all along that this moment was inevitable.

He hesitates momentarily as his squinted eyes lock with mine and I see his enormous hate for me. Strong hands take my shoulders and he lifts me completely in the air. "Enough of this shit," he hisses. He picks me up physically, easily, and carries me to the kitchen sink, right in front of the table where everyone can see and enjoy the show. I feel confused and terrified, with no idea of what he is about to do. I say nothing; I make no sound at all. He is so strong. He takes my head and forces it into the sink, turns the tap full blast. Water floods my head and sprays everywhere. Laughter. My father laughs too. The force of the laughter brings more force to his hand. He holds my neck and head, strong and firm, under the flood of water. I cry and make no sound at all. Dramatically he lifts my head from under the tap and carries me wet and dripping to a kitchen chair.

"There you go, Randy," he states, giggling. "Fix that up, would ya?"

Apparently, the vision of a pathetic child with a cap of dripping wet hair is a cause for complete hilarity. They cannot contain themselves.

I surrender limply and Randy cuts my hair while everyone watches and chortles. I cry nonstop. When he finishes, one of the jailbirds makes an assessment: "Well that's better, aye? Now ya gotta do somethin' about those teeth and she'd be a beauty."

Finally released, I run to my grandmother's bedroom. My mother follows me. She kneels down in front of me with tears in her eyes. "Don't you listen to them," she says. "Just don't listen."

But I did listen. I listened and absorbed every word. I was ugly. As ugly as sin.

X I X

"DO YOU THINK THAT I COULD GET MY TEETH FIXED, MOM?" I asked her sheepishly one morning as she applied her makeup in the hallway mirror.

"What do you mean?" she asked.

I laid it out for her as plainly as I could. "Well, just take a look at my mouth. My teeth are all crooked and growing one behind the other. There are huge gaps between them. I've got a dent in my tongue from the one that's growing underneath it. I look like some kind of wild animal. Dad says that I have summer teeth: "some are here and some are there." That's really not funny. I don't even smile for pictures anymore. Sean starts crying when I grin at him in a dark room. That, by the way, is the only fun part of having these ugly teeth."

"Are you telling me that you want braces?" Mom asked.

"Yes! Something has to be done. Everyone thinks I'm so ugly." I choked; tears appeared. "I really do want them fixed."

"Braces are really expensive, Lynn, and you're not ugly."

"Oh come on, you know the truth. I know they're expensive, Mom, but I could work more around the house to earn them. My friend Dana has braces and her teeth are going to be gorgeous. I always have to hide my mouth when I say anything because the kids at school make such fun of me. Some of the boys tell me that I look like a lion," I told her in a low voice. I could feel the stinging in my eyes. "It's so humiliating."

She looked at me for a least a whole minute before saying anything. "I'll make an appointment for you and we'll see what we can do."

"Oh thanks so much, Mom! That would be great! I can't wait! Will you phone today?"

"I'll make some calls when I get to work, but remember, no promises. If I can't afford the payments, you won't be able to have the braces."

"Fair enough," I said, completely overjoyed.

My mother took me to see Dr. Ed O'Leary, an orthodontist in Kingston. He convinced her to make the investment in my smile and self-esteem. I loved him for that. He fitted my mouth with the metal, glue, and elastics that I would wear for the next four years. I knew this was a frightening financial investment for my mother, who could barely keep us in groceries and, to this day, I see it as the kindest thing she ever did for me. I think she did it, in part, to make up for that terrible night at 16 James Street. My father made me believe that I was ugly; she wanted to do what she could to undo the damage.

I couldn't wait to show my new braces to Dana. Even though she was at a different high school, my parents gave me permission to attend a dance there. We had kept in touch by letters and cards, but as time wore on, they seemed to dwindle and made me worry that I was going to lose her friendship. In my heart, she was the best friend I had ever had in my first fourteen years and I loved her. Even though it was a long distance call, my mother let me phone her to tell her I would be coming to the LaSalle dance that Friday night. She seemed as excited as I was and she told me that she would wait for me inside the main doors.

All that week I had a difficult time concentrating on my schoolwork and chewed my fingernails to the quick wondering what I was going to wear. My clothes weren't even remotely fashionable. Every evening after school, I tried on my available combinations of old Howick jeans that were either too short or too tight, frilly out-dated shirts that made me look like a ten-year-old, and the plaid shirts I was so fond of, which had suddenly gone out of style. No matter what I put on, I looked like what my sister and I referred to as "Bagot Street trash".

I decided to approach my mother with my fashion dilemma hoping that she would take me out and buy me a new outfit. No such luck. She found a burgundy and beige blouse in her closet that was too small for her and figured it would look spectacular on me. It had large black buttons, hung down to the hips, and had a tie at the waist and was clearly too big for me. I put it on with a pair of my old Howick's and figured that this was going to be as good as it got. I completed the ensemble with a pair of my sister's black cloth Chinese shoes. I tried the outfit on several times before the dance and thought that it looked better and better each time, even though I wouldn't score any points on a runway.

That Friday night, my body became a bundle of nerves; butterflies flitted around my stomach. This was to be my first high school dance and I was going to see Dana! I worked for hours on my hair with Annie's curling iron and Mom let me use some of her purple eye shadow and mascara. I donned my outfit and thought that I looked okay. My father took me on the long drive to LaSalle Secondary and Sean came along for the ride. He dropped me off outside the main doors, told me to have a good time, and to stay away from the boys. I knew that wasn't going to be difficult.

"The dance is over at eleven, Dad," I reminded him.

"I know. I know. I'll be here. Me and Sean are going to visit one of my pals and we'll pick you up afterward."

After my father and brother drove off, I nervously approached the doors and the crowds of teenagers standing in groups under the lights, laughing, smoking, and flirting. I scanned the crowd for Dana but did not see her. Slowly, I walked up the steps and joined the line going into the dance. There was still no sign of Dana. I could feel the music booming and throbbing:

Oo my little pretty one, pretty one,
When you gonna give me some time, Sharona?

The Knack, *My Sharona*

I showed my student card, paid the fee, and entered the dark gymnasium lit only by flashing lights coming from above the DJ booth on the stage. Completely self-conscious, I wanted to jump out of my own skin. Then I saw her. Dana. She smiled, grabbed the arms of two girls on either side of her, and made her way toward me. The trio looked like *Charlie's Angels*, only prettier. I pulled nervously at the tie belt around my waist. They walked up to me and all three gave me the once over glance from head to toe. From the looks on their faces, including Dana's, I could see that they thought my outfit was all wrong and that Dana was embarrassed. They were wearing new Rainbow jeans and Sergio Valente. Their tops were cute and form fitting. They had eye-catching necklaces and bracelets. Their shoes appeared to be real leather and were new and stylish. They each had a small purse with a shiny buckle slung over one shoulder. They looked like gorgeous triplets that had momentarily walked out of a teen magazine.

"Hi Dana," I said with a smile. I was so happy to see her face.

"Hi," she said, "Girls, this is Lynn. Remember I told you about her. We went to Holy Name."

"Hi," they said in unison. One of them smiled weakly and the other, the one with long dark hair, looked downright disgusted.

"It's great to see you again," I told Dana.

"Yeah, you too," she said. After a short but uncomfortable pause, she added, "Well, you have a good time, okay? I'll talk to you later."

Then the three of them turned around and walked away into the crowd in the center of the gym. As they did, the one with the long dark hair turned her head around to look back at me and burst out laughing as she pulled on Dana's arm. I was devastated. My heart jumped into my throat and I knew I was going to cry. I found the washroom and entered its overly bright fluorescent light. There were girls laughing, fixing their hair and makeup, and a group in one corner smoking hash from a bong. I shut myself in a bathroom stall and quietly wept. I kept it brief because I knew the mascara would run down my cheeks. I waited until the outer room was mostly silent before leaving the safety of the stall. There, in the mirror, I saw myself. I saw the truth of me, my life. I didn't fit anywhere. I stared at my image until it was a blur. *That's better.* I turned and walked out.

I bravely went back into the gymnasium and leaned against the wall. Gloria Gaynor was just finishing *I Will Survive* and the dance floor was packed. The DJ took the crowd right into the Bee Gees:

> *Nobody gets too much heaven no more*
> *It's much harder to come by*
> *I'm waiting in line*
> *Nobody gets too much love anymore*
> *It's as high as a mountain*
> *And harder to climb*

The Bee Gees, *Too Much Heaven*

Couples filled the floor in their close rhythmic embrace. I saw Dana in the arms of an attractive, athletic guy and my heart broke again. Suddenly I realized just how much I loved her.

No one asked me to dance. No one else said hello to me. No one even looked at me. I realized that I was completely alone. Before long, I made my way outside and sat on the steps away from those who were getting some air or contaminating it with marijuana smoke. I looked down at the black cloth Chinese shoes on my feet and I wanted to scream.

As 11:00 PM rolled around, I felt like I had been there for a lifetime. I had no further contact with Dana and hadn't danced even once. Cars rolled in en masse to collect sons and daughters. I kept an eager eye out for my father's vehicle and went to the entrance of the lot so that he wouldn't have to drive all the way in. I waited and waited and waited. I went up on the steps of the school and waited some more. Every one of the hundreds who were there were now gone. The only other human presence was the two custodians who were mopping the floors of the school's foyer. I walked back inside the school to check the time and to escape the chill of the night air. It was 12:00 AM. I wanted to cry. I didn't know how I was going to get home. Inside my guts, I started to panic.

"Hey there," one of the custodians said. "How come you're still here? Don't you have a ride home?"

"Yes," I replied with embarrassment. "My father is coming to pick me up."

"Well, doesn't he know the school dances end at eleven?"

"Yeah. He knows."

The custodians looked at each other. One shook his head and continued mopping the floor. I put a quarter into the nearby vending machine and pulled out a bag of salt and vinegar chips. I walked outside, embarrassed that these men knew that I was abandoned. I knew that I was on my own. I waited a little longer, until the custodians disappeared, and then peeked through the front doors at the clock. It was 1:30 in the morning and still there was no sign of my father's car.

I started walking Hwy. 15. I had no idea how long it was going to take me to walk to Inverary; I did know that it would take me well into the next day. As I put one foot in front of the other, all I could hear was the sound of stones crunching under my cheap cloth shoes and the chirps and hums of night bugs. The only interruption to these sounds and the blackness of the cool night were the infrequent headlights of a passing car coupled with the whir of its engine. Whenever a car passed from behind, I could see my long thin shadow in front of me, numbly reminding me that I was still there. I gave up looking closely at the cars and figured my father was never going to surface.

It didn't take long before fear started to get the better of me. I began to weep softly. The later it got, the further I traveled toward the ditch in a feeble attempt to hide as I journeyed, knowing that I would be easy prey for any of the psychos I had seen in the movies. In my mind, I started to think that this was far worse than the other time my father had left me on the side of the road. I sat to rest for a bit at the edge of the gravel and grass and remembered.

"Why don't you get your dad an ice cream cone with all that change that you have?" Dad says as he parks the car at Code's Corners.

"That's my money from babysitting," I tell him. "I'm saving it for something." I was eleven years old and wanted to buy myself a small chemistry set.

My mother says, "Don't worry, Wade, I'll get you a cone. What flavour do you want?"

"I didn't ask you to get me one. I asked her," he tells Mother. He is drunk. He has been drinking all day at the cottage on the Isle of Man. We go to Code's Corners to get some hotdogs for dinner and more mix for liquor.

I tell him that I'm saving for the chemistry set and don't even plan on buying anything for myself at Code's.

"You selfish little bitch," he says, laying his arm over the seat and turning toward me. "You won't even buy your old man a cheap ice cream cone?"

"She's worked hard for that money, Wade. She's saving for something. I'll get you the ice cream cone. What do you want? Chocolate?" Mom asks.

"You shut the fuck up," he tells her, spit flying onto the car seat.

He turns his head again and looks at me with disgust and hate. "You," he says, "you get the fuck out of my car."

"Oh, Christ, don't be ridiculous, Wade!" Mom yells, looking around frantically with her eyes bulging, "You can't just leave her here, this far from the cottage!"

"The fuck I can't," he replies. "Get out, you little shit, before I drag you out."

I know that he is serious and look to my mother for help. She stares straight ahead through the windshield, silent, mouth and shoulders drooping. I open the car door and step out. I don't expect that they will actually leave.

My father says, "Have fun finding your way back," before the car speeds off in a large cloud of dust and gravel spit.

I stand there, stunned, for what seems like hours. I see the car grow smaller and smaller, becoming wavy fluid gold metal in the bright sun, as it travels down the highway to meet the vanishing point on the horizon. I cannot believe that my parents have actually left me here, this far from home. For some reason, a ludicrous survival instinct kicks in. I walk into Code's Corners, not to report my abandonment, but to purchase a drink to quench the thirst that I will surely have on my long walk back to the cottage. It never, even for a moment, occurs to me to tell anyone that I have been left there on the side of the road. I already know that my family's behaviour is not only embarrassing, but that it is an ancestral crime to rat them out.

I partly enjoy the peacefulness of my trek down Hwy. 15 to the Isle of Man Road. The day is bright and full of sunlight, heat, and wildflowers. I hum one of my favourite songs: Band on the Run by Paul McCartney and Wings. I fully expect that my mother will come to retrieve me after my father passes out at the cottage. She never shows up. But someone else does.

He pulls his pale blue car over onto the gravel shoulder ahead of me. I slowly walk up to the driver's side to see a man who is older than my father, with thinning white hair, a huge red nose, and deep pock marks peppering his face. I think to myself that he looks like he was once hit with buckshot. I notice a tackle box and fishing rod on the backseat of the car, but not before I smell the whiff of booze on his breath. It is a smell that I know well.

"Can I take you somewhere, little lady?" he asks with a yellow-toothed smile.

"No thank you," I reply politely. "I just live down the road from here."

He says, "Well, I'll take you there."

Somehow, I know he is not to be trusted. It's the smell of alcohol that saves me.

"Really, no thanks mister, I don't need a ride." I continue walking and waving at the next few cars that go by, as if they are close friends of my family.

"Fucking little tease," he hisses as he drives off.

I have lost my ease and arrive at the cottage in a full trot hours later. My mother is in the kitchen cleaning the countertop.

"Why didn't you come back and get me?" I ask her, winded.

"Because your father was so pissed off. He told me not to. He said that if I went to get you, then I would get what was coming to me."

I slowly walk by the bedroom they share at the cottage. My father is in there, asleep and snoring loudly.

"He's asleep, Mom," I say softly. "You could have come. At least I wouldn't have had to walk the whole way."

She doesn't look at me and continues cleaning the countertop.

I don't tell her about the man in the pale blue car.

This memory plagued me as I walked the very same highway on the night of my first high school dance. The memory intensified my fear. My heart raced with every sound, every shadow, every rustle in the brush, every car that passed by. I began to cry from terror, exhaustion, and the realization that I was nowhere near a telephone. The fear replaced my intense sadness about Dana. Just as I started to consider knocking on the door of the next house, a car slowed down behind me, passed, and parked on the side of the highway. It was my father's car. I walked up to the passenger side and saw that my father brought his friend along, Bobby. Both were drunk. I could smell the alcohol as soon as Bobby rolled down the window. In the back seat was Sean, shirtless, half-asleep, and shivering. I began to cry harder.

"Well, what the hell are you waiting for? Get into the goddamned car," my father said.

I yelled at him. "You're drunk! I'm not going anywhere with you!"

"You get into this fucking car now! If I have to come out and get you, you'll find out what's good for you!"

I was far too tired. I slipped into the backseat beside my shaking brother and slammed the door as hard as my weary arms allowed.

"Do you have any idea what time it is?" I asked him, sobbing.

"Yeah. It's late." He and Bobby started laughing.

I tried the guilt approach and asked him how he'd feel if I had been abducted, or worse.

"Like that would happen," he slurred back at me. "You're not much to look at." More laughter.

I didn't have the energy to fight back. I leaned my head against the window and cried silently until I slept.

* * * * *

I woke up the next morning to sunshine filling my room, warming the cool blue walls. Lifting myself from the bed, I caught sight of myself in the mirror above my chest of drawers. The image was ghastly. My eyes were swollen almost shut, tracks of mascara beneath them; my thin hair was separated to reveal my scalp in some places while it stood on end in others. There was a scab of white crust at the corner of my mouth. I looked just like my mother after one of her nights of heavy drinking.

Memories of the night before struck my brain with the force of a rocket. Dana was now dead to me. She had bitten my red heart in two. The subsequent humiliation from my father and his friend only served to fuel the frying pan where my broken life-organ laid, simmering. I climbed slowly out of my bed, changed my clothes, and loaded my brother's pellet gun.

With the gun in hand, I walked, trance-like, into the nearby woods. I didn't plan on using this gun on myself. I wasn't an idiot. A pellet gun could only do surface damage to my body, but it could do plenty of damage to a small animal.

I walked slowly through the trees, watching the dappling light under my feet. I stopped. This was the spot. Quietly, I stood there. The branches of the trees waved gently in the breeze. This day was beautiful. I looked up, closed my eyes, and felt the warmth of the sun on my face.

My eyes opened and I saw it. My target. It was a small sparrow resting on the branch of a diminutive birch tree. I watched it make its tiny, quick movements for a few moments before aiming the weapon. Once I had eyed the bird confidently in my sight, I fired the gun.

As soon as I took the shot, I hoped that I had missed. Instead, I watched as the sparrow fluttered and spiralled to the ground. I ran to it. There it lay, flapping one wing, its body jerking under that birch tree. I could see the growing red spot on its neck, the terror in the little eyes that eerily looked up at me.

I gently lifted the wounded sparrow up and cupped it in my shaking hands. With one finger, I petted its head until it closed its eyes and died. Then I wept uncontrollably. Using a stick, I dug a small grave and buried my crime. "I shouldn't have done this to you," I said, patting the soil, neatly and delicately.

Somehow, I knew I had killed more than the sparrow. As I placed a rock upon it, I told the little mound that I wouldn't let myself feel the way I felt about Dana ever again.

X X

"HEY, YOU, WHATCHA READIN'?" HE ASKED AS WE RODE THE bus to high-school.

I was partly annoyed by the interruption, considering that this was one of the more private and quiet times I had to read. Invariably, my face was within a book on every bus ride to and from school. This was *my* time. I wanted him to get lost, but knew how unfriendly I would appear if I ignored him.

"It's an edition of *Alfred Hitchcock Presents,*" I told him, smiling weakly.

"Oh yeah. Hitchcock. Is it any good? I've seen the movie *Psycho* that he directed."

I was impressed that he knew Hitchcock was even associated with the movie, let alone that he directed it. But everyone knew about *Psycho*. I figured I would entertain myself by testing his knowledge.

"Have you ever seen *Rope* or *Strangers on a Train*?" I asked him smugly.

"No. Never heard of them. What are they about?" he asked, genuinely interested, leaning over the seat toward me.

"Forget it," I said, turning back to Hitchcock, "It would take too long to tell you about them."

His name was Marc Gatien. Until that moment, all I knew about him was that he was in my art class and his graphic ability was impressive. While I took advanced level classes, he took general level courses, meaning that our contact was minimal. I had begun to forge a friendship with his sister, who rode the same bus, but was in a grade below. Catherine was intelligent, moody, and absolutely beautiful. She reminded me of Botticelli's *Primavera*. I had seen a colour plate of the painting in art class during a study of early Renaissance art. I didn't have the courage to tell her that every time I looked at her, I saw the gorgeous *Primavera* with spring flowers in her hair. As for her brother Marc, he struggled with a bad case of acne and was known by most other students as a class clown followed by resident expert, in no particular order, on the rolling of perfect joints, the qualities of hash oil, and the superior homemade bong.

"Oh, what? Do you think I'm too much of an idiot to understand those movies? I'm not asking you to tell me the entire plot, you know," Marc continued.

"I'm sorry," I replied, smiling. "I didn't mean to imply that you wouldn't understand. It's just that I'm at a really interesting part of this story and I want to finish it."

"No problem. Sorry I bothered you," he said, leaning back in his seat.

As soon as I finished the story and closed the jacket of the book, he said, "Do you want to read a really good book?"

"Like what?" I asked with the snide tone that indicated I wouldn't wipe my ass with a book that he would read.

"Oh, so you think you're the only one who can read and tell a good book from a bad one?"

"I'm not into *Penthouse*, if that's what you're going to suggest," I told him with a laugh.

"I wasn't going to suggest *Penthouse*, Miss Priss, though I think you could benefit from some of its educational merits."

Asshole. I made a twisted face at him but at the same time, I was intrigued.

"The book I'm trying to tell you about, Miss Know-It-All," he added, "is *'Salem's Lot*, by Stephen King. Have you read it?"

I hadn't and hated to admit it.

"No I haven't," I explained, "but I have read *Carrie* and I loved it!"

"Hey, let me tell you, that if you loved *Carrie*, you'll be blown away by *'Salem's Lot*. I have the book. I'll bring it for you tomorrow, okay?"

"Sure," I replied enthusiastically.

This was how it began. The catalyst for our young love was a mutual adoration of Stephen King.

* * * * *

Marc was true to his word. The following morning, he eagerly and immediately joined me in my seat, the second last one on the bus. Catherine gaped with her mouth hanging open. It was usually she who joined me for the early ride before I opened a book.

"I brought the novel," he said. "You're going to love it." He handed me the dark coloured *Signet* paperback of *'Salem's Lot*. I read the caption, "*A town possessed by unspeakable evil...*" and wanted to begin reading right then and there.

"Thanks," I said.

"Let me know what you think," Marc said as he left my seat and slid into his at the very back.

As soon as he sat down, Catherine joined me. "What the hell did my jerk of a brother want?" she asked with total disgust.

"Oh, he just gave me a book to read. *'Salem's Lot* by Stephen King. I really liked his book, *Carrie*, so Marc figured that I would enjoy this one."

"Listen," Catherine said seriously. "Marc is a fucking dickhead and I would steer clear of him if I were you. God, I can't stand him. Looking at his face makes me sick."

I laughed. "He's not that bad, Cath. He's your brother. Of course you can't stand him! I think that my brother, Wally, is an annoying turd."

"Look, Lynn," Catherine continued, "I can tell that Marc likes you. He asked me a million questions about you last night. Take my advice. Don't get involved with him. You'd regret it. He's a complete loser and you deserve someone better, someone more like you."

"I wouldn't say that I was a winner, Cath," I said, laughing.

She latched onto my arm. "You're smart, talented, and pretty," she told me, "and he is fat, pimply, and dumb. I should know. I have to live with the asshole every day."

She was the first person, besides my cousin Darren, who ever called me pretty. Though I had a tough time believing her, her words were more sonorous than *Vivaldi* to my ears.

"What are you telling her about me?" Marc asked with a shout, breaking my reverie.

Catherine answered, "I'm telling her the truth about you, you slime!"

"Don't believe a word she says, Lynn," Marc told me. Turning toward her, he spat the words: "She's nothing but an uptight little bitch!"

I hated that word. Bitch. I had heard it so often from my father.

"Okay, guys, calm down," I said, looking at both of them. "You'll end up getting kicked off of the bus." It was the only thing I could think of to say.

It seemed to work. Marc muttered one last retort, "bitch." She hissed, "faggot." That was the end of the first of many brief and hurtful battles between Marc and Catherine in my presence.

I read *'Salem's Lot* in two nights and couldn't sleep for several nights thereafter. The novel incited the terror and excitement that came to me comfortably and served as a vessel to ride out my fantasies of rage. I couldn't wait to talk to Marc about it. I told him how I looked out my window every night to terrify myself, heart pounding, waiting for the blood-sucking ghoul to appear on the other side of the glass. What I didn't tell Marc was that if the monster appeared with his garish pointy-toothed smile, he would be no scarier than the bloodsucker that shared a bed with my mother across the hall. I would be ready for him.

'Salem's Lot was just the beginning of a long book sharing venture between Marc and me; over the years we bought and traded the entire works of Stephen King. I bought *Firestarter* and he bought *The Dead Zone*. When the *Creepshow* series began, we could talk about little else. He drew amazing images of the characters we read about and we compared our sketchbook drawings. I admired that he could so aptly capture the essence of "The Dark Man" in *The Stand,* and I impressed him with my meticulously detailed drawings of birds and plant life. His drawings were filled with provocative darkness and devilishness and mine were filled with feathers and leaves, yet we each admired the other's work. Soon, I took a constant seat beside Catherine so that I could talk to her *and* Marc. With my aisle seat, she was on one side of me and he was on the other. My position between the two reduced their fighting somewhat, but it never ended.

"Look at this drawing that Marc did," I said as I held his sketchbook toward Catherine.

She looked at it for exactly one second, turned her head to the bus window, and said, "Who cares what he does."

"You have to admit that it's a good drawing, Cath," I said.

"You're entitled to your own opinion," she replied coldly.

I tried the same tactic with Marc. Catherine showed me a science test with a mark in the nineties. I grabbed it, aghast, and congratulated her. I held the test toward Marc.

"Look what Cathy got on this friggin' test!" I yelped.

He replied, "Big deal," as Catherine ripped the test from my hands and told me not to show him because he wouldn't know the difference between a plant and animal cell if they both bit him on the ass at the same time.

I finally conceded that bringing them together was completely hopeless. I didn't get it. I could punch my brother Wally in the head, he could chase me with an axe, and we would play road hockey together an hour later.

The more interested I became in what Marc had to say, the more Catherine withdrew. I certainly valued her friendship above Marc's, at that point, and was always trying to smooth out her ruffles of discontent. I did a good job of keeping the peace until Regi's Student Council organized a Sadie Hawkins Dance.

At first, I had no idea who the hell Sadie Hawkins was and why the school council would name a dance in her honour. A girl named Lana in my math class made it all clear for me:

"Are you taking anyone to the Hawkins dance?" Lana asked.

"Not yet," I answered. "I don't even know what a Hawkins dance means."

Lana laughed good-naturedly. "It's a dance where the girls get to ask the guys to go as their date. It's kind of a nice change. Usually it's the guys who ask us," she said.

Even though her explanation didn't tell me who Sadie Hawkins was, I did finally understand the purpose of the dance.

"So, is there anyone that you'd like to ask?" she inquired, smiling, all of her white teeth visible.

"Are you kidding me?" I replied, blushing. "I'd rather have a Pap Test." As young teen girls enduring the onset of menstruation, we were all terrified of our first examination and joked about it frequently. The truth was that I hadn't even started my period. Annie had started so young, and here I was, approaching my fifteenth birthday without nary a spot in my underwear.

"I happen to know that Marc Gatien thinks you're pretty cool," she whispered to me.

"How do you know that?" I asked, blushing even more, to the point that my head started to ache.

"'Cause he told me so," Lana answered with a wide grin.

Just then, Ms. Chandler's voiced boomed: "Lynn Hellers, I take it that you've already solved this equation for X and Y. Would you mind giving us the answers please?"

I blushed even harder. I thought that my head was definitely going to explode, blowing blood and brains all over the room.

I liked Ms. Chandler and thought that she was brilliant and that it was a shame she was so fat. Walking always seemed to be an exasperating chore for her. She had to prop herself against her desk to pull herself out of her chair. She consistently wore stretchy fabrics, misshapen skirts that covered the substantial expanse of her ass, and jackets that she compulsively tidied and closed across the bulging front of her body. I respected her as my teacher and for her obvious high intelligence; I didn't want her thinking that I wasn't paying attention to her lesson.

"Yes," I replied, head pounding. "I have the answer. X equals 2 and Y equals 5."

"Uh, yes, uh, that is correct," she said with complete surprise, looking at me suspiciously above the dark rims of her glasses. "I'm happy that you are still with us. Perhaps you should save your conversation for after school so that you don't fall behind."

I took Ms. Chandler's advice and waited to discuss the matter after school. It filled my mind for that entire afternoon. The answers to my math equations came easy. The answer to the matter was a whole other ball game. Every nerve in my body felt like it had a pin sticking in it.

That afternoon on the bus ride home, I sat literally on the edge of the green vinyl seat. Marc sat in his usual spot behind me. Thankfully, Catherine was not on the bus; had she been there, I would never have had the courage to talk to him.

"So, Marcus, have you been asked to the Sadie Hawkins dance yet?" I asked, trying to be nonchalant.

Laughing, he replied, "No! I'm not the kinda guy that girls ask to dances."

"Why do you say that?" I really wanted to know.

"Because I don't really fit anywhere," he said. "I'm not good-looking enough for the pretty girls; I'm not smart enough for the smart girls; I'm not a jock, and the rest of the girls are too shy to ask."

I absolutely *loved* his answer. I smiled at him.

"Well, you could go with me," I said bravely. An electric current shot through my body.

He looked at me for what seemed like an hour. "Are you frigging kidding me?" he asked with a twisted face.

I wanted to die. My heart sank and I wished that the bottom of the bus would give out and drop my sorry ass onto Latimer Road and drag it for miles. Marc must have noticed the stricken look on my face.

"Oh, Lynn, don't take this the wrong way! I just can't believe that you are asking me. Somehow I think this must be some kind of cruel joke. Did my sister put you up to this?"

"Catherine didn't put me up to anything," I answered as I looked away from him.

"Well, then who did?" he asked.

"Nobody. I just thought that maybe you would like to go. I don't know. Maybe it's a bad idea. I'm not much of a dancer and I haven't asked my parents about it yet. I take it back. It's a stupid idea."

"It's not a stupid idea," he said, "I just can't believe that someone like you would want to go with me without it being some kind of joke on me."

"I wouldn't do that," I told him. "Let's just forget about it, okay?"

"I can't forget about it," Marc replied. "Is this invitation for real?"

The bus slowed as it approached the driveway of my house. "I was just messing around," I answered with a smile. Walking down the aisle of the bus, I finished, "I probably wouldn't be allowed to go anyway."

I had let the idea go until Catherine called me on the phone later that evening. "Hey, Lynn, it's me, Cath. I can't believe what my fucking asshole of a brother is saying. Did you ask him to go to the Sadie Hawkins dance with you? I know that it's a pile of bullshit, but I thought that you should know about it. He told my mom and dad while we were having dinner. What the fuck is he talking about?"

"I asked him as a joke," I told her. "I shouldn't have done it. It was a mean thing to do. Please don't tell him that it was a joke."

"Thank God!" Catherine said. "I thought that you might have taken leave of your senses! Fuck! You and my brother together... now that's a joke!"

"Marc isn't so bad," I said.

"He's a fucking idiot and a drug head," Catherine said. "He's a pig and an ignorant asshole. I don't understand why you even give him the time of day."

"You don't like him because he's your brother. He's not as annoying to me as he is to you. You can't stand him because you have to look at him every morning, afternoon, and night. I want to puke every time I set eyes on one of my brothers. It's really quite normal."

"Okay, you can try to argue the truth away if you want. If you're as smart as I think you are, you will be able to see through my brother; you'll be able to see what a fraud and a shit he is."

"Wow. You can be nasty when you want to be," I said with a laugh. "He doesn't talk about you this way."

"That's because he's too stupid to think about it," she replied. "He doesn't think about anything beyond comic books and masturbation."

I howled, unable to contain my laughter.

"It's the truth! If it doesn't involve drugs or his dick, then he's not interested."

I laughed harder. Catherine was always a hoot. I loved her smarts, her honesty, her tragic self-loathing, and her deadpan humour. I often thought what it would be like if she were a boy; I would have been madly in love with her. I endured moments of panic in which I thought I could be a lesbian. *No fucking way, that's not it,* I thought. I knew all the "homo" words: *dyke, fag, lez, muff diver, dick licker.* Each was a frequent put-down of choice in the school halls, on the street, and in my house. At the same time, society was being bombarded by a new term: AIDS. It was the Black Plague of the eighties and was ravaging the gay male community. There was continuous talk about the virus being God's determined will to rid the world of homosexuals. There were very few people who were willing to argue with that one. Within every sphere of my life, I had been taught that it was wrong to have feelings for another girl; one more detail to add to my ongoing argument with God. I felt like a complete fucking oddball, an aberration, a cosmic blunder. Still, when I looked at Catherine's lips, I wanted to kiss them.

My cousin Regan had set the precedent in the family. She knew that she was into girls by the time she was sixteen. The entire family, including her own parents, joked about it and alienated her. She looked like a boy and was considered by some as the family freak. She dove into drugs and left home early, heading for western Canada. I thought that Regan had guts of steel, yet I did not feel a kinship with her. I had no guts. I adored Dana, adored Catherine, but I would make myself adore Marc. It was what was supposed to happen.

X X I

THERE WE ARE, THE TWO OF US, IN ONE OF THE FEW PHOTOS
ever taken during our time together. Marc is dressed in black pants and a gray
pinstripe shirt, well pressed and clean. His lips are pursed together in a tight
smile above his pimply chin; it does not reflect the truer smile in his eyes. I stand
beside him, thin, wearing jeans that are too short and a well-worn white shirt,
my eyes squinting in the setting sun, and no smile. I'm sporting the bad perm
that I continued to wear in the eighties, the hairstyle that turned my fine hair
into a brown ball of fuzzy split ends. This picture was taken as we stood on the
concrete front step of my house in Inverary. I cannot recall the photographer.
Marc's tense smile beside the absence of mine indicates that it probably was my
father. The fact that Marc found himself at our house at any point is miraculous.
Even more miraculous is that my father sealed one of our moments in a snapshot. Miracles do happen.

As Marc and I got to know each other better and became more interested in
each other, he came to the conclusion that it would be a great idea if he accompanied me off the bus one Friday after school. I was not accustomed to having
friends as guests at my house. The living room was a minefield, the kitchen a
frontline trench. Subjecting anyone to life in my house was unthinkable. The
unpredictable blitzes were not worth the risk.

I protested politely with Marc, but he was insistent that I ask my parents for
permission. I held him off for as long as I could and was soon running out of
excuses. Marc said that he was getting the impression that either I didn't like him
or that I was embarrassed to introduce him to my parents.

"That's not it, Marc, really," I explained. "It's just that my father might have a
hard time with it."

"Well, you could come over to my house," he replied. "I've told my parents all
about you and they would love to meet you."

"Oh, no, no way," I said laughing. "My father would never go for that!"

"That settles it then," Marc added. "Ask your parents if I can come for a visit. My father would come to pick me up afterward. The worst your parents could do is to say no."

You don't know my father, I thought, *he could do a lot worse than say no.*

"Okay, I'll ask them."

I was terrified. Now I was committed to asking and giving him an answer. My stomach rolled over and my head started to ache. Upon arrival home, I diligently began all of the chores that were daily left to my sister and me. We were expected to clean the bathroom, vacuum all of the carpets, and cook dinner every afternoon after school. I made sure that Annie and I did an impeccable job that evening. She vacuumed while I took control of dinner, making fish sticks, creamed corn, and Rice-A-Roni. I made certain that dinner was ready as soon as my parents walked in the door. For that, the two of them were very grateful and the six of us sat down to our usual silent dinner.

There was never much said at our dinner table unless my father decided to initiate conversation. Otherwise, talking was mostly forbidden. It all depended upon my father's particular mood. If he wasn't in the mood, we could count on a fist slammed on the table, a serving utensil thrown across the room, or a wounding of his own fashion.

On this evening, having been served his dinner so promptly, my father was sedate and quiet. After dinner, I began to clear the table and run the dishwater, another of the chores shared among the four of us children. My mother usually assisted with the cleanup while my father plopped his ass in front of the television with a cigarette and a bottle of beer.

I decided to test my request on my mother first; she was safer and would give me her honest opinion about asking my father.

"Um, Mom, can I ask you something?" I must have sounded like I was on the very brink of doom, because she completely stopped what she was doing and turned her entire body toward me, apparently ready for my request for birth control or my declaration of suicidal intent.

"What?" she asked with a serious face.

"Um, well, I was wondering if I could have a friend over for dinner."

"Who?" she asked, shocked. I rarely asked to have friends over who were not family members.

"His name is Marc," I told her. "He's in my art class and he rides our school bus. He's really nice and polite. We're just friends."

Mom stared at me. I turned away and continued washing dishes.

"Is he your boyfriend?" she asked slowly.

"NO!" I answered too loudly. I lowered my voice to a whisper and said, "I told you. He's just a friend."

"Good," she said. "Your father would have a shit fit if it was more than that. I'm fine with it, Lynn, but you will have to ask your father."

Fuck. She always said that. Just about anything was fine as long as we asked Dad.

"Thanks," I said.

I walked quietly and carefully into the minefield where my father sat on the piss-stained couch, staring at the tube while slurping on his bottle. He was watching *WKRP*, one of the family favourites. I sat on the carpet near him and leaned one elbow on the coffee table. I wasn't stupid. I waited for the commercials. As he lit another cigarette, I took the plunge.

"Hey, Dad, I want to ask you a question."

"Ya, what?" he asked, still staring at the television.

"Well, I already asked Mom and she said it was okay if it was alright with you." No response.

"Um, I was just wondering if I could have a friend over for dinner on Friday. His name is Marc and he's really nice and polite." I thought I sounded like a desperate ass.

"A boy?" he asked, slowly turning his head away from the television and toward me.

"Yes. But he's only a friend. He's not my boyfriend or anything," I said, anticipating that he would think the same as my mother did.

"Well he'd better not be your boyfriend, for Christ's sake. And it better stay that way. I don't need a pregnant daughter. You end up that way, and I'll shoot you myself. Do you hear me? Are you fucking him?"

"NO, Dad! He's just a friend. I'm not interested in him that way," I replied, blushing.

"You better not be. I won't allow any slut to live under this roof," he said with bulging eyes. "Well, I suppose he can come over, but no messing around."

I was bewildered. He was going to allow the visit.

"Thanks," I said with a strained voice. I left the minefield, only slightly wounded, to do my homework in my bedroom.

* * * * *

That Friday, Marc stepped off our school bus, exuberant, and entered our house with complete bodily ease. He was bouncing joyfully from wall to wall while every muscle and nerve in my body was bound tightly with elastics and twine. I could not relax and my parents' impending arrival would only make things worse.

I started dinner by browning hamburger and chopping vegetables for spaghetti sauce. It was one of the dishes that I did very well and would be hard to fuck up, even though I was nervous. Marc assisted with the vegetables. He managed to put me at ease as he chopped onions and faked losing his digits.

While the sauce simmered, Marc and I took a walk down Latimer Road. We talked about the books we were reading and the movies that we couldn't wait to see. Marc wanted to take me to see *Conan, the Barbarian.* I wanted him to read *The Picture of Dorian Gray* by Oscar Wilde. Each told the other that we couldn't wait to do so.

Back at the house, my brothers ran circles around us, whistling and making kissing noises. Marc and I retreated into a metal catering unit that my father kept in the backyard in his hopes of transforming it into a camper. We sat there, staring out the door windows and laughed at my brothers. Finally, they left.

Marc and I sat there nervously. My parents would be home soon and we would no longer be alone. We both felt that anticipation. The charge in the metal box could not be ignored.

"What would you do if I kissed you?" Marc asked.

Oh, God, here it comes. I couldn't think of anything romantic or intelligent to say.

I opted for, "I don't know," as I stared straight ahead.

Marc placed his gentle hand on the side of my face and turned me toward him. He leaned into me and touched his full lips to mine. My body tingled pleasantly and I thought the top of my head was going to blow off. His kiss was so soft and his tongue flickered knowingly across my lips. It felt wonderful.

In an inexplicable instant, it felt so wrong. My stomach rolled and I thought I might vomit. I pulled away from him and held my hand over my mouth.

"Did I do something wrong?" Marc asked softly. "Didn't it feel good?"

"Oh, Marc, no. It felt very nice. It's just new to me, that's all," I replied.

Marc kissed me again. It was smooth, moist, and soft. My tongue touched his. Again, my body tingled and then fought the urge to barf. I didn't understand it. How could something that felt so glorious make me want to puke?

I told Marc that we needed to go in the house and check on the sauce. He was clearly disappointed at the end of skin on skin. My legs straightened abruptly and carried me awkwardly into the kitchen. Marc followed, saying nothing. I continued to fight the urge to toss my guts as I stirred the red concoction in the saucepan. He leaned over my shoulder and placed his hand gently on my waist as he watched the spoon swirl in the pot.

"That smells really good. You're a great cook," he said, still holding my waist. I was grateful for the compliment, but I quickly slid away from him to get the noodles from the cupboard. The truth was that I didn't want to be seen with his hands anywhere upon me; I didn't want my sister or brothers to see and I certainly didn't want to be caught in that position by my parents. I knew that it wasn't out of the realm of possibility that my father would take our sharpest butcher knife and hack off Marc's hands.

Marc was anything but shy. After I had removed the plastic bag of spaghetti noodles from the embarrassingly messy cupboard, he took them from my hands and rested them gently on the counter. He moved in close to me and took me by the waist.

"You're so pretty," he said and kissed me softly. This kiss was longer and quickly grew more passionate. My face felt hot. I immediately knew that he was a good kisser and hoped that he didn't notice my inexperience. Within an instant, I was terrified of getting caught, and that my father would find out that a boy's tongue was in my mouth. Again, I pulled away from Marc and excused myself to the washroom. As I walked away, I noticed that his face was flushed a brilliant red.

Once in the washroom, I took deep breaths and tried not to throw up. If there had been more food in my stomach, I'm sure that I would have spewed all over the place. The glands under my jaw tingled and a sour taste filled my mouth. I felt dizzy and it took all of my strength to remain on my feet. I sat down on the toilet, dropped my head between my legs, and tried to control my breathing and my body's urge to purge.

I kept talking to myself, telling myself to pull it together fast. I didn't want Marc to think I was in there having a shit—or worse, the truth: that I wanted to barf every time he touched me. I brushed my teeth with my old frayed toothbrush, primped my hair, and left the safe haven of the bathroom.

Back in the kitchen, Marc was sitting in my father's chair at the kitchen table with a huge smile on his baby face. "You okay?" he asked. "Sure," I answered weakly. All I could think of at that moment was that he had better get his ass out of my father's chair before he got home. How was I going to tell Marc this politely? I sat down in my usual chair and we chatted about school that day and seeing *Conan* at the big theatre. For a few moments, I felt like we were together in our own place, enjoying the smells of dinner simmering as we had pleasant conversation topped with a huge dose of sexual tension.

Then my parents' car rolled into the driveway. I jumped up so swiftly that I startled Marc. "What the hell's the matter?" he asked, very concerned. "Oh, ah, nothing," I replied, lying. "My parents are here. I should tell you now that you are sitting in my father's chair. That wouldn't go over very well with him."

"Oh. Okay. Where should I sit?" he asked as he respectfully placed my father's chair the way he had found it.

"You can sit across the table from me, beside my brother Sean. I don't know if my dad would appreciate us sitting beside each other when he is just meeting you," I told Marc, being as upbeat as I could.

"Your old man is a strict one then, is he?" Marc asked with a sly smile.

"Oh, you don't even know the half of it," I said, looking out the window at the Buick.

As the side door opened and my parents entered the kitchen, I felt my heart jump and thought I could literally hear it beating. My ears were filled with the sound of waves crashing against a shore. I felt I might faint. *Okay, get a grip on yourself; you haven't done anything wrong and he's not going to kick your ass in front of a new guest.*

I approached my parents almost too quickly, being so self-conscious. "Mom, Dad, this is Marc," I said hastily, as I began to fidget with the small buttons on my shirt. Marc leapt from his chair to greet my parents with a handshake. "It's such a pleasure to meet you, Mr. and Mrs. Hellers," he said, as he pumped each of their hands enthusiastically. My mother smiled at him. "It's nice to meet you too, Marc," she replied. My father just stared at him and gave a short nod. "What's for dinner?" my father asked, turning toward me.

"It's spaghetti," I replied, my voice quavering.

"Well, get it on the table. I'm starving," he said.

Annie quickly set the table with our best chipped plates and dull, bent cutlery while I drained the spaghetti. As we all sat down to eat, I had a sudden moment of dread. *What if Marc puts his elbows on the table? Shit. I forgot to tell him how particular Dad is about that. Too late now.*

The meal began quietly with only the clinking sounds of metal on glass and the familiar *glug, glug,* of my father sucking on his brown bottle. That was usually the way my father preferred it until he felt he had something to say.

"So, Marc? Is that your name?" he asked looping noodles over his fork.

"Yes," Marc replied, smiling.

"Do you hunt?" father asked.

Marc looked at me. "No sir," he replied.

"Do you fish?" my father asked earnestly and disgustedly, taking his eyes off his plate and fixing them on Marc.

"Uh, no, I don't," Marc answered.

"What the hell?" father asked with a snort of laughter. "What are you? Are you some kind of faggot?"

"Dad!" I yelped.

Wally and Sean exploded with laughter. Wally sprayed some of the red sauce from his mouth onto the table. Nothing sprayed from Sean's mouth. He ate his spaghetti noodles plain, with a little butter. He couldn't stomach the sauce; he said it always made him think of blood.

Father continued. "Well, I gotta say that most guys I know who don't like hunting and fishing are usually a little fruity. Nice catch, Lynn."

"Wade, don't," Mother said in a low voice.

My face burned and my throat closed as my brothers continued giggling.

Starting to laugh, Marc said, "I'm not gay, Mr. Hellers. I just don't like shooting animals or going fishing. I'd prefer to draw or paint pictures of them."

Oh, God, here it comes.

"Really?" my father said. "You might want to take a long hard look at yourself then. That all sounds pretty faggoty to me."

More laughter erupted around the table. "Trust me, Mr. Hellers," Marc said, grinning. "I'm not a fag."

Father asked, "So then, are you interested in my daughter?"

"I think she's amazing," Marc replied as he looked at me with a gentle smile.

"Yeah, right." Father paused momentarily. "Well, if that's the case, you'd better keep your dick in your pants if you want to keep coming around here… so to speak."

Oh God, I need to get off this fucking planet. Is this really happening? I was horrified and paralyzed beyond the nature of embarrassment.

I looked to my mother for some help, but she just stared into her plate, as usual, looking like she was about to find some buried treasure. Crossing my father was one thing, but crossing my father at the dinner table was an invitation to personal humiliation and doom. If you wanted to finish the meal you were having, you had best keep your big mouth shut.

"Marc is a really good artist, Dad … just like Lynn," Annie said. How I loved my sister then and always. She had a way of spinning some of the most mind wrenching situations into something positive. She never gave up her search for the goodness in everybody and everything. My sister was always true to her name, Annie. She was, and is, gorgeous and kind-hearted. For the most part, my parents found a way to clear their heads and listen to her.

"Really?" Father asked, facing Marc again. "Do you have any of your art here with you?"

"Yes, I do," Marc answered. "I can show you my drawings after dinner if you would like."

"Let's see them now, if you're that good."

Marc looked around the table and rose slowly from his chair to retrieve his sketchbook out of his knapsack. Once Marc was out of earshot, my father couldn't resist the temptation to humiliate me further: "Looks like you found yourself a little fag, Lynn."

My brothers and my mother smirked and giggled. Annie looked down at her plate.

"He's not a fag, Dad," I said. "Just because he's artistic and can make a sentence without using all four letter words, doesn't mean he's gay. Remember Jack Reynolds? He wasn't artistic at all and said "fuck" and "cock-sucker" all the time, and he *was* gay."

Everyone, including my father, laughed.

Marc returned with his sketchbook opened to one of the pencil drawings he was most proud of. It was the dark man from *The Stand*. He placed the book gently beside my father on the dining table.

"Well, well, well, that *is* quite good," my father said in a surprised tone. He set down his fork and continued to turn the pages of Marc's visual journal. He stopped momentarily to praise certain drawings for their detail or deftness with pencil values.

Closing the sketchbook, my father remarked, "These are very well done, Marc, but they're not near as good as Lynn's work."

"I know," Marc said. "Lynn is the best artist at our school."

I was both embarrassed and delighted: embarrassed for my father's obvious insult toward Marc and delighted by his compliment toward me. It struck me then that I deeply craved my father's approval. I wanted him to disappear, but I also wanted him to love and respect me. Somehow, I knew that it was an internal conflict that would plague me for all my days.

After dinner, Marc, who managed to keep his elbows off the table, assisted Annie and I with cleaning the dishes. Annie washed while we dried. The rest of the family retired to the living room to watch television. We were grateful for the noise from the TV.

"So what do you think of our Dad, Marc?" Annie asked, giggling.

"Well, he certainly is… interesting," Marc replied, laughing out loud.

"He's an idiotic asshole," I added.

Marc whispered back, "He can be pretty funny at times."

"Funny? Funny?! You've got to be joking," I said. "He's a fucking brute."

"He's not too bad if he hasn't had a lot to drink," Annie said.

With the dishes done and put away, Annie and I were permitted to join the family in the living room. Marc, Annie, and I formed a small arc on the carpet in front of the television. I cannot recall what we watched. Maybe *Dallas* or *Knots Landing*; everybody was enraptured by these night-time soaps. One of the grander media puzzles to eventually taunt the public was to figure out who had shot J.R. Ewing. Whatever was happening that night, whether it was Sue Ellen getting pissed on cocktails on *Dallas* or Abby seducing every man but her husband on *Knots Landing,* I was too focused on the way the light from the

TV accentuated the bones of Marc's face. I watched his hands on his knees, his thick thumbs sliding back and forth in small movements on his dark, pinstriped dress pants. His large shoulder leaned into mine and I felt the heat and the shock allowing me to consider that I might not be a lesbian after all. I thought that I might spontaneously combust when I felt his thumb brush against my thigh. He had to be pretty ballsy to do this in the presence of my father. I admired that. Having no fear.

By 11:00 PM, Marc's father had arrived to pick him up. Mr. Gatien waited in the car in the driveway, never coming to the door to introduce himself. For this, I was thankful because my father had entered his familiar alcoholic oblivion as he lay sprawled on the Couch of Piss.

I rose from in front of the television and walked Marc to the side door. From this space we could not be seen by anyone in the living room. The kitchen was dark. Mother had turned off all of the lights before retiring to her bedroom. As Marc bent down to put on his shoes, he looked up at me.

"I had a really great time tonight."

"Yeah, it was fun," I replied. "Except for my father's remarks. He seems to enjoy embarrassing me."

Marc laughed softly. "He's not that bad, Lynn."

"You don't have to live with him."

Marc rose from below. He took me by the waist, causing me to flash freeze like a lobster cornered in a refrigerator for transport. My brain screamed silently: *Don't you know that my Dad is in the next room and if he catches us he'll commit the most diabolical homicide?* I didn't have time to say a thing. Marc moved his face toward mine and kissed me passionately. He pulled my body closer and I felt the hardness in his pants press against my pelvis. Marc started to gyrate and my body exploded with excitement; I felt a gush of moisture in my underwear and gasped so loudly that I was sure my family must have heard. Marc pulled away from me whispering, "I'll see you on Monday," and then rushed out the door.

I was momentarily spellbound, stunned, and gasping for air. I quickly rushed into the bathroom after a fleeting glance at my father, who was now asleep on the couch. As I lowered my pants, I felt the sticky wetness in my underwear as I pulled them away from my body. *What the hell is that?* It was a clear, slimy mucous, like snot. *Oh my God,* I thought, *that's come.* I had heard enough about it, especially that year. One of my friends, Terri, talked about a guy coming on her stomach after which she played with the fluid, forming small pools inside and outside her bellybutton. When she told me this story, I fought the urge to vomit. Looking at my own smears of sexuality made me feel even sicker. I gagged and heaved, trying to be as quiet as possible. It just wasn't fair. Marc was smart, kind, cute, artistic, and what happened with him felt exhilarating, but now I was releasing sour spaghetti mush and sauce into the toilet. The truth was that being close to Marc made me equally excited and revoltingly sick to my stomach.

Suddenly, I had a profound need to see the one man in my life who didn't make me want to expel my meat and vegetables.

XXII

"MOM, I WANT TO GO VISIT GRANDPA CARRON," I TOLD HER that morning as I packed my knapsack full of texts and notebooks before the arrival of the school bus.

"Well, I think that he would probably like that. Why don't you call him at your Uncle Harland's? Do you want to go for the whole weekend?"

"Yes, I would. I haven't seen him in such a long time."

"Well then, give him a call," Mother said.

"Um, Mom, could you call for me? I don't want Uncle Harland and Bertha to think that I'm imposing."

"Sure. I'll call them from work. How was the rest of your evening with Marc?"

"Oh. Yeah. That was fine," I replied feeling the flush of heat rise from my neck to my face.

With a sly smile, she asked, "Do you like him?"

"He's okay. I wish Dad wouldn't embarrass me though. Calling him a fag. Dad can be such a dink sometimes."

"Just ignore him," she said.

"You know that's easier said than done."

That weekend my parents took me to see Grandpa. Marc was quite disappointed in my plans; he wanted to see me again. I couldn't imagine going through that torture again so soon. Besides, I needed to digest a decent meal. My mother and father spent a few hours visiting, just long enough to drink most of Harland's case of beer. I couldn't wait for them to leave so that I could have some time with my grandfather.

Before they left, some snapshots, sandwiched among the multitude that I carry, were taken. In one of them, my father stands beside my grandfather and my uncle, flashing a broad white smile, thanks to his false teeth, as he wraps his arm around Grandpa and lays his hand on Harland's shoulder on the other side. Standing against the wood paneled wall, my father is clearly blitzed on beer and is relishing the special moment far more than the other two. Harland has a tentative half smile, while my grandfather has no smile at all. Grandpa has a serious look, the same one he always held when he talked about the war and how he tried to feign his death lying beside dead German soldiers full of maggots, while the live Germans passed by the ditch that cradled their bodies.

It is the other photograph, taken afterward, that I treasure. In it, Grandpa has a broad smile, displaying some of his pink gums. He is standing behind me and has his thin arms wrapped around my shoulders, his damaged hand resting on my left shoulder like a soft yellow hook. My smile is genuine. He is dressed in one of his freshly pressed white shirts, carefully starched. I am wearing a new navy, red, and white striped hooded sweater and my clean, fine hair has been styled with my sister's curling iron. I tried to feather it after curling it and I look like some poor little bird caught in a wind tunnel. I had wanted Grandpa to see me at my best.

During that visit, after a dinner of pork roast and potatoes, my parents took their leave. Father only picked at the meal; he would be looking for another drinking hole on the way home. As soon as the front door of Harland and Bertha's house closed, with my parents on the other side of it, I relaxed.

"Hey Grandpa! Do you want to play checkers, just like old times?" I asked.

"You bet I do," he answered. "But you better have some slick moves because your old Grandpa has improved! I'll fix us some tea and a plate of cookies and you set up the board, okay? It's on the bureau in my room."

Oh how I love you, Grandpa.

We sipped tea, chewed peanut butter cookies, and played checkers on the small coffee table in my uncle's cozy cottage home. I hadn't felt so good in a very long time.

"So, honey, you're in high school now. What do you think you might want to be when you're finished school?" he asked as he made his next move, jumping one of my red playing pieces.

"Good move, Grandpa!" I said. I hesitated for a moment before answering his question.

"Well?" he prompted.

"Well, I'm not one hundred percent sure, but I think that I might want to be a teacher," I told him.

His wide smile immediately told me that he was pleased. "I think that you would make an amazing teacher, Lynn. Do you know what you would like to teach?"

"Definitely art," I replied without hesitation. "But Mom thinks I might be too shy to teach."

"Nonsense!" Grandpa said firmly. "Don't you ever let anyone tell you that you can't do something. Shyness, of all things, you'll grow out of that. I'm going to tell you a secret. I think that you are the smartest and most talented young girl I have ever known. Your Nanny thought so too. You make wonderful pictures that make me so proud. I would love to see you show other kids how to do what you can do. Someday, you'll do great things. I know it."

I almost wept. Having received relatively few words of encouragement, I was starving for recognition and my grandfather had just filled me.

"Thank you, Grandpa," I said in a quiet voice.

"Just don't get yourself involved with some boy too soon. Boys can ruin your life. I should know, aye."

"I'm not involved with a boy, Grandpa."

"Your Mom says that you brought a fella home some nights ago. Who is this boy?"

"He's just a friend," I said. "He draws, paints, and reads cool books. He does things that I like to do. He's just easy to talk to."

"Well, that's fine, honey, just don't get too serious when you're so young. There's plenty of time for romance and marriage later on."

"Oh God, Grandpa! I'm not going to get married!" I yelped, laughing.

"Oh you will someday, but all I'm saying is that there's a whole lot of time for that business."

This conversation provided the groundwork for a question that I had always wanted to ask him.

"Hey, Grandpa, can I ask you something?"

"Sure, hon," he replied, peering at me over his glasses.

"Is it true what Mom told me? That you didn't like Dad when you first met him and that you threw him down the huge flight of stairs at the apartment on Princess Street?"

Grandpa lowered his eyes and spat into his tobacco can. "Yes. That's true. I didn't figure that your father was good enough for your Mom. He came from trash, what we often called 'the other side of the tracks'. But your Dad works hard and does his best."

"But you moved away from our house because of him," I said with a serious tone.

"I know that, dear," he said. "I just couldn't stay there anymore. It wasn't doing anyone any good."

As I shifted my weight and looked him directly in the eye, I said, "I know what you mean. I can't wait to get out of there. I can hardly stand him."

Grandpa looked right back at me. "You need to hang in there, honey, for just a little while longer. With him, you just need to stay out of his way when he gets ugly."

"I try, Grandpa. Really, I do. When I try to get away from him, he just follows me to my room and won't leave me alone."

Grandpa looked down for a moment and then turned to stare out the window. His face drooped and his eyes watered.

"It's your move, sweetheart," he said. "I'll pour you some more tea."

The following day, Grandpa took me fishing on the shores of the cool dark green stream that bordered the cottage property upon which he lived with my uncle. He fixed us a large bag of food for lunch: roast beef sandwiches, cookies, and oranges. He made a thermos of tea for me and slipped a bottle of Bacardi white rum into the bag for himself. A large tomato can covered with tinfoil and an elastic band was the prison for our live bait; Grandpa always insisted on luring fish with something alive and smelly. Earlier that morning, he arose before anyone else in the house and dug for worms on the shady side of the cottage. He proudly revealed the contents of the tomato can under my nose as I awoke from a sound sleep. The pinkish brown squirming cords scared the shit out of me and I squealed loudly, much to the delight of my grandfather.

I will never forget that morning and afternoon with him. Someone should have taken a photograph of that, freezing and preserving the moment: the two of us sitting on the shores with sunlight spraying through the trees dappling our faces, Grandpa's smiles, inspired by rum and my newly developed girlish squeamishness, as he baited my hook because I couldn't bear the thought of it. I couldn't tell him the reason for my alteration. I couldn't reveal that I had brutally shot a small beautiful bird; for me, it was criminal behaviour and I could not risk my grandfather's disapproval. As he baited my hook, he told me to "toughen up" if I was going to survive.

We arrived back home with a large bucket filled with good-sized perch. Though he had an apparent glow on from the rum, Grandpa Carron cleaned the fish, and made a divine dinner of battered fried perch with home fries and creamed corn. I helped him as he made his own special rice pudding for dessert, loaded with cinnamon. Uncle Harland and his girlfriend, Bertha, raved about the fine meal we had created.

After helping with the dishes, I wanted to give something back to my grandfather for providing a most wonderful weekend.

"Before I go tomorrow, Grandpa, I want to draw a picture for you. Anything you want. I brought my art book and my materials. What would you like me to draw?" I asked.

"Oh, sweetheart, I would love any drawing you did for me."

"I know that, but I want to do something just for you, a picture that you might like to put on your wall."

"Well," he said as he cocked his head to the side, "I would really like a picture of a deer. I see them around here all the time and they're so beautiful."

"Okay!" I said eagerly. "I'll start right away. I think I will use charcoal pencil."

Since I was uncomfortable rendering such a perfect and majestic creature from my imagination, I searched through Uncle Harland's *Field and Stream* magazines to find the perfect photograph to inspire my drawing. I began work immediately and stayed up late into the night to complete the piece. I chiselled the end of the charcoal stick several times with the penknife Grandpa had given me years ago. Everyone eventually went to bed while I continued to work by the light of a small lamp near the pullout couch. I finished the charcoal drawing on thick beige paper, to my satisfaction, and fell asleep almost immediately.

That morning, I presented my gift to Grandpa Carron. He looked at it, gasped, and began to cry. "Oh, Lynn," he said with a shaky voice. "This is amazing. It looks so *real*. My God, you are talented. Harland, Bertha, look at this."

"Wow," they both said in unison. "You are a great artist, Lynn," my uncle said, smiling. "We need to find a frame and put that up right away."

"I know where there is one," Bertha exclaimed as she ran to a closet. "Here it is."

Grandpa took the frame and removed the backing with shaking hands. Bertha helped him place the drawing carefully inside. The frame was made of oak and seemed perfect for the subject I had rendered. I had to admit that it did look pretty good. My grandfather scanned the final product and wiped his pale blue eyes and then his substantial nose with the white handkerchief that he pulled from his back pocket.

"Thank you for this, darling," he said. "I will never take it off of my wall. You know that your grandmother is watching you and she's just as proud of you as I am."

153

X X I I I

I WISH I HAD KNOWN. I WISH I HAD KNOWN THAT THAT weekend would hold the last moments of true clarity that I would share with Grandpa Carron. The illness seemed to strike him instantaneously and ran its course swiftly. He was diagnosed with prostate cancer, complicated by emphysema, black lung, his incessant smoking, and alcoholism. That one time that I saw him in the hospital, I knew that he was dying. It was in his laugh and the stories he needed to tell. My parents, aunts, uncles, and I surrounded his bed as he gleefully and tearfully told only the funny stories about his friends in the war, stories of friends who had died and those who had survived. I had never heard him speak of them before. He entertained us with anecdotes about boot polish spread inside his friends' footwear, blackening their socks before inspection, toothbrushes used to clean toilets and then left for use by some poor sod, Vaseline on toilet seats causing late night curses, and the successful theft of bottles of booze from mess tents. It was the stories of these sophomoric pranks that he chose to tell as he lay dying. He needed to talk about his life during the war but clearly understood that no comfort could be garnered from the endless horror stories. Foraging for humour would provide comfort, not only for him, but his family as well.

When the other relatives left, my grandfather wasted no time making a serious request of my father.

"Hey, Wade, do you think you could sneak a little Bacardi in here for me? I'd really appreciate it," he said with his pink, gummy smile. "It's the only thing that really steadies my nerves. I asked one of the really nice nurses if she would sneak me a beer and she brought me goddamned apple juice. I told her that I'd rather drink my own piss."

We all laughed. "I'm glad you guys think it's funny. She didn't think so," Grandpa said. "She said that I needed to take care of myself, to make myself stronger. I told her that the white rum and beer always took really good care of me."

"The nurse is right, Dad," my mother cut in. "You need to build your strength up again."

"Oh, good Christ, Margaret," Grandpa added, shaking his head. "I couldn't change years ago when it actually mattered. How do you expect me to change my habits now?"

Mother lowered her head and said nothing. What could she say to that?

"For fuck's sake, Marg, he's only asking for a little rum. He's not asking for a forty ouncer or for us to build him a goddamned still," Father said.

Grandpa's eyes lit up and he sat upright for the first time that evening. "Hey, Wade, do you think you could get a forty ouncer in here? That'd be great. I'd find a way to hide it."

"I'll see what I can do, Earl," he replied.

On our way home, my mother chastised him for agreeing to bring alcohol into the hospital. Like it mattered.

"Margaret, get a grip on yourself," Father said. "Earl is dying. Your father is dying. Do you think he gives a witch's tit about getting caught with rum in his room?"

Mother responded with her usual worried tone, "Well, we could get in trouble for bringing it to him."

"Again, Margaret, I'm going to tell you that your father is *dying*. If he wanted a prostitute brought in, I'd find a way to do it."

I couldn't believe it. For once, I completely agreed with my father. My lovely grandfather should have anything he wanted and we should do our best to provide. Right then, I realized one of the few true moments of connection with my father. I had hated the way he had treated Grandpa while he lived with us, but now he rose to the challenge and displayed a level of selfless graciousness as Grandpa journeyed through his final days.

* * * * *

Oh, how I wish I had known. That weekend at Uncle Harland's cottage as we fished the stream. I would have told Grandpa how much I loved him and how pivotal he and Nanny were in shaping my young life.

After that night in the hospital, I saw Grandpa Carron only one more time. Again, like my last moments with Nanny Carron, I was not prepared for what I saw. My mother told me that Grandpa was in a "very bad way" and that she, Annie, and I were going to visit him at my Aunt Mary's house.

When we arrived, we were greeted by my heavily intoxicated aunt who clumsily ushered us into the living room where Grandpa sat, almost catatonic, with a half consumed bottle of beer in front of him. Immediately, I pondered the words, "living room". What the hell kind of description was that for a room? My grandfather was sitting in the *living* room and he was *dying*, rotting from the inside out, just like Nanny. Houses had kitchens, bedrooms, parlours, living rooms, dens, foyers, dining rooms, and even nooks. There were no dying rooms. I guessed that would be a waste of space, as if a nook wasn't.

There in Mary's living room, my grandfather sat staring at his hook hands, hands that were a sickly combination of the colours yellow and violet, complimentary colours, but not on this day. Mother leaned down to him and kissed him on the cheek. "Hi, Dad," she said softly. It seemed to register only slightly.

Annie made the next move. "Hello, Grandpa," she said as she placed a gentle hand on his shoulder. Again, no response. She became so upset that she rushed to the kitchen. My mother and aunt followed her, wiping tears from their eyes.

I sat down on a shabby La-Z-Boy chair and peered out the front window for a moment before turning my head toward Grandpa. I looked at him closely. He still stared at those hands. His hair, usually combed back with Brill Cream, was now just unruly gray wisps, appearing to grow in all directions from his shrunken head, reminding me of a coconut. He was incredibly thin. Through his unbuttoned plaid shirt, his once broad, hairy chest looked as if it was on the brink of caving in. I swore I could see his heart struggling to beat under the paper-thin skin that held that fragile chest together.

"I'm here, Grandpa," I said. "Can you hear me?"

No answer.

"Can I get you anything, Grandpa, anything at all?" I asked.

His hands moved and he slowly lifted his head to look at me. He began to weep, heavily. He put his hands to his face and cried loudly. I politely looked away and out the front window, not knowing what to do or say. My heart broke.

In an instant, my mother and Aunt Mary, carrying those familiar brown bottles, entered the room and tried to comfort their father. "What did he say?" Mother asked, looking at me.

"Nothing," I replied. As his two daughters held him and cried with him, I rose from the chair and joined Annie in the kitchen.

"This is fucking crazy," I told my sister through my sobs. "He should be in a hospital."

"Come on, Lynn. Really? What would be the point?" Annie gasped. "At least he's with his family."

"Fuck," I hissed, unable to contain my anger. "He deserves better than this."

A few days later, the telephone rang at our house during the early morning hours. My mother's sobs said everything. I wept only for a few minutes. Grandpa's brutal suffering was over. I tried to imagine him greeting Nanny somewhere, anywhere, and reminiscing about their times beside Grandpa's tomato plants on the sun-filled deck that was attached to the back of the apartment building at 187A Princess Street.

That was in June, 1982. My grandfather's retreat from this world was tethered in time to Israel's invasion of Lebanon and the sentencing of John Hinckley for the attempted assassination of President Ronald Reagan. Exactly seven years after Nanny, Grandpa Carron died. This time, I was permitted to attend the visitation and funeral, to say goodbye to him formally and properly. I guess at the age of seventeen, I was considered of fit mind.

He was laid out at the Gordon Tompkins Funeral Home in Kingston. Annie and I walked in together. We both wore a dress. I borrowed a lavender coloured one from Mom. I hated dresses but it was the least I could do for Grandpa; he always loved it when I wore a dress; he would tell me that I was as pretty as my mother. As soon as Annie and I entered the room and saw our once colossal grandfather physically diminished and squished into a coffin, we wept and gasped for air. Uncle Harland attempted to comfort us, but his attention only made us cry harder. It took everything I had to muster the strength to regain my composure. Annie and I sat down for a few minutes before approaching the coffin. We held hands as we drew toward him. As I looked carefully at my granddad, I noticed a cut under his hairline, visible even beneath the heavily caked makeup; it seemed to run around toward the back of his head and out of sight. *Oh my God, somebody cut him open!* I almost screamed it out loud. I didn't have to. Aunt Sheila noticed the slice at the same time.

"Jesus Christ," she sobbed loudly. "He's been cut open. Someone cut his head open! Who did this?! Harland, who cut our father and why? Tell me why!" Harland and my mother carefully drew Sheila away to sit on a sofa. I couldn't hear what they were telling her. Whatever it was, it made Aunt Sheila hide her face in her hands and shake her head violently.

I turned back toward my grandfather. I decided to focus on his hands, his beautiful large hands. One was placed over top of the other; the unmarred hand covered the nicotine-stained one with the hooked finger. Those hands had carved mini hockey sticks for me so that I could play games on the apartment floor on Princess Street. They had banged wooden spoons against pots on New Year's Eve inciting squeals of delight from my brothers and sister. Those hands had made the best donuts and meat pies in the world. They cultivated prize tomatoes, played expert checkers, and baited our hooks when we went fishing. Those big lovely hands held mine with care as we walked to the A&P or The Smoke Shop. Looking at those hands always made me feel so safe and content. I decided to keep a permanent picture of them in my brain. I reached out and touched them.

I didn't expect them to be so cold, even though I knew they wouldn't be warm. I then promptly turned around and left.

I walked out of the funeral home into the sunlight and the intense heat of a gorgeous June day. Annie met me outside. Our brothers decided to stay with our parents.

"I can't take this situation for much longer," Annie said.

"I hear that," was my reply, "Let's get out of here. We'll say goodbye to everyone and then let's go."

"Where do you want to go?" Annie asked, looking at me like I had suddenly taken a dangerous leap off the deep end. We were miles away from home with no money and the only ride to be had would be from our grieving parents.

"Let's go back to school," I said. "We can take the bus home from there. Then we won't have to deal with Mom and Dad for the entire day. You know they're all going to end up plastered down at Nanny Ida's. I can't take that, not today."

"Me neither," she added.

Upon our arrival at Regiopolis, Annie and I were greeted by various friends, teachers, and classroom acquaintances who all gave their heartfelt condolences between classes. One of them was Marc Gatien.

"Hi Lynn. Hi Annie," he said, exchanging glances with both of us. "I'm so sorry to hear about your grandfather. The office staff announced it over the P.A. this morning. How are the two of you doing?" *He is so nice,* I thought.

"We're okay," Annie replied. "Considering."

"I hope this doesn't sound wrong," Marc continued, "but the two of you look very pretty in those dresses."

"Thank you," we said in unison.

"Well, I've been thinking about you guys all day. Would you like to go to the cafeteria with me? I've got a little money. I could get us some chips and a drink."

"That's very considerate, but you don't have to do that, Marc," I said sheepishly.

"Oh, but I insist," he protested in a firm voice. He put his hand gently on Annie's shoulder, and then on mine, and directed us toward the cafeteria. In my mind, I was determined not to fall for Marc, but these small gestures and his tremendous empathy began to chip at my formidable wall. In the cafeteria, Marc pulled out a chair for both of us and then paid his visit to the vending machines, returning with three pints of chocolate milk and two bags of cheese balls. I wondered how he knew to choose chocolate milk, that sweet elixir that always calmed my stomach when I was upset.

Both Annie and I thanked him wholeheartedly. We were famished and wobbling at the knees, having had nothing to eat all day. We gulped our milk, while Marc politely sipped his. We munched on the cheese balls, saying very little. Moments later, Annie's best friend joined us to offer her sympathy; Lisa asked

Annie if she might like to take a walk. She, having decided to go, took a handful of cheese balls, thanked Marc again, and told me that she would see me later.

"So, are you really okay, Lynn?" Marc asked with concern.

"Sure," I answered.

"Well, you were really close to your grandfather, weren't you?"

"Yes, I was. I will always feel close to him. He is the best man I have ever known," I told Marc. Suddenly, I blurted it out, without even thinking: "Somebody cut his head open, Marc. Somebody was poking around in his brain."

"What?" Marc asked, coughing on a cheese ball.

"He was cut open," I continued through tears. "There must have been an autopsy. What I can't figure out is *why*. I also can't understand why nobody mentioned it, as if it wasn't important, like he just suffered a paper cut on his way from the hospital to the funeral home."

Marc put his hand over mine. "What exactly did your Grandpa die of?" he asked.

"He had prostate cancer and emphysema. His lungs were fucked. The cancer wasn't the thing that killed him. His lungs collapsed."

"Well," Marc said, "I'm no doctor, but I don't think that calls for an autopsy. His cause of death would be pretty obvious."

"That's what I think. He had suffered so much after my grandmother's death and then with his own horrible illness. I don't know why they had to make things worse by carving him open. It doesn't make any sense at all." I began to sob.

Marc took my hand and walked me out into the sunlight. We sat under the trees beside the school property and waited for the bus. Marc continued to hold my hand and rubbed my back in an attempt to comfort me.

It was days later that I found out why my grandfather's head had been cut open. He had been taken back to the hospital just days before he died and the hospital staff determined that there were some grounds for suspicion in his death. Some of the nurses or doctors figured that my grandfather had been "helped along" with his dying. The evidence: empty beer and rum bottles found in a drawer. The hypothesis was that the cocktail created with his medication and the alcohol somehow led to the collapse of his lungs.

There, alone on the firing line, was my father and mother. Mother's prophecy came true. There was a short medical investigation, questions about my father providing alcohol to a dying man, accompanied by reprisals from family members leading to bitter battles, both in person and by phone. My parents drank and fought even more and my mother withered like a fragile flower in an October wind. Then, just like that, it was over. No more talk of Grandfather's autopsy, or the bottles found in his room, no more talk about a mystery surrounding his death. I think it became abundantly clear that my parents had only sought to comfort Grandpa; he asked for alcohol and they fed it to him because he was on his deathbed. Who could fault them for that? Grandpa begged and they provided. I saw it as no different than juicing up a terminal cancer patient with morphine. My grandfather *was* terminal. If he had begged me for Bacardi, I would have stolen it and fed it to him with a syringe.

Like my grandmother's prayer book, I wanted, needed, a tangible object to hold near, something that Grandpa had touched and reflected some part of his living years. I remembered his war medals. I remembered those colourful badges and ribbons, the symbols of his courage and unwavering dedication to his country and the army. I also recalled his wishes, repeated on several occasions while we played checkers, that he wanted me to have them after his death.

"Hey Mom, can I talk to you about something?" I ask as my mother applies her bright red lipstick, a ritual that completes her face before leaving for work at the bank.

"What?" she says through her puckered lips before blotting them with a piece of toilet paper.

"Remember Grandpa's medals from the war? Did he ever tell you that he wanted me to have them? He always told me that he wanted them to be with me after he died."

She turns toward me, her lipstick still in hand, and stares at me as if she has just laid eyes on the alien that will suck out her brain.

"What the hell are you talking about?" she asks, almost in a whisper.

My blood rushes and my face burns. "He wanted me to have those medals. You know, as a remembrance. I told him that I would treasure them and take really good care of them."

"Listen you," she replies through clenched teeth, "those medals are never going to be yours and you have no right to them. You weren't one of his children, for fuck's sake."

I never saw my grandfather's medals again.

X X I V

"We must not look at goblin men,
We must not buy their fruits:
Who knows upon what soil they fed
Their hungry thirsty roots?"

Christina Rossetti, *Goblin Market*

FOLLOWING THE DEATH OF GRANDPA CARRON, I WITHDREW
deeper and deeper into myself and found it difficult to give two shits about
anything, especially the mundane routines around daily living. In a strange and
inexplicable way, I felt parentless. I sought solace in novels, art, poetry, horror
films, and the arms of Marc Gatien. His arms and hands, as I soon discovered,
held an abundance of comfort, whether they were wrapped around me or feeding
me drugs.

Marc introduced me to what he felt were true rites of passage: the use of marijuana, hashish, hash oil, and acid. Almost daily, he tempted me with something
new and I did very little to protest. Soon, I stopped even asking for my parents'
permission to have him over to our house; eventually, he just joined me off the
school bus and his parents picked him up later in the evening.

Once off the bus, we entered the house, followed by my sister and brothers, threw down our books, and made sure there was something that we could
prepare for dinner. I always told Annie that we were going for a walk and that
we would be back later to help her with the cooking. Then Marc and I headed
into the farmer's fields that surrounded our property on almost every side. It was
there, in one of the fields of hay, wheat, or apple trees, that Marc would entice
me with his fruits of pleasure. They came in the form of plump joints, sweet hash
brownies, a remarkably tasteless dot of paper, or thick, syrupy oil glazing the

161

bottom of a glass bong. We brought my old transistor radio from Uncle Harland; the red one that looked like a battery. It was fully charged:

> *"Come on home girl,*
> *He said with a smile,*
> *You don't have to love me now,*
> *Let's get high awhile,*
> *But try to understand,*
> *Try, try, try to understand,*
> *I'm a magic man,"*

Heart, *Magic Man*

After enjoying the delights of Marc's market, we would roll around on the ground together, kissing passionately and rubbing against each other to the point of heated and exhaustive orgasm. No clothing was ever removed. Marc tried to loosen buttons and pull down zippers, but I would always move his hands elsewhere. I could not bear the thought of being penetrated, especially by the sizeable pipe he had lodged in his pants, but I was even more terrified of possible pregnancy. I had finally started my period the year before, the onset of the bloody curse. For me, it was unbelievably sporadic, making its appearance every four months or so. Regardless, I wasn't stupid. I was aware that I could still become pregnant, and that it would be a fate leading to certain death. I knew that my father would remain true to his words: *If you or your sister ever come home pregnant, I'll shoot you right in your slutty fucking heads with my deer rifle. And don't think for a minute that I don't know how to get rid of a body.*

From the creative and colourful stories spoken by my father, uncles, Nanny Ida, and her friends, I knew fine well that crimes could be committed and no justice paid, bodies could be hidden, and that the family loyalty code was all-powerful. I caught only glimpses into this aspect of their criminal world; words and statements were cloaked and disguised, whispers and hisses usually occurred late at night when they thought no one was listening. They were naïve enough to think that the kids wouldn't bother listening or wouldn't understand. They weren't aware that I heard and digested the stories about the bodies weighted down in the pea green swamp, or the two men who, while still alive, had been encased in a metal barrel that was welded shut and thrown into a local lake.

I don't think for one minute that my father and his brothers did any actual killing, but they knew who did. The elimination of certain people worked so much to their benefit that they took the stories on as if they were the main characters that had lived up to their roles and had enacted the plots exceptionally well. Fearing them was healthy.

Savouring Marc's market was treading on very thin ice. If my father even once discovered the two of us grinding together or sucking smoke from a glass pipe, I knew that we would join the ranks of the barrel boys. Still, I was willing to take the risk. With Marc, I was finding ecstasy and comfort, both so new to me.

I became so immersed in the chemical euphoria that Marc provided, that my performance at school began to weaken. My previous pathetic entry into grade nine soon turned around. By grade eleven, I had become an "A" student in the advanced level program and seemed to be respected for academic prowess, respected by everyone, that is, but my father. Faced with my typical report card containing seven marks over 85%, he would focus on the one grade of 74% in physical education.

"What the fuck is this?" he would ask. "All these A's and a B in gym. It's fucking *gym*. How hard can that be? You run and throw baseballs. Big fucking deal. I thought that you were supposed to be a good athlete."

"I'm not very good at gymnastics. I can't do a cart-wheel or a round-up," I said.

"A cart-wheel?! You got a fucking B because you couldn't do a goddamned cart-wheel? Jesus Christ, that's pathetic. Why don't you do something useful, like practice?"

"Oh, sure," I answered. "This coming from a guy who couldn't get through grade nine." *Oh God, did I just say that out loud?*

He glared at me with his black eyes. He grabbed my arm and squeezed. "You fucking bitch," he spat. "You've got a death wish."

"Let go," I pleaded pitifully as I tried to loosen his grip.

His grip tightened. "I'll let go when you learn some respect, you little whore. How dare you talk to your father that way?"

"Let go of me," I said firmly.

In an instant, he freed my arm and used the same hand to swat my face.

"Now get the fuck away from me!" he screamed.

I slipped into the safe closet of my bedroom and pounded my head against the frame of the door. I wept as quietly as I could. I wept until I heard the boom of my father's voice break the silence.

"Jesus fucking Christ. What the hell is this? Have I raised a bunch of god-damned retards?" he yelled.

I stealthily slipped into the hallway to listen.

"What do you mean?" Annie asked.

"This fucking report card. Most of these marks are B's. What are you, a fucking idiot? Why don't you go and take a look at your sister's report card."

I heard the sound of paper waving through the air.

"Now that's what a report card should look like," he said.

"I did the best that I could!" Annie screamed. "You're never happy!"

My sister came running down the hallway, crying. She glanced at me and ran into her bedroom. I immediately wanted to go to her, but I wasn't sure that I could. How was I going to tend to her wounds when I, too, had a sword in my side? I took a few deep breaths and entered her room with my fists clenched. She looked up at me with her wet, bloated, and blotchy face. I wanted to hug her.

"Don't listen to him," I said. "He's a fucking asshole and a loser."

"You got a better report card than I did, as always," she said, sniffling, as she looked out her window.

I went and sat beside her on her bed. "Listen," I said, "he gave me shit right before you for getting a B in Phys. Ed. He's a fucking lunatic. That stupid fuck never even finished grade nine and he's riding us for getting B's." Annie started to laugh.

I kept going with it.

"He can't even keep the simplest fucking job," I said. She laughed harder.

"You know what we should get him for Christmas?" I asked. Annie shook her head, laughing.

"A package of fucking extra large baby diapers. The pathetic shit can't make it through one night without pissing himself. Mom's gotta be pretty turned on by that, aye?"

She fell over laughing, hanging onto her stomach.

* * * * *

"Uh, Lynn, could you stay for a minute? I'd like to speak to you." It was Mrs. Garry, my chemistry teacher. The bell that signalled class change made its annoying chime and she practically blocked me bodily as I attempted to immediately scurry out of the classroom. I stayed behind as she waited for every student to leave the room before she spoke again. My stomach turned over and bile oozed up into my mouth.

"I just want to talk to you for a minute," she said, "and don't worry about being late for your next class because I'll write a note for you." This sounded awfully serious. She stood there across from me at one of the lab benches, wearing her narrow black skirt and her tiny gray sweater. Her hair was perfect, a tidy brown bob; not one of her hairs straggled away, trying to escape the skull, like mine did. She wore no make-up and had crystal blue eyes that stared right into me. I always noticed that affect when a woman didn't wear any face paint.

No clumped mascara, no heavy, uneven blush, no sickly lipstick bleeding into the lines around the mouth, those cosmetic blunders that allowed the silent pondering and laughter that gave me some sense of comfort in the light of my monstrous insecurity. I knew that she was brilliant; I admired her deeply; I was terrified of her.

Without looking directly at me, she slowly opened her mark book on the ebony counter of the lab beside one of the pristine stainless sinks. I turned away and focused my attention on the eyewash station, longing to drown myself with it.

She began, seeming to choose her words carefully:

"Lynn, I want to talk to you about...your academic performance... for starters."

"Okay," I replied, glancing up at her face only briefly. I knew what was coming.

"Well, I just don't understand how a student who is in the top three of this class, with marks in the nineties, can suddenly drop to marks in the sixties. Could you please explain that to me? I really do want to understand." She paused. "Are you bored or tired?"

I felt my face flush with almost suffocating heat. My chin dropped, as usual, into my chest.

"No, it's not that," I replied.

"Then what is it?" she asked, leaning toward me, obviously concerned.

"I don't know," I answered weakly.

"Well, there has to be something wrong," Mrs. Garry continued, "Your marks are dropping drastically and you just don't seem to be interested. You have such enormous potential." *Blah, blah,* the words I had grown so tired of hearing.

Without raising my head, I tried to explain, "I guess I have to study more. I'll work harder."

"Uh,huh," she said, nodding her head slowly. "Can you tell me what happened to your face?"

What the fuck?! "What do you mean?" I asked.

"You have a cut on your lip and a bruise on the side of your face. What happened to you?" she asked in a quiet, gentle, voice.

I had no idea that these minor injuries were visible to others. I had tried to cover them with make-up and I had gone almost the entire day without anyone mentioning them.

"I fell while playing tag with my brothers," I told her. *Wow, that's a good one, she has to believe that one for sure.*

Mrs. Garry stared at me and paused briefly before asking, "Do you have a boyfriend, Lynn?"

"Yes," I answered shyly. Being caught off guard made me blush again.

"Did he do that to you?" she asked.

"No!" I answered quickly. "He would never try to hurt me. I told you. I had an accident while playing a game." I couldn't believe that she suspected Marc. He was the gentlest boy I knew. Still, I could not fathom telling her the truth, that my father had caused the cuts and bruises. I could not face the shame and embarrassment of that revelation. I didn't want Mrs. Garry, or anyone else, to know about what happened in our house; people like her would be disgusted by the way that we lived. Trash.

"Okay," Mrs. Garry said. "I'm just a little worried, that's all. You're an excellent science student. I don't know what you're considering for the future, but you would do very well in the sciences at university. But, marks like this," she continued, while pushing my test paper toward me with 62% neatly printed in the top corner, "will not get you there. Do you understand what I'm saying to you?"

I nodded and turned my gaze toward the comforting eyewash machine.

"Do you have any idea what you would like to do after high school?" she asked as she leaned her elbows on the lab bench.

"Well, I was thinking of going into art and maybe teaching."

"Really," she said. "I don't know much about art and I don't think that I've seen any of your work yet, but I do know that everyone thinks you are a terrific artist."

"Thanks," I said.

"Look, Lynn, the truth is that you have the ability to do anything you want. But if you continue getting marks like this one," she said, waving the test in the air, "you will limit all of your options. This paper in no way reflects what you are capable of achieving."

"I know," I conceded. "I'll work harder. I promise."

"Don't do it for me, Lynn. Do it for yourself, for your life. And I want you to know," she finished, while writing an admittance note, "that you can come and talk to me anytime you want…about anything, okay?"

"Thank you," I replied. "I *will* make things better, Mrs. Garry."

"You take care, Ms. Hellers," she said with a wide smile.

I left the chemistry lab completely dumbfounded, because she seemed to actually give a shit. She was the first and only educator to ever draw attention to any visible wounds on my body and yet, over the past three years, I had gone to school with deep violet shadows under my eyes, swollen pink lips, green and blue bruises, and blackish-red blood on my white cloth Nike sneakers, all seeming elements of a spattered Jackson Pollock painting, all tidbits of a dark life that I attempted to conceal in one way or another.

Later that very week, I was taken aside by another teacher, the one who was teaching me how to really paint. The long, lanky, eccentric Mrs. Hagen asked me if she could eat lunch with me in the cafeteria. "I want to talk to you about something," she said. I told Marc that our art teacher wanted to speak with me and that I couldn't spend the lunch period with him. "Gee, what do you think that's all about?" he asked. I told him that I had absolutely no clue. The truth was that I had some idea about my art teacher's knightly manoeuvre. I figured that she and Mrs. Garry were working together on the same side of the chessboard and that they had discussed my situation.

I sat across from Mrs. Hagen at the wide brown veneer slab in the school cafeteria. I tried to ignore the stares from other students who certainly wondered why I was sitting with a teacher during lunch. Mrs. Hagen opened her brown paper bag and released a Kaiser bun full of ham, cheese, and lettuce wrapped sloppily in plastic. She opened a Tupperware container with a beautiful, fresh green salad with cherry tomatoes and shredded carrot. *What an exquisite lunch,* I thought, suddenly embarrassed by the fact that I had nothing to bring to the table.

"Aren't you going to have your lunch?" she asked, smiling. "I thought that we could eat together while we have a chat."

"Oh, I already had a snack earlier. I'm really not very hungry," I lied.

"Well, my dear, I refuse to sit here and eat alone. You are going to at least have half of my sandwich."

"Oh no, that's okay. Really, I'm not hungry," I said.

"Oh, yes you are. Now here," she said cutting the bun in half and handing it to me. "You are going to eat this and you will love it. I've been using this different mayonnaise that is so tasty."

"Thank you," I said softly while the familiar heat flooded my face.

I took a bite of the fresh puffy sandwich and felt my stomach immediately rise upward, like some separate uncontrollable animal, to receive the gift that was being sent. It *was* exquisite. Saliva filled my mouth to the point that I thought I might drool all over the table. This had to be one of the best sandwiches I had ever had.

"How do you like it?'

"Oh, thank you so much, Mrs. Hagen. It's absolutely delicious," I answered awkwardly, covering my full mouth with my hand to keep the food and saliva from spraying all over her like a Vesuvius eruption.

"I'm sure that you are wondering why I called this little luncheon," she began.

"Yes," I replied simply, having finally swallowed the gob in my mouth.

"I want to talk to you about your future plans. I want to talk about what you would like to do when you leave Regi."

I stared at her.

"You must have some idea about how talented and intelligent you are," she said.

"Not really," I replied flatly, wiping crumbs from my face.

"Well, if you don't know it," she continued, leaning toward me, "I'm here to tell you that you are. You are one of the most gifted students that I have ever had the pleasure to teach."

"Okay," I said even more flatly.

"But you're not doing your best," she said. "You're far too cautious artistically and you're not reaching your creative potential."

What?! Fuck you, bitch! I'm working my ass off here! "I'm trying my hardest," I said.

She continued, "I don't think that you are. I've noticed a recent decline in both your interest and your artistic production. Tell me, what do you want to do after high school?"

"Well, I was thinking that I might go to St. Lawrence College for art," I told her.

"St. Lawrence College," she repeated, staring off into space. "You went on the day trip we had there, right? Remember what you said to me about the assignment you saw those college students doing?"

"No," I answered.

"I'll remind you then. They were drawing a Canadian dollar bill in detail. Remember? You said, 'What's the point of that, copying a dollar? Are they trying to make a bunch of counterfeit artists?'"

I laughed. "Yes, I remember," I said. "There could be a future in that." I giggled.

A stern look took control of Mrs. Hagen's lined faced. It made her hair look even stringier.

"Lynn, you do not belong in a college. You belong in a university. If you don't explore university options, I think that you will regret it. I'm not putting down the colleges. It's just that people who have your capabilities can end up being extremely bored there. You need to push yourself...and your ideas."

"Going to university means spending another year in this place," I said as I spread my arms out and looked around with rolling eyes. What I really meant, and didn't say, was that it meant spending another year in the house of my parents and the thought was like a knife in my temple. I wanted out as soon as possible.

"It's only one more year, Lynn! I really want you to reconsider. You can do this. Please don't waste your gifts."

Where had I heard that before?

"I'll give it some thought," I told her honestly. "I don't really know how I could afford university."

"Can your parents help you?" she asked.

I laughed out loud. "No, that won't be possible."

"Then consider OSAP, student loans and grants. Believe me, there is a way to do this."

"I'll think about it," I said, as I prepared my books to leave.

"Can you wait just a couple of more minutes? There is one more thing that I want to discuss with you."

"I don't want to be late for class," I told her.

"Don't worry. I'll give you an admit slip."

Oh, Christ. What now? I thought.

As I folded my kilt under my ass and sat back down in the orange plastic chair, I could see that Mrs. Hagen was clearly nervous about something. She rubbed her large hands together, attempting to impossibly smooth the dry, cracked, parchment skin that covered the bones.

"I'd like to talk to you about Marc Gatien," she said.

Oh, fuck. She has *been talking to Mrs. Garry.*

I stared down and rubbed at the scratches in the table and asked, "What about him?"

"Well...how serious is it between the two of you?"

"I don't really know," I answered.

"This is difficult for me to say to you, Lynn, but I think that he is holding you back."

I managed to open my mouth and that was all. She continued on a roller coaster of words, a continuous run, a breathless rant designed to avoid any interruption: "Marc is a really nice boy but he's not the right one for you. Sure, you have art in common with him, but that's all! He's just a boy. You are a high level thinker and he's satisfied with making the guys in the class have a big laugh. He can't even come close to you. You probably don't know it yet but you will soon grow extraordinarily bored of him. He isn't even close to being in your league."

I grinned and stared at her.

"Well, I don't plan on marrying him tomorrow, Mrs. Hagen," I said with a smirk.

"I know that dear," she said, smiling wanly. "I just want you to think about whether you want to stay in the place that you are or if you want to move on."

Oh God, what am I going to say to that? I want to move on and have a better life. She thinks my life is fucked because of Marc. She doesn't know the truth.

"I do want to move on, but you're mistaken when you think that Marc is a problem," I told her.

"Then please tell me, what is the problem? I hope that you feel that you can talk to me."

"It's okay, Mrs. Hagen. I'm fine. Really. I've been slacking off a little bit, I know. I will work harder and I will think about university."

Mrs. Hagen stared at me with a look of skepticism that made me blush. She didn't believe me. "Alright," she said with a heavy sigh, slapping her hands down on the brown veneer. "I'll trust that you will make the right decisions for yourself. But listen to me: I want you to come to me with any questions, thoughts, fears, *anything*. I think that you are a person who finds it difficult to trust. You might think that this sounds typical and empty, but I want you to know that you can trust me, okay?"

"Sure," I answered. "I had better get going. I'm already late for French class." Mrs. Hagen wrote a note and sent me on my way. While leaving, as I waved back at her, I noticed her strained and worried smile. How I would hate to disappoint her.

Later, as I sat there in French class, engulfed in an immense fog, I thought about what my two teachers had said as I conjugated verbs and pluralized a word list. Part of me felt that they should fuck off and keep their pasty faces out of my business and another part of me revelled in the fact that they even cared and dared to speak to me about such personal matters. If I could see myself as worthwhile, even for a second, it was because my grandparents and these teachers made me think so. If I could contemplate a future at all, it was because of them.

X X V

MARC AND I SAT ON THE DAMP GRASSY FRINGE OF A FIELD lined with funky smelling earth mounds, the remnants of the hayfield from the previous season, near my house on that cool spring afternoon. He pulled a blue Bic lighter from his pocket and fired up the chubby joint sandwiched between the thumb and index finger of his right hand. He took a couple of long draws from the wrinkly white tube before handing it toward me.

"No thanks," I said, rather matter-of-factly.

"What?" Marc asked, with his eyes already red and confused.

I lifted my head and looked at him directly. "I don't want to do this anymore, Marc. It's making my head foggy and I don't like it."

His mouth dropped open. "What the hell happened? Have I done something wrong? Does this have anything to do with your talk with Hagen? What the fuck did she say to you?"

"She didn't say anything that didn't make sense. She talked to me about the drop in my grades and how I don't seem to be all that interested in school anymore," I said.

"Who the fuck does she think she is?!" Marc countered. "It's none of her fucking business what you do or what marks you get! Fuck her and fuck Regi!"

"I don't want to live a life like my parents; I want something better for myself. Don't you?"

"Listen to me, Lynn," he said as he leaned toward me. "You are an amazing girl and you're going to be successful no matter what any teacher says. They always want to poke their big fucking noses where they don't belong. What the fuck do they know about you?"

"Mrs. Hagen thinks that I should go to a university."

"Wow, that's big news," he said as he stared off into the sun-filled field. "Of course you could go to a university. So what? Big fucking shit. The point is that you can do whatever you want to do. You don't need some teacher to tell you where you should go. I'll bet that she talked to you about me. She did, didn't she? I know that she thinks I'm a piece of shit. I'm not in her group of chosen ones,"

171

he continued, waving his hands in the air and rolling his eyes. "I can tell that she disapproves of our relationship. Have you noticed how she always tries to keep us apart in art class?"

I sighed heavily, hanging my head to one side, as I thought about what I should say next.

"She thinks that I'm a little distracted, like I'm in some kind of coma, like I'm wasting opportunities," I said softly.

"Oh right," he yelped, clearly angered. "And I'll bet that she thinks that this is all my doing, that I'm dragging you down into some sucking pit of swamp shit!"

"No Marc! That's not it at all!" I couldn't let him think that he was a negative component in Mrs. Hagen's scenario. I was desperate to find a way to live the world that Mrs. Hagen and Mrs. Garry saw for me, but at the same time, to have Marc Gatien be a part of it. Why couldn't I have both?

"I love my times with you, Marc. You help keep me sane. It's just that I have always done well in school and I know that it's my ticket out of the Hellers-hole. If I keep pumping drugs into my face, I'm going to screw all my chances. These teachers haven't told me anything that I don't already know. I guess that I've just needed a little push…maybe even a big one." I put my hand gently against Marc's face, leaned into him, and kissed his lips. "You should do this with me," I whispered into his ear. "We need to stop this shit and pull it together or we're going to end up like Margaret and Wade. We could have a great life if we would just work at it."

"What if I can't quit?" Marc asked, very seriously and sadly.

"Then I will have to quit you," I said as I dug my hand into the moist soil.

He asked in a fevered shocked voice, "Are you fucking kidding me?"

"No," I answered calmly. "I need to change my plans. I'll understand if you don't want to come along. Don't get me wrong, I don't want to lose you in my life, but I'm telling you now that I need to change things or I'm fucked. If you're going to keep laying a flame to this stuff," I picked up his clear plastic baggie of pot, "then we aren't going to make it as a couple."

Marc's mouth dropped open and he stared at me as if confronted with a tribal warrior who apprised him of the fact that his balls would be perfect for a souvenir necklace.

"Oh fuck. You're serious, aren't you? Jesus, Lynn, I don't know if I can quit cold turkey like that. You know that I love you and that I want to be with you always. All that I can say is that I'll do my best. Is that good enough?"

"That's good enough, honey," I said. "I know that you can do it. Don't you want a better life for us?" He nodded robotically. At the time, there was no doubt in my mind that Marc would alter his habits and behaviour if only for his love for me.

I was a fool.

X X V I

I FOUND NO DIFFICULTY IN WITHDRAWING FROM THE FRUITS of Marc's goblin market. It hadn't appealed to me much to begin with. For me, it was a forbidden social activity that would have sent my father into a bulging eyed, vein popping homicidal frenzy, regardless of his own addictions. That was just enough to make it appealing. The only thing that could top that would be if Marc were black or Asian.

I quit. Just like that. No problem, no withdrawal, no aching yearning or desire to light up one last doobie. To be honest, the forbidden fruit made me loathe the earthy grittiness in my mouth and I became nauseous at the taste when Marc and I would kiss. It was easy. I immersed myself into my schoolwork, completing every assignment, formulating all mathematical and chemical solutions, actively planning and articulating every response, every literal and visual passage to pave my way in paper to a future beyond the scarred and tattered walls of the house I lived in.

The story for Marc would be vastly different. He didn't give a shit about school and academic success; the only course of study that received his half-baked attention was visual arts. Even there, he didn't try to experiment or take any risks suggested by our teacher. He wouldn't listen to any of it; he did what he wanted to do, reluctant to follow any formula, defined task, or teacher suggestions for further discovery. At first, I admired him for his determination and his faithfulness to what he called *his* art. The more I delved, investigated, experimented, researched, and shared ideas and concepts with others, I saw how artistically constipated Marc was. He never pushed himself beyond his small pencil sketches, which all started to look the same; he drew the same male face, like the Dark Man in *The Stand,* over and over again. The face varied only in terms of its stage of completion; the whole face soon gave way to half a face, smudged away with a finger over a 2B pencil. He failed to finish any major piece of work outside of his sketchbook. Even so, it took a good space of time before I realized that his battle with drugs was more like a love affair. He wasn't only into pot and hash; I eventually discovered his lust for cocaine. There was no way that I could compete with that succulent lady.

Learning the truth was a devastation that defies words, even if I carefully tried to piece the words together with a whole year's time to do so. Marc's journey into the sinister and criminal world of substance abuse and drug sales coincided with the arrest of my grandmother for theft that was on such a grand scale that it blew the minds of all who knew her.

Marc started to miss our small customary meetings at school, the quick touch of hands by my locker and the sweet stolen kisses in a vacant corridor. Then he began to make excuses about why he couldn't join me for lunch; even so, he handed me a bag of goodies every time, sent from his mother. He was losing weight and his face became a map of sores, zits, and pocks. Wally started to joke that he wanted to play "connect the dots" on Marc's face but that it would be useless because his face would eventually be a complete inkblot. I told Wally to go whack off to one of his magazines, even though I knew he was right.

After one particularly gruelling bus ride with Marc, after chastising him for his bloodshot eyes and telling him not to call me that night, I walked into our house to find my mother frantically yanking her genuine leather coat with the real fur collar out of the closet.

"What are you doing, Mom?" I asked, "What's the matter?"

"Nothing," she replied abruptly, without even looking at me. There was a pause as she held the coat in the air and rolled it into a ball. I gasped. This was a cherished cloak purchased by my father from the expansive mountain of stolen goods littering Nanny Ida's bed. My mother loved that coat. I gaped at her as she stuffed it haphazardly, without emotion, into a black garbage bag.

In an instant, she stopped and stared at me. "Lynn, go get those new Jordache jeans that you got from your grandmother."

"What?!" I screamed. I couldn't believe that she didn't notice that I was wearing them. Of course, why would she? I had received several pairs of authentic Jordache and Sergio Valente jeans from Nanny Ida's stash. It was wearing Jordache that garnered for me the most suspicious looks from schoolmates and even teachers. Everyone knew that no Hellers kid could afford such fashion fineries; they knew that we were wiggling our asses in stolen denim.

"I'm wearing them," I told my mother.

"Oh fuck," she said. "Get them off NOW!"

That was it. I needed to know what was happening. "Jesus, Mom, what is going on? Have you just suddenly lost your bloody mind?"

"Your grandmother has been arrested," she blurted out, dropping the garbage bag on the floor. Her eyes were dark and huge.

"Oh, God," I whispered. I couldn't think of anything else to say. To me, Nanny Ida was immortal and untouchable. For as long as I had a memory, she had committed infamous acts and always managed to evade the law. As a young child, when I tore open the numerous gifts that she scattered under her crystal white imitation Christmas tree adorned with those plastic balls covered with spun threads of blue nylon, I hoped to be instilled with her fearlessness so that I could erect such a shiny tree, complete with countless gifts for my siblings' future children, as I still planned to not have any children of my own. She never failed to pull out all of the stops to create the most festive moments for her family. Unfortunately, she had to steal and play games with numerous demons to make it happen.

"It's worse than you might think," Mother continued. "The police raided 16 James. They have surveillance tapes and phone recordings. Every fucking person who's been around there for the past six months is on them, including us! Jesus, I need a cigarette. Where the fuck are they?" she asked, as she spilled the contents of her purse onto the kitchen table.

She fumbled with the package of Player's Light and lit her soothing stick with a shaking hand. After sucking on it as if she were taking her last breath, she hacked and stared out the patio door.

"Where is Dad?" I asked.

"Uh, he's getting some stuff out of the basement. We've got to get rid of all this shit. Get rid of anything that can be linked to 16 James. Like I just told you, get those jeans off and bring them to me."

"But Mom, what are you going to do with all this stuff? There's so much stuff here! What's going to happen to it all?"

She took another long puff before answering. "It's all going into a deep fucking hole in a farmer's field. Your father already has it dug. Everything's going into garbage bags and we're just going to have to hope for the best. Hopefully the bugs don't get at that coat. I'll flip my goddamned lid."

I walked slowly down the hall and into my bedroom. I searched for something that I could actually wear, something that hadn't come from 16 James and my grandmother's den of thieves. Here my grandmother was facing prison and I was actually worried about what I was going to wear the next day; my stomach acid splashed and burned as I considered the reality of wearing my shitty old denim "floods" to school.

But I was even more worried about my father. How was he going to react to the fact that his mother was in police custody, that our family had become a group of guest stars on police video, and he was preparing to leave our house under the seemingly safe blanket of darkness to bury practically everything we owned in a hole somewhere. I knew that the man was going to be positively wretched.

I handed my new Jordache jeans to my mother just as Father ascended the basement stairs carrying two garbage bags. He looked stricken, frightened. The man was scared shitless. I couldn't believe it. The monster was sweating with fear. I couldn't help but feel some measure of smug pleasure in the face of his obvious shock and dread. *Not even remotely pleasant, is it, you bastard?*

"Is that all of it?" he asked, looking at my mother and nodding toward the bags on the kitchen floor.

"Ya, I think so," she said. "Do you think the coat is going to be okay, I mean, you know, buried in the ground like that?"

He glared at her, his mouth a thin, taut line. "You're something else," he said. "Just don't fucking worry about it. I think there's a hell of a lot more to be concerned about right now. Don't you?"

Silently, she lit another cigarette.

The bags were loaded into my father's car and he left without saying another word. Later that night, he walked into the house, sweaty, weary, and dirty. He didn't even tell us where he had buried the loot. There were deep soil marks on the knees of his work pants. He opened a bottle of beer and retreated into the basement. Even Mother knew better than to even blink in his direction.

XXVII

MY FATHER HAS BEEN CAUGHT COMPLETELY OFF GUARD IN THIS snapshot. He has always hated being caught like this, totally unawares, as if his pants are down and he's wearing frilly underwear. His face registers such surprise and alarm that I almost feel sorry for him. He has been jostled into fear by a camera's flash, captured while reading the newspaper. He's reading about his mother, Kingston's newest jailbird.

Wade Stanley Hellers looks out at the photographer with apprehension and a hint of fear. I wonder who took this picture. I can tell that it was taken in our kitchen; he is sitting in his usual spot at the old wooden table within the paneled walls of that small violent room in Inverary. He wears a plaid shirt with earth tone colours. He always wore plaid. Anything else could be confused for "fag rags". Any garment with bright colours, pinstripes, dots, or paisley was a fag rag in my father's estimation. Of course, he wasted no time in pointing out that my boyfriend Marc had a closet full of fag rags and wasn't I the lucky girl.

What I find particularly humorous about this snapshot is that Wade S. Hellers is also sporting a fairly nasty permanent wave. With the 1980s came a fad that found men getting perms in their hair and afros became vogue. The puff surrounding his tense face looks like something a cat might cough up. At the time, I couldn't help reminding my father, with sheer delight, that chemical alteration of the hair was a fashion whim with women and most gay guys and that afros came from the black population and a fascination with Stevie Wonder, Jimi Hendrix, and Diana Ross. He told me to bite his even hairier arse.

The emotional strain on his face, like any face that can be found in an Ensor painting, is more distinctive than his hairball. My grandmother was facing serious charges. In the newspapers, she had been identified as the Kingston contact in a huge theft ring that ran from Toronto to Kingston, and then to Montreal and back again. She and the notorious site of 16 James Street had been under surveillance for months; no one knew exactly how long. One could only estimate from the amount of videotapes and phone tap logs that were made available to my grandmother so that she could prepare for her defence. There were countless phone tap books and each one was at least four inches thick. When the mountains of pages were presented to her, she just stared at them and said, "Fuck me."

The phone tap books contained every single conversation that went to and from 16 James. There had been no attempt to delete the extraneous material from the criminal negotiations:

Hey Betty, you old slut, what the fuck are ya doin'?

Ha, ha, you crazy bitch. I'm just watching the fucking Young and the Restless.

Oh yeah, what the fuck is goin' on today?

Oh, that cocksucker Jill is making life hell for Mrs. Chancellor again. Fuck that Jill is a slut. Can't keep her hands off Chancellor's husband. Chancellor's diving back into the fucking sauce again because she can't handle it.

Jesus Christ, why the hell do you watch that shit?

Beats playin' with myself, Idie, ha, ha, ha.

Ha, ha, oh my God, ha, ha. You're one loony bitch. Listen, why don't you get your fat ass over here and join me. I just opened a nice bottle of whiskey.

Oh, now that's my fucking language! I'll just grab some butts and I'll be right over.

My grandmother Ida did her time in prison. Before heading off to the big house, she took one last swing at a police officer, one of her unlucky escorts. She cursed every one of the "cock-suckers" into an "early fucking grave" before they could finally be rid of her and drop her into the hands of the prison staff. Despite this tumultuous entry, she became a model prisoner who bonded well with her fellow inmates and joked with guards. She learned how to knit and crochet and told my father that they were actually turning her into a "real fucking grandmother". She was allowed to work in the kitchen and perfected her already masterful culinary arts. As a result of her impeccable behaviour, Ma Barker was released from prison early, after a little over a year.

Upon her release, Nanny Ida presented everyone in the family with either a piece of knitting or a crocheted doily that she had made while incarcerated. There was a mountain of these handmade goods as high as the one that used to rise above her bed, created by layers and layers of stolen property. In prison, she had fashioned images of puppies, kittens, hearts, and cottages. She gave me a pair of knitted slippers made with stripes of turquoise and white yarn. At the same time, she flung me a piece of her crochet.

"Here you go, Lollipop," she said, tossing a wadded chunk of cloth in my direction. "Take this one too. I'm so sick of these fucking purple puppies. I don't know what I'm going to do with them all."

Grandma Ida's rehabilitation was like an egg that couldn't hatch. The core, the yolk of it was there; she wanted to live a better, proper, crime-free life, but its development was hindered by external forces. The core of the egg did not receive enough tender loving care, enough warmth and nurturing. The yolk was a cold, gelatin glob that refused to grow; her cycle would not be complete.

Nanny Ida continued to dabble in the criminal world that she knew so well. She even managed to add a few bodies to her crew of thieves, having met them while she did her time. She tried to moderate the goings on at 16 James; the bed was only piled half high with jeans, shoes, blouses, boots. Nanny decided that furs were too risky so they were virtually eliminated from the pile of loot. She had become far more careful and rarely discussed any of her activities on the phone. Ma Barker started to move away from the bootlegging and kept her business fairly small time. She was determined to never crochet another purple puppy in her lifetime.

Marc, on the other hand, was riding a slippery slope toward purple puppies or whatever crafts, if any, were done in prisons for men. The first time that Marc was arrested, I was with him. I knew that he had developed a habit of stealing audio equipment; he stole tape decks, stereos, speakers, headphones, wires, absolutely anything and everything to do with fine music equipment. He started out by taking small things, like cassettes of his favourite bands. He became obsessed with The Clash and made me listen to *Rock the Casbah* at least one million times:

> *The shareef don't like it*
> *Rockin' the casbah*
> *Rock the casbah*
> *The shareef don't like it*
> *Rockin' the casbah*
> *Rock the casbah*

I didn't understand the song, nor did I want to. To me, it was an indicator of Marc's decline. I unfairly came to associate all English punk bands with excessive drug use. Whenever he played a new cassette for me, I knew two things for sure: he was high and he had been stealing. There was no way that the jobless Marc could afford to purchase all of the new cassettes that he carried in his knapsack.

On the day of Marc's arrest, we left our high school and walked all the way out to Sears, the huge department store located within the Kingston Shopping Centre. We had planned to get a ride home from his father after his shift at Weston's Bakery. As we entered Sears, I was immediately captivated, as I always had been, by the beautiful house wares, linens, and furnishings, so beyond mere contrast to the shit we had at home. Marc finally grabbed me by the arm and impatiently said, "Come on, let's get going."

"Let me guess," I said as I followed behind him, "we're going to the music section."

"You got it, baby! Wait until you see this set of headphones that I've had my eye on."

"Marc, you already have several sets of headphones. Why the hell do you need another set?"

"Oh, now listen. This isn't just any set of headphones. They're top of the line and made by Sony. I don't know anybody who has a set of phones that good."

"Yes, I'm sure they're just spectacular," I said sarcastically.

"Look," he screeched excitedly, leaping toward the shelf that held the prize. He handed the headphones to me. They were encased securely in hard plastic and even though I knew very little about such things, I had to admit that they looked pretty cool and seemed to have all the bells and whistles.

"They are really nice, Marc," I admitted as I turned the package to look at the price. They were well over $50. There was no way that he could afford them even if I had offered to pool my money with his.

I looked at him with a stone face. "These are expensive. Do you actually have the money to get them?" I waited for his response as my skin prickled with rage at the thought that if he had that kind of money, why wasn't he taking me to a movie or offering to buy me a Snack Pack from Kentucky Fried Chicken.

"Oh, I don't have the money yet," he answered. "I'm in the process of trying to save for them."

"Uh, huh," I grunted.

Marc hung the package back on the shelf, back in its home beside all the other black, silver, and white tech equipment. "Hey, Lynn, why don't you go look at that bedding that you really liked. I'm just going to fish around here for a bit. I need to buy some new speaker wire. It's only a couple of bucks."

"Alright," I said. I did want to look at those pristine sheets and comforters again. I wanted to dwell in the rooms of my imagination, rooms that were filled with shiny glass, new pots and pans, crisp sheets on a new soft, thick mattress, and a sofa that didn't stink like piss.

I left Marc to his wires and went to view the house wares first. My distorted face stared back at me from the convex silver surface of a new toaster. Our toaster was a square block full of stains, grease spots, and had long lost its ability to pop up the toast. I looked at the price: $24.99. How was I ever going to manage it? How was I going to get out of my parents' house and be able to afford to live somewhere else? Even if I could do it, the place would be empty. *I can't afford this fucking toaster. What the hell kind of life am I going to have?*

Engrossed in my own misery and sense of future doom, I turned my head to something that I might be able to afford: a potholder. It was quilted with a simple, opaque design: black cows and chickens on a white background. It was $2.99. If I saved my babysitting money after paying high school tuition, then I could afford that. *Fuck.*

As I stood there in the Sears department of luxurious small appliances, I contemplated my future life, a life endlessly repeating the trashy cycle I had already lived. I actually smelled my fate. I smelled the dirt because I wouldn't be able to afford the good cleansers; I smelled my body because I couldn't bathe every day; I smelled the foul desperation coming from my breath as I craved the next meal; I smelled sour milk.

My shoulders slumped and my vision blurred as I entered what seemed like a catatonic state. I came to find solace in a self-imposed prison cell where I could temporarily feel safe and untouchable. My detached mind floated like a helium-filled balloon above my body and watched the world below, the world of all the pleased and sometimes disgruntled consumers shopping for little kettles, toasters, and dishtowels. How I envied them and wished to weight myself down with irons, griddles, and that fucking toaster, to join them in the real world.

"Hey, Lynn, let's get moving." I barely heard Marc's plea as he hooked his hand like a clamp around my upper arm.

"What, huh?" It was all I could manage to say.

"We need to get going, sweetie. We need to get to Weston's to meet my father."

"Uh, right," I said, trancelike. "Weston's, right. We're at Sears. We should get going, right?"

"Jesus, are you okay?" Marc asked.

"Sure!" I answered excitedly, having snapped out of it. "Let's go."

Marc put his right arm around my waist while the other expertly swung his knapsack over his left shoulder. He quickly ushered me to the exit doors, constantly looking over both shoulders.

"What the hell's the matter with you?" I asked him.

"Oh, uh, nothing. I just don't want us to be late when we meet Dad after work. He'd be really pissed if he had to wait around Weston's after a long day."

"Of course," I said, taking his hand.

Marc and I approached the exit doors and opened them to a gorgeous sunny afternoon. I enjoyed the thick blanket of heat that engulfed us as we left the overly frigid air-conditioned interior of Sears with its shiny, stainless toasters. We took maybe two steps before a large hand planted itself upon Marc's shoulder, stopping us both in our tracks.

"Excuse me, sir," he said officially, looking at Marc. "I saw you take something from this store."

My blood went cold blue and Marc's face went blood red.

"Uh, I think that you're mistaken, sir," Marc said, looking at me nervously. "I didn't take anything from this store."

"Listen, son, take a look at me," the man said. "Do I look like an idiot to you?" The man was wearing a crisp white shirt with a grey and blue striped tie, tightly knotted, founded by stiff grey pants that were too tight and too short.

Marc was shaking. "No, sir."

"Then cut the crap and give it up. You've got Sears merchandise in that knapsack."

"No, sir, I don't," Marc said.

"Well then, son, you will have no problem with me looking in your bag. You were on store property and I can search you."

Marc blanched. His hot pink pimples became even more visible against his parchment skin. He trembled and gave me a look that said, *Sorry Lynn, I fucked up.*

Marc tilted his head sadly to the side and handed his knapsack to the striped tie. He took one look inside and ushered us to a small office inside Sears. At that point, I decided to float above the scene and watch from the ceiling. I could barely hear a thing. The room vibrated lightly with mumbles and tiny echoes. Words bounced around. *Right. Wrong. Theft. Headphones. Wires. Cassettes. Police.*

The entire scene became a huge blur to me. I thought that I might be losing my eyesight. My ability to focus had vanished. My hearing was so strangely affected. Nothing really registered coherently in my brain until Mr. Gatien arrived. When I squinted and saw his stern but sad face moving its lips slowly in front of the uniformed officer, I wanted to die. He had been called to pick up our sorry asses after Marc had been officially charged with theft under $500.00. *Fuck,* I thought, *you're an amazing kisser but you can't steal worth shit. How could you be so stupid?*

In Mr. Gatien's small car, nothing could fracture the eerie silence. Mr. Gatien started the car without looking at either of us and stared at the long highway for the entire trip to my house in Inverary. Marc sat in the front seat, offering only a few fleeting glances toward his father before setting his gaze upon the road as well. As for me, I sat numbly in the back seat hoping that Mr. Gatien would say something, anything. I was ashamed of Marc and ashamed that I was with him. I wanted Mr. Gatien to know that I had not been a party to this crime in any way; I worried that he might think that Marc stole the headphones as a gift for me. In retrospect, Mr. Gatien probably didn't give a shit. The raw truth was that his son was charged with theft and I was free to go without repercussions.

When Mr. Gatien finally dropped me off at my house, I was grateful to exit his car where the air was thick and heavy and the absence of sound made my skin prickle.

I said, "Thank you for driving me home, Mr. Gatien."

He did not respond. He continued to stare ahead out the windshield at the view of one of my father's countless metal wrecks that littered the yard and driveway, a blue half-ton truck with no tires and the box removed. *I'm so sorry, Mr. Gatien. Your son is a criminal and is dating true trash.*

I closed the car door gently and walked toward my house without looking back. I expected to hear the sound of swiftly spinning tires and spitting gravel. Instead, Mr. Gatien left our driveway as serenely as he had entered it. *Oh, you're in for it, Marc.*

There was no telling my parents. I knew that my father would take this opportunity to underline all of Marc's flaws and failings and I didn't want to hear it, especially from a pot so black that it needn't talk about the kettle.

Later that evening, Marc phoned my house. Father answered and, without confirming my presence, handed the phone to me. I shook my head "no" and stared at the greasy doily in the middle of the kitchen table. I heard my father tell Marc that I wasn't available at the moment. He opened the fridge, removed a beer, and asked why I wouldn't accept the call.

"Usually I have to threaten you with a good swat just to get you off the phone with that little fag," he said.

"I really don't want to talk about it," I told him.

"Well, well, well, isn't this interesting," Father said, smiling wryly. "What did that little geek do?"

"Nothing," I answered, seething with anger.

"Well, it must be something." He laughed. "Usually that fucking phone needs to be surgically removed from your ear."

"Could you just leave me alone, Dad, please?"

His smirk faded and he stared at me. "Well, you're obviously upset about something, Lynn. What happened? Has he met another girl?"

I tentatively turned my head and expected to see his sick, grinning face taking its pleasure in my pain. But he wasn't grinning, smiling, or laughing; he looked concerned and borderline protective.

"If he messes things up with you, he's a fucking idiot," he said, leaving the room to descend the basement stairs.

I sat there at the kitchen table, stunned and silent. I wasn't used to having support from my father, not used to him caring about me at all. If we weren't spending our time consumed by our ongoing vicious battle and tearful, tired retreats, we were ignoring each other completely. He saw me as a wallpaper pattern and I saw him as a turd on the floor. His sudden concern made me weep until my shoulders shook and my body heaved. I shut myself in my bedroom closet and let my snot drop in gobs onto its small, carpeted floor and my latest copy of *Mad Magazine*.

X X V I I I

AT THAT TIME, I FELT THAT I WAS DONE WITH MARC. HE HAD crossed the line and I was sour and disappointed. I was relying on him to hold my hand and help me lift myself out of the trashcan, but he was sinking so deep into the garbage that I was standing on his head. The vision I had of future romantic bliss to be shared with Marc narrowed into a tiny black dot.

I immediately called him on the phone. I couldn't wait to drop the bomb on him. My skin was crawling with the anticipation and I sucked on my fingers.

"Hello?" It was Marc.

"Hi, Marc," I said flatly.

"Oh, hey, Lynn! Oh, I'm so glad that you called. You must be pretty pissed at me, aye?" I winced at the sound of fear and panic in his voice.

"That would be putting it rather mildly."

"Listen, please. I am so sorry for everything that happened. It was a dumb ass thing to do. Dad's so mad at me that he's still not speaking to me. I'd much rather it if he just kicked me in the ass. His silent treatment is giving me an ulcer. I just hope that we're okay and that you will forgive me for being such an idiot."

Oh, God. Here it is. The moment.

My heart pounded so loud that I could hear it banging on my eardrums. I deftly glided my imaginary plane over the Gatien house in Perth Road and pushed the button that would release the explosive shell.

"I need to take a break away from you, Marc," I said, my voice beginning to crack.

Boom! There it is, devastation and smoke. I did it.

"Oh, God, please don't say that. We can work this out." He started to cry.

Hearing him sob made me feel even stronger, even more in control.

"There's really not much to work out. It is what it is. I can't be with someone who reminds me of the junkies and thieves in my own goddamned family. I want a better life for myself." I hated the sound of my holier-than-thou voice.

"Oh, I get it," he said through his tears. "Now you suddenly think you're better than everybody else. Is that it?"

"No, I just don't want to end up like my parents and so many others in my family. I don't need another druggie and thief in my life."

"I am NOT a druggie!" he shouted.

"Oh come on now, Marc. Let's cut the shit," I spewed back. "I know for a fact that you can't keep the fucking bong from your lips. Half the time when I see you, you've got bloodshot eyes and some new zits to add to your ever growing collection!"

He cried harder and I was pleased.

"Wow, I didn't realize that you could be so cold," he sobbed.

"Get used to it," I said calmly. "I've learned it from the best."

After a short pause, he said, "I think I should go now."

"Yep, I suppose you're right," I said, quite proud of my handiwork.

He whispered, "Bye." I heard the phone click in my ear before I could say goodbye back.

I smoothly placed the handset back onto our cruddy yellow telephone and sat down at the kitchen table. I gazed out the patio door. I stared at an evergreen seedling until my vision faded and everything went misty. I slipped into one of my comforting, numbing trances to avoid any physical or mental sensation. Quite suddenly, my hypnotic reverie was ruptured by a loud, dull thump and the dark coloured flicker of a small bird flying into the glass of the door.

The bird was fine. I was not. Once out of my trance, my stomach turned, my heart fluttered, and my hair felt like wires charged with electricity. I had ended it with Marc. It was over. My whole body shivered and instantly seemed infused with ice. I staggered to my bedroom and crawled under the dirty white blanket that covered my bed. With my face buried in my pillow, I howled and bawled until everything went black.

That following morning, I nervously boarded the school bus and took one fleeting glance at Marc before setting myself and my knapsack four seats in front of him. He looked almost fatally wounded. It was obvious that he had been crying. My missile had found its mark.

It didn't take long before kids on the bus started asking why Marc and I weren't sitting together. I overheard one annoying kid question him. Marc told him to mind his own fucking business and leave him alone. It was Catherine who came to interrogate me.

"Hey, Lynnie. What the hell is going on?" She plunked herself down in the seat beside me. She had a slight grin and I knew that she was enjoying herself.

"Oh, nothing much," I answered as I turned away and stared out the window.

"Come on, Lynn. I know you. I know when something is wrong, even beyond the obvious fact that you're not sitting with my dick of a brother." She paused. "Does this have anything to do with that asshole getting caught for stealing?"

"Somewhat," I answered, still facing the window.

"I knew it," Catherine said. "What a retard he is. No one can blame you for being pissed off at that."

"I broke up with him," I blurted out.

Catherine gasped. "Holy shit! Really? That's fucking great, Lynn! Wow, there really is a God. It's about time. You deserve way better than that friggin' loser."

"I'm really not in the mood to talk about it right now, Cath. I'm not ready to celebrate quite yet."

"Oh, I know that. But soon you'll see that it really is the right thing. He's a shit skid and isn't going anywhere. Listen, I'll call you tonight and we'll talk. Maybe we could hit a movie this weekend…*blah, blah, blah*."

Catherine continued talking in my ear but anything else she said did not register in my brain. Sometimes I would nod to give her the illusion that I was listening. She was far too enthusiastic about excavating and cataloguing the ruins of my relationship with her brother.

During my attempts to push Marc and his kisses from my mind, I worked even harder to achieve good grades. I also started to spend time with a girl whom I had originally met in my Grade 10 geography class. Aisling Gowan had sat in the desk in front of me and cracked me up with her stories about the devious tortures visited upon her three siblings followed by her animated imitations of her "lunatic" mother, Fiona. I spent more time laughing at the drawings of her mother wearing flared polka dot pants and her stories of butter sandwiches placed in the lunches of her sisters and brother than any time spent on class notes about the Canadian Shield and glaciers. My favourite story, which I had her repeat on numerous occasions, relayed the terror of her baby sister, Erin, who she chased around the house with a cold iron, pretending that she had just unplugged it.

Prior to my deepening friendship with Aisling, I had only a few female alliances formed earlier in elementary school. Before I gradually separated myself from them after meeting Marc, we would hang out in the halls between classes and in the cafeteria. At Regi, there were countless cliques and these girls had certainly developed a forceful one. Katie, Megan, and Casey were considered three of the coolest chicks in the school. They were pretty, had just the right amount of brains, and laughed easily. The trio took Terri and I into their fold more to keep the elementary school group together and for the fact that we contrasted them nicely. Terri and I had mediocre looks, even more mediocre clothing, and were rarely asked to go to the roller rink, Studio 801, by any of the boys. Terri and I knew our place. Unlike the three prima donnas, Terri was the group slut who would screw anything and entertained us all with her stories of the perfect blowjob, coitus interruption, and the odour of semen. I, of course, was considered to be the smart, geeky, least interesting one.

I soon grew tired of this group and their obsession with lip gloss, eyeliner, and hairspray. The most intellectual conversation I had with them was about the best Loreal perm and how to make the curls last. Though each one of us was adorned with a true 1980s perm; theirs looked thick and gorgeous, like Abby's on *Knots Landing*, while my thinning mane resembled tumbleweed.

When I met Marc and started spending my free time with him, it didn't bother me at all to ditch my clique; however, it bothered them a great deal. When they passed by us in the halls, they would literally grab my arms and pull me away from Marc so that they could whisper their mundane confidences in my ear, just rude enough to cause Marc to turn away.

"Hey Lynnie. What the hell are you doing with him?" Katie asked.

"Talking to him," I answered, smiling.

"That guy's a big loser," Terri added. "He has zits and a wide ass." The group erupted in laughter and each gave Terri a high five.

I stared at them and said nothing.

"I heard that he's a major druggie." It was Casey.

"Yeah, well, whatever you guys think," I said. "I like talking to him."

"Well, he certainly doesn't look good for much else," Terri howled. More laughter exploded in my ears.

"I'll see you guys later," I ended politely.

"Right," Katie said. "Maybe you will if you could pull yourself away from super freak over there."

My so-called friends moved on, still laughing, looking back enough times to let us know that they thought we weren't worth any more consideration than a wad of gum stuck to their Nike running shoes.

Conversely, Aisling was a breath of fresh air. She didn't give a frog's fat arse about lip gloss or hairspray. Her hair was naturally curly but unruly. She thought that she looked like a poodle with the mange. She told me that kids at her elementary school in Ireland would throw bits of pink eraser in her hair and it would take her several tearful days to get them out. Sometimes her mother had to cut chunks out of her hair to finally remove the bits of rubber. I thought that this story was both hilarious and dreadfully sad. At the same time, I was elated to have finally found a girl I could relate to.

Aisling also had to withstand the cruel scrutiny of my former clique. When Katie and Terri heard that I had dropped Marc and was hanging out with her, they hunted me down in the hall after my French class. My recollection is as vivid as if the meeting happened yesterday.

"Okay Lynnie," Katie says, chewing on her gum like a cow grinding its cud. "What's the deal? Have you suddenly taken leave of your fucking senses? What the hell are you doing hanging out with that scuzz bag, Aisling Gowan?"

"Yeah," Terri chimes in. "You're sinking to the bottom of the swamp with this one."

"You don't even know her," I say firmly. "She's hilarious. I like her."

"She's a huge friggin' loser, Lynn. Gawd. Don't be so fucked in the head," Terri says.

"I'm not fucked in the head," I tell them both as I swing my knapsack over my shoulder. "You guys won't give anyone the time of day who doesn't want to bend over and fix their lips on your ass."

Both their mouths gape and I can see Katie's blue gum nestled inside her cheek.

Katie closes her mouth, breathes deeply, and crosses her arms across her chest. "Look Lynn, you can hang out with that skid Aisling if you want. But how can you just dump your other friends? Don't we matter to you?"

"Sure you do," I tell her, touched by her seeming vulnerability. "I just wish you guys wouldn't be so judgmental."

"Well maybe we wouldn't be if you actually spent some time with your old friends," Katie says. "When you got together with Marc, you just ditched us and now you're pushing us aside for that skidder, Aisling."

"Okay," I concede. "The next time that you guys are doing something, let me in on it and I will try my best to go. Alright?"

"Sure," Katie answers. "Actually, we're going to a party at Elizabeth Merry's house this Friday night."

"I'll ask my parents," I tell them with a smile. "The only problem is that I won't have a ride. Mom and Dad don't venture far from their beer case on Friday nights."

Katie provides the solution. "I'll have my Dad's car that night. I can pick you up and drive you home."

"Cool. I'll let you know tomorrow," I tell them, somewhat excited by the prospect of the party.

"Try to convince your parents to let you go," Terri finishes. "It's going to be a blast."

I walked away feeling quite jolly, having placated my old posse and I couldn't help the skip in my step, the result of the clear fact that they wanted to spend time with me after so much absence and the truth that it was my doing that we had lost touch after I met Marc. My joy was rather short lived once I met Aisling at her locker.

"Do you want to know who just walked by me and gave me the snottiest look?" Aisling asked.

"Who?"

"Your old buddies, Katie and Terri," she said.

"Oh, them." *Godammit, are they ever going to change?* "Listen, don't pay any attention to them. I think that they're a little jealous of you."

"*Them* jealous of *me*? You mean the bitches who think that they fart perfume? What the hell for?" she asked.

"Well, I've been hanging out with you and not them since breaking up with Marc."

"Ah, that would probably do it," Aisling said with a giggle. "Gee, I think that I might actually enjoy this."

"They *are* odd ducks," I offered.

"Yeah," she said. "Hey, have you heard about some big party at Elizabeth Merry's house this weekend?"

"Um, yeah," I answered as I dropped my gaze from her eyes to the tops of my shoes..

"Everyone is talking about it," Aisling continued. "Sounds like the kind of gala that we wouldn't get invited to. Rob Derocher is going. Fuck he's hot."

I decided to tell her. "I think that I'm going to that party. I mean, I still have to ask my parents, but I'm probably going with Katie and Terri."

"You got invited?" Aisling asked curiously.

"Yes."

"That's great. I'm sure it'll be a great time." Every word dripped with sarcasm as she slammed her locker shut. "Make sure that you remember everything so that you can tell me all about it. Oh, and you might want to watch your back lest somebody there puts a dagger in it."

"Don't worry," I laughed. "I'll be careful."

I should have been more careful about a lot of things. First, I stole a cute purple sweater from the mall to wear to the party, the perfect accompaniment to my not so old jeans, so terrified at the prospect of wearing one of my shabby, outdated rags, or worse, something my mother found in her closet. Amazingly, there was absolutely no guilt about stealing the sweater, though I felt like a mammoth hypocrite for the way I had lectured Marc about his sticky fingers. In fact, I experienced exhilaration and empowerment. In an instant, I understood why my grandmother Ida did what she did, why Marc couldn't seem to help himself. Successful thievery was a rush, a shot in the arm. At that same moment, I also sadly recognized that I was living up to my family name.

That Friday night, Katie rolled into our driveway in her father's blue Chevy, Terri in the passenger seat. Though I had been given their permission, my parents weren't home yet, a detail that rendered me enormously grateful. Had they been there, my father would have been impelled to check out the old Chevy and would have discovered that Terri was nursing a bottle of Molson Export in the front seat. This was a ritual that was fine for him, but for anyone else, would have sent him into one of his bloated, red-faced tirades that would have landed me back in our house and my friends packing it back down the Latimer Road.

I slid easily into the rear seat and said, "Hey girls, are we ready for some fun?"

"You bet!" they chimed in unison. "This is gonna be great," Katie barked excitedly. "It's good to have you back with us."

"Hey Lynn, would you like a beer?" Terri asked.

"No thanks," I told her. "I don't much like beer." The truth was that I hated it. Drinking beer would be like drinking my father's sweat. The mere thought made me gag.

"Jesus Christ, you don't like beer? Well, did you bring anything else to drink?" Terri asked, flabbergasted.

"No."

"Well holy shitballs, Lynn," Katie said. "What the hell are you going to have to give you a buzz?"

"Nothing, I guess."

"Oh, wait a minute, I get it," Katie added. "You brought some weed with you."

"Nope girls, sorry to disappoint, but I don't do that anymore," I stated proudly. "I guess I'll have to go without."

"Fuck that!" Terri said. "We'll find something there that tickles your fancy."

Upon arrival at Elizabeth Merry's house, the three of us walked up the front steps, arm in arm. The stereo boomed with the sound of the J. Geils Band:

> Years go by, I'm lookin' through a girly magazine
> And there's my homeroom angel on the pages in-between
>
> My blood runs cold
> My memory has just been sold,
> My angel is the centerfold.

Elizabeth Merry greeted us in her kitchen. She was impeccably dressed with a tight white sweater over her substantial boobs, glittering hanging earrings in her ears to match her necklace, and designer jeans that fit like a loving glove. Her long, shiny hair flowed smoothly over her round shoulders. Elizabeth Merry was gorgeous.

She gave each of us a polite hug and directed us to the basement stairs that led to the party. Desperate to say something, I said, "You have a really nice home, Elizabeth."

"Thanks," she said. "Oh, and please call me Liz."

I was ridiculously and pathetically thrilled. It seemed that only her closest friends called her Liz. Temporarily, at least, I was accepted into the pack.

We descended the carpeted basement stairs and entered a large room filled with endless clouds of hairspray, bad cologne, and pimples. I became instantly anonymous. The place was packed, wall to wall. Throngs of shouting teenagers filled every space and there was no place left to sit or breathe. I opted for planting my ass on the second last step of the staircase while Katie and Terri ventured off to say their hellos to everyone they knew. I squirmed nervously on that step for about a half an hour before Terri came up, sat beside me, and handed me a glass of dark brown fizzy fluid.

"Hey, thanks," I said, relieved that I was no longer sitting alone. "What is this?"

"It's rye and Coke," she answered. "You'll like it, so you'd better drink up."

I took a small sip and I had to admit that it tasted pretty good. I continued sipping and I could feel the heat slide down my throat and diffuse through the rest of my body. Terri kept up with me and it didn't take long before we were both giddy and euphoric. Everything became a source of side-splitting humour. The pattern in the carpet made us laugh until our bellies hurt. We thought that it looked like a bunch of dicks growing out of flowers.

"Gee, looking at this carpet is making me horny," Terri yelped and fell forward. I went into a new bout of hysterics and helped her back up onto the step.

"Who do you think I should set my sights on tonight?" she asked.

"Oh, how the hell should I know?" I offered. "I don't even know most of these guys."

"I'd like to try for Rob Derocher. He's amazingly gorgeous, but I know he probably wouldn't give me the time of day."

"Now how do you know that unless you try?" I said encouragingly.

"Fuck, you know, you're right. I think I'll go have a little chat with the Robster."

"That's it girl! You can do it. Good luck," I said as I patted her on the back.

While Terri headed in the direction of Rob Derocher, I took my empty glass up to the kitchen. I didn't have to look far for my next drink. The kitchen counter was littered with bottles of liquor and pop. My shoes stuck to the floor in the inch of gunk created from spilled beverages.

After I poured myself another rye and Coke, I staggered up against the refrigerator to make the room stop spinning. Within minutes, I noticed a guy staring at me from a stool across the room. Even in my drunken stupor, I could see that he was extraordinarily attractive. He had dark curly hair, dark intense eyes, and a body like a football player.

I took a leap from the cliff and smiled at him. He smiled back, showing perfect white teeth, and then moved from the stool toward me.

"Hi," he said. "My name is Mike."

"Hi Mike, I'm Lynn. Nice to meet you." I revelled in the absence of my usual shyness.

"Who did you come here with?" he asked.

"With Katie and Terri. Do you know them?"

"No. I don't know very many people here. Everyone is mostly from Regi or KCVI. I go to Sydenham High. Liz invited me because I'm friends with her brother."

"Oh."

There was a short, awkward pause before he said, "You have really pretty eyes, you know."

I smiled, grateful for the compliment. "Thank you."

"Why don't we get out of this shitty little kitchen and go into the living room and sit down," he said, taking my hand in his.

"Sure. I've been sitting on a friggin' step all night."

Mike Davis and I sat on the sofa that had a large print of red roses and dark green leaves. Looking around Elizabeth Merry's house, one might think that a florist had thrown up in it. Mike immediately put his large hand on my knee and turned my face toward his gazing eyes.

"You're so pretty," he softly whispered.

"Thank you." I was truly flattered and my friends were going to think that I had struck gold.

He leaned in and kissed me gently on the mouth. When I showed no resistance, he kissed me harder and more passionately. Other than the fact that he had beer on his breath, I was enjoying myself. He put his hands into the hair at the base of my neck and made me shiver. After only a few minutes of kissing, he stood up, took me by the hands, and helped me lift myself from the rose covered cushions. He kept hold of my left hand and guided me knowingly down the hallway of Elizabeth Merry's house. He opened one of the doors and ushered me into a dark room. I could see from the moonlight through the small window that there was only a single bed and a tall chest of drawers decorating this tiny box.

He gently pulled me down onto the bed and started kissing me again, even more passionately. *I don't want this,* I thought, *I don't want this, I don't want this, I don't want THIS.* He moved his right hand up under my stolen purple sweater. I wanted to puke. *Please don't. Please don't.*

Expertly, he undid my bra and began massaging my breast. I began to panic and finally said, "Mike, could you please stop. I don't want to do this. I need to get going and find my friends."

"Just relax," he hissed in my ear. *Oh God, help me, I can't take this. I'm going to scream.*

He pressed his mouth hard against mine and I could feel the rigid lump of his cock against my thigh. While on top of me, he moved his hand down and unzipped the fly of my jeans. My heart pounded and no matter how much I moved my head, I couldn't get his mouth away from mine. He lifted himself up and placed his right hand over my mouth while his left hand undid his own pants. *No, no! Oh God, please, no!*

I squirmed and struggled and used every bit of strength that I had in my 102 pound body. He pushed his one knee up between my legs and told me to stop fidgeting. I started crying.

"What did you think was going to happen when we came in here? Just relax and you might enjoy yourself," he said directly into my mouth.

I managed some more words under the immense weight of his body: "Mike, don't, please." I was begging.

He pinned my arms down and pressed his lips to mine and began to grind his lump into my crotch. Pulling at my jeans, I felt his fingernails sink into my hip. *Oh God, why is this happening to me?*

Suddenly, the door to the bedroom burst open and almost broke from its hinges. It was Katie.

"Get off of her, you fucking perverted cock-sucker!" she screamed.

Oh dear God, you finally listened to me.

"Hey, we were just having a little fun," Mike said. "You need to chill out."

"Fun?! Fucking fun?! I know her, you dick. She wouldn't think this was fun," Katie screeched shrilly. "Look at her. She's crying you fucking asshole."

"Ah, you're both a couple of frigid bitches," he said as he left the room.

Katie came to me and refastened my bra. She helped me with my sweater and my jeans as I sobbed. Terri entered the room.

"Thank Christ you found her. Lynnie, are you okay?"

I nodded.

"That was a close call, Lynn," Katie said as she fixed my hair. "That fucking asshole deserves to die choking on his own dick."

Terri slung her purse over her shoulder. "C'mon, let's get the hell out of here."

We three jumped into the blue Chevy and said goodbye to no one. The drive home was mostly silent and I shouldered the responsibility of the damaged evening. I urgently wished to change the foul mood of the situation and light-heartedly flicked Terri on the shoulder: "So, Ter, what became of your little adventure with Rob Derocher?"

"Oh, that. What a fucking joke. I practically threw myself at him and made it pretty goddamned clear that I was good for a lay and he just laughed at me, spat out his beer, and dismissed me like some pesky insect. Stupid fucker doesn't know what he's missing, aye girls?"

We all laughed loudly and each took turns at verbally carving everyone that we could think of who had annoyed us at the party. We giggled uncontrollably like little schoolgirls and I know that we all felt a good deal better.

Katie and Terri dropped me off at my house around midnight and I couldn't wait to lay my head on my dirty pillow. I needed to forget the events of the evening and hoped for my favourite dream of flying with arms wide open over lush green fields divided by crystal blue streams.

I was sitting on the edge of my bed, in the midst of removing my socks, when I sensed a presence in the doorway of my bedroom. *Oh God, please don't let it be Dad,* I thought, as my internal organs did their familiar tumble. I slowly lifted my head and turned my attention toward the doorway and braced myself for whatever was coming.

It certainly wasn't something that I would ever have expected. There, with one arm braced against the doorjamb was my brother's friend, Roy Connor. He was completely nude; his hips were tilted and framed his large penis that was half erect and heading skyward. He was stationed in a perfect *contrapposto* pose, worthy of any I had seen carved in marble by Greek masters.

My first thought: *This can't be fucking happening. This night has to be a fucking nightmare. I must be hallucinating.* But it was happening. Roy Connor was standing at my bedroom door, naked, with one of the biggest cocks I had ever seen.

"Uh, hey, Lynn," he began. "How was your night? How was the party?"

I laughed and ran my hands through my hair. "Swell."

"Did you go with Katie and Terri?"

"Yes, Roy, I did. Look, what do you want?"

His face turned blood red and I swear that his penis took a slight dip south.

"Oh, nothing, uh, um, I just wanted to say hi to you because I was still awake."

"Well then, hi back to you. Listen, I've had a long night and I'm really tired. I'm going to hit the hay, okay?"

"Oh, sure. I hope that I didn't bother you."

"It's okay. Goodnight."

"Sweet dreams," he said, and walked down the hall, slowly enough that I could watch his ass if I wanted.

Wow. You've got some serious balls, I thought. Not only did he think that he could score with me, but he thought that he could do it in a bedroom adjacent to my homicidal father. I thanked God, aloud, for not having my father wake up in time to see Roy's naked ass and huge dick in such close proximity to his daughter. We both would have been flayed to within an inch of our lives.

X X I X

MY PARENTS WOULD NEVER KNOW ANYTHING ABOUT MY ordeal that night. Telling them was ridiculous to conceive. Though I had surfaced relatively unscathed, my mother would have taken me for a pregnancy test and my father might have knocked out my teeth. The one person that I did want to talk to was Marc. He would never behave like the boys I had met that Friday evening. I figured that I had been completely unfair to him. He loved me and treated me with respect, two levels of affection that I craved deeply.

The following Monday, I took a seat beside Marc on the bus. He blushed and stared at me. "What gives?" he asked with only the hint of a smile.

"Oh, I don't know. I miss talking to you."

That was all it took. Everything was forgiven and we almost instantly resumed our relationship, much to the disappointment of his sister Catherine and my old posse of friends. At that point, I didn't care what anyone thought. With Marc, I felt safe.

The one assurance I asked of Marc was that he lay off the dope. I didn't dare mention the stealing, considering my own recent crime. He vowed that he would be a good boy, that he was finished with his self-inflicted medicinal wounds. Naively, I believed him.

Once again, we became inseparable. That summer, we both took jobs at Lake Ontario Park in Kingston. Annie and I had been working there every summer since the age of thirteen, quite illegal at the time, or so I was told. My father insisted upon it since we needed the money to pay our tuition at Regi, with enough left over to buy school textbooks, our Kotex pads, shampoo, and underwear. We were hired by my father's pal Will Vallier; this kind man managed the seedy park complete with his open barbeque of roasted pig. I recruited both Marc and my friend, Aisling Gowan, to the shoddy amusement park, situated ironically and appropriately beside the Kingston Psychiatric Hospital on the shores of Lake Ontario. Marc took his position at the Tilt-A-Whirl ride where he cleaned up floods of puke; Aisling worked the Longhouse canteen slinging

196

greasy hamburgers and fries, while Annie and I shared duties in a miniscule booth making popcorn and pink or blue candy floss.

It was the summer of 1983. Thomas Dolby blinded us with science and Michael Jackson was pretty pissed at Billie Jean. Every teenage girl tore into her sweatshirt, exposing one skinny shoulder, the look made famous by Jennifer Beals in the movie *Flashdance*. The USSR became the evil nation to be feared by all, sparking political premonitions of a new Star Wars. It was then, the summer of 1983, the summer that I really fell for a girl, while the scrawny shoulder that held my purse strap poked out of my ripped, pink sweatshirt.

Tammy Collins was one of the countless teenagers that were employed at Lake Ontario Park. Like my friend Aisling, she worked The Longhouse and was up to her ass in grease and cheap condiments. She was older, quiet, and drew my attention immediately. Tammy seemed so unaffected by anything. She was wholly aloof, almost disconnected from the world. She didn't participate in the moronic banter that loosely flew around the grounds of the park; she rarely smiled and she didn't respond to the hormonal pleadings from the boys. Even I smiled shyly when they told me that I had a nice ass. Her ability to completely ignore them made me feel embarrassed, common, and juvenile. Tammy soon earned my deepest admiration.

I took quick advantage of my half hour breaks from the popcorn and Slush Puppies to make my way to her. I always spent the first five minutes chatting with Marc at the Tilt-A-Whirl and spent the remainder of my break near Tammy. I waited at the Longhouse until she wasn't busy so that she would be the one to serve me a Coke. If I was fortunate enough to have my break at the same time she did, I would casually take a seat beside her at one of the picnic tables. Sometimes we slurped our Cokes in complete silence. She didn't seem to mind talking to me, except that it was I who, in the beginning, had to initiate all conversation.

"Hi Tammy." My usual greeting—short, sweet, and full of nerves.

"Hey," she answers with a brief glance at my face.

"How is your shift going?"

"Oh, the usual bullshit," she says. "Grease, grease, and more grease. Don't ever buy one of those burgers. They float them in oil. How's life in the popcorn booth?"

"It's a fucking Mardi-Gras. I treasure every moment."

She laughs loudly, spitting out some of her Coke. Making her laugh makes me euphoric.

"Ya, I hear you," she adds. "This place is something fucking else. I get zits from just looking at the sludge on the grill."

There are no zits, no blemishes whatsoever. Her skin is clear, white, and lightly freckled, and stretches flawlessly over her square jaw. Her eyes are large almonds, dark brown. She has a long mane of chestnut hair that is so straight that I think she must iron it on a board. The other girls at the park call her Snotty Plain Jane behind her back. I disagree. I laugh along with her and think that she is extraordinarily beautiful.

Spending time with Tammy became all important; however, I was at the mercy of Annie who drove me back and forth to work, which was at least forty minutes from our house. She had been given a car, a gift from our father, and she wasted no time in getting her driver's license. The same privilege was not offered to me. My sister's chauffeur act lasted until she quit working at the park and took a job at the McDonald's on Division Street. My rides to work stopped, just like that. No one seemed particularly concerned about me, or the job that I needed to pay for my schooling and Kotex pads. Annie didn't care; she had her own life of responsibilities. My mother didn't care; she just didn't have the energy, and my father told me that if I was so smart I could figure out my rides some other fucking way.

That is exactly what I did. I started by hitchhiking. I didn't have much trouble getting rides. My last was with an elderly couple who lectured me on the dangers of hitching and wondered what I was thinking as a seventeen-year-old girl thumbing for rides in the dark. They insisted upon driving me right to my door. Unfortunately, Father, gassed up on beer, witnessed the event.

"Who the fuck was that who just dropped you off?" he yelled as he rose from his favourite kitchen chair.

My body felt wired; my scalp tingled while my stomach pitched and turned over. "Two old people," I answered. "I needed to get a ride home from work."

He moved unsteadily toward me. "Did you fucking hitchhike?"

"Um, well, ya. Look, I didn't have any choice." My voice sounded desperate. "Nobody would come and get me and you told me to figure out my own rides."

"I didn't mean that you get into cars with strangers, you stupid bitch!" He screamed it as he staggered toward me. I had exactly two seconds to brace myself before he planted his fist in my mouth. After the familiar white explosion, I fell to the floor, shaking my head to regain my bearings. Slowly, I crawled up the kitchen wall to stand on my feet. My lips felt stuck to my braces. Warm fluid ran down my chin. He had already gone back to his chair and his soothing Molson Ex. I placed a hand to my mouth, turned toward the hallway and walked to the bathroom in silence, taking careful steps as if I had suddenly found myself atop thin ice.

The mirror reflected the bloody mess. My top lip had snagged on my braces. Carefully, I pulled the flesh from the metal as blood splashed into the sink. I cleaned my wounds with cold water, wiped the sink, and went quietly to my room.

Behind the door of my bedroom, I did not cry; I did not hide in the closet; I did not hit myself, or the walls. All I thought about was how I was going to get to Lake Ontario Park the next day.

In the morning, the lip was only slightly swollen. I asked Annie if she would drop me off in Kingston before her shift at McDonald's. I explained that I needed to get to a Canadian Tire store.

"What the hell could you possibly want at Crappy Tire?" she asked with a furrowed brow.

"I need to buy a bicycle," I told her. "To get back and forth to work."

"Are you kidding me? That's nuts! You're going to ride a bike all the way to the park and back? Your shifts are nine hours long. It's too far to ride."

"It's not like I have a choice, you know. You can't drive me because your shifts are different and you're being a bit of a bitch lately. On top of it all, Mom and Dad don't give a shit about me and my summer job. The whole thing cuts into their boozing hours at the cottage. I can't hitch any more rides or Dad is going to remove my friggin' face with his bare hands. What the hell else am I supposed to do?"

"What about Marc?" she asked. "Can't his father drive you to work with him?"

"No, Annie, he can't. Marc's shifts are completely different from mine and I could never ask that of him. He only works a couple of days a week."

"Okay fine. I'll take you to Canadian Tire. I still think it's crazy. Why don't you apply for a job at McDonald's? Maybe they could arrange shifts for us together." She pushed her cruddy brown and orange McDonald's uniform into her knapsack.

"I don't want to work in that grease pit," I answered. "Everyone who works there ends up fat with clumps of boils on their ass."

Annie glared at me and I regretted the looseness of my tongue immediately. She had already begun to gain more weight while working there. With the lack of food at home, she took to having several meals a day at McDonald's. With a Big Mac here and a Quarter Pounder there, it didn't take long for her adolescent body to expand.

"Thanks, bitch," she said.

"I'm sorry, Annie. It's just that I can't work there. McDonald's is like a fucking cult." Plus, I thought, I wouldn't get to see Tammy.

"Sure. Right. Get in the goddamned car because I'm leaving."

That day at Canadian Tire, I purchased a sparkling red Raleigh ten speed bicycle, my very first brand new bike. I bought a silver wheel-powered head-light to mount on the front for my night rides and a chain lock to protect my new vehicle from theft. In an instant, I felt a surge run through my entire body, the electric current of freedom. Even though the purchase cut into my tuition money, I shook with the excitement of finally being mobile. I took the Raleigh smoothly over the store lot and began my proud, determined ride to the popcorn booth at Lake Ontario Park.

The ride from Canadian Tire to LOP was a comparative breeze to the pedaling home from work. My shift ran from noon until nine o'clock at night. It was amazing to me how many people wanted to ride the Scrambler and barf up their candy floss at those hours of a summer night, but they continued to come in droves. The insidious carnival music continued to play interrupted only by the sporadic squeals and screams of those riding the nearby Ferris wheel.

At nine o'clock, I closed the sliding windows and cleaned the booth with a bucket of water and bleach. By nine-thirty that night, I was able to happily board my bike and head home. I had no idea how hard it would be nor how long it would take. By the time I reached the end of Portsmouth Avenue, I was utterly exhausted and still had to get all the way to Inverary. I had eaten only popcorn from my work booth. Annie was quite right. I was fucking nuts.

I pushed myself, pedaled and pushed. When I arrived home, it was after midnight. It had taken me almost three hours and my shift for the next day started at nine in the morning and would be twelve hours long. My siblings were asleep and our parents were partying at the cottage. Throwing myself upon my bed, I cried. I set the alarm to give myself enough time for a quick shower and the three-hour ride to work; the bike ride would totally negate the shower, but I just couldn't deal with sweat on top of sweat. I set the time for 5:30 AM. Falling back onto my pillow, I slipped into a solid sleep, fully clothed.

Though I was physically used up from daily labour and biking, I enjoyed the short freedoms I had to get to know Tammy better. After work, we would meet at the picnic tables or by the beach to talk. She lived within walking distance to the park. We would joke about the events of the day, how funny Aisling was, and how idiotic the guys were. Then Tammy would have to make her way home. We would say goodbye and make a plan to meet on our break the following day. I never told her that I was stupidly cycling the distance from Kingston to Inverary. I told her that I was waiting for my ride and it always took a little more time than our moments together.

After one late night of chats with Tammy, I discovered that my new bike had a flat tire. I thought that I was wholly alone in the outside darkness of The Longhouse, with only two lights casting eerie rays upon the asphalt and empty picnic tables. That night was the blackest black that I have seen and I felt a moment of panic. I mounted the red Raleigh and made an attempt to ride; it was like pedaling through quicksand. My heart rate accelerated and my panic increased, but it was nothing compared to the panic I was about to experience.

Suddenly there were voices. Male voices. I turned my head slowly to see five teenage boys approaching me under the lights of The Longhouse.

Fuck, this can't be happening. Please God, don't let this be real.

"Hey there," one of them said. Tall, thin, curly blond hair.

"What are you doing out here alone?" asked another. Striped t-shirt and dirty jeans. They laughed in unison.

Oh shit. "I'm, um, waiting for, um, my ride home. My father is going to be here any minute." Even I think it sounds like a lie.

"Is that your bike?" asked the one with the blue ball cap.

"Yes."

"Well cutie, you have a flat," the ball cap continued, giggling.

Oh God. "I know that," I answered. "I've called my father and he's on his way."

"Ya, sure he is," laughed the fourth, the one with crooked teeth and a face peppered with brilliant red pimples. "I'm sure your old man will be here any second." More laughter.

"He *is* coming," I said desperately. "I just called him on the payphone."

It was crooked teeth. "You're pretty," he said.

"Great eyes," added the ball cap.

Striped t-shirt: "I'll bet your lips are really soft."

The fifth boy never said a word and I wasn't really aware of him until the group started to form a circle around me. I looked at him and could see that he was not comfortable with the obvious plans of his friends. I tried to communicate my pleading with my eyes on his, but he turned away.

"Look, guys, I just want to go home," I said. There was a few seconds of more giggling before a booming voice broke the air.

"What the fuck is going on down here?!" It was Will Vallier, the manager of the park, my father's friend. He had a large wrench in his hand.

"Jesus Christ, Lynn, is that you?" he asked squinting at me.

"Yes, Mr. Vallier," I said relieved and smiling, "I need a ride home."

He scanned the group of boys. "What the fuck do you think you assholes are doing here?"

"Um, nothing, sir. We were just leaving," ball cap answered.

Mr. Vallier grabbed his scrawny arm. "Right you little bastard. Do you think that I was born yesterday? If I ask her and you little shits laid one fucking hand on her, you're going to deal with the wrong end of this," he said, shaking the long wrench at them. "Lynn, did any of these grimy fuckers touch you?"

"No, sir."

"Are you sure honey? Just nod your head if that's all you want to do."

"No, sir, really, they didn't touch me."

"Alright. You fucking creeps get the hell out of my park and I don't want to see hide nor hair of your sorry asses or you won't be able to sit down for a month."

After they scattered, Mr. Vallier asked me what the hell I was still doing at the park at that time of night. I showed him the flat tire.

"Do you mean to tell me that you are biking from Inverary?" he asked.

I just looked at the ground.

"Okay. Let's take your bike and put it into the back of my truck. I'll drive you home. Lynn, does your father know that you're riding a bike this far to work?"

"Yes."

He shook his head and lifted my bike into the back of his pickup.

My exhaustive footwork on the Raleigh didn't last much longer. One morning I awoke to the 5:30 AM alarm and puked all over my bedroom floor. In the mirror, I saw an unrecognizable version of myself. My eyes were almost swollen shut and my neck bulged hideously on both sides. *What the hell is that? That's not even me.*

After tossing my guts a second time and coughing up blood, I phoned my mother, who was savouring her perpetual party with my father and his family at Nanny Ida's cottage on the Isle of Man. In a rare moment of true motherly concern, she told me not to go to work and that she would get Annie to take me to the hospital. I could tell that she was actually frightened.

At the hospital emergency, I was weighed, measured, and inspected by a doctor. The immediate diagnosis was a serious case of mononucleosis. I was not to work, play sports, or exert myself in any way for at least three weeks. My spleen was enormous and the slightest poke could rupture it. I was given a prescription but the doctor wanted to have a word with me.

"Hi, Lynn. I just have a couple of quick questions for you before you go."

"Okay."

"First of all, are you one of those young girls who thinks that it's attractive to be quite thin?"

"No, I don't think that at all." I was amazed at the question.

"Do you eat regular meals?" he asked.

"Most of the time," I lied. I could not tell him the truth, that especially during the summer while my parents were away, I scraped for meals, ate vegetables directly out of the garden that were baked in the sun; hot tomatoes and punky cucumbers. I ate fried zucchini at least three times a week. I ate handfuls of popcorn at work because it was free. Every cent I made went to tuition and books. I could not imagine attending a different school. Starving was more acceptable than leaving the familiar halls and faces of Regi.

"Do you play a lot of sports?"

"Well, I bike a lot." *Like I have the time and energy for sports, buddy.*

"Do you get regular periods?"

I wondered immediately how he could know anything about that.

"No," I replied. "I get one maybe every three to four months."

"Listen, Lynn," he said. "You are seventeen, five foot six inches tall, and you weigh just less than 103 pounds. What I'm telling you is that this is unhealthy. You are slightly malnourished. That's why you don't have regular periods and why you're getting so sick. You need to eat more. It's as simple as that."

"Okay." *Right pal, and how am I supposed to get all this food?*

When my mother heard the details of my emergency room visit, she had Annie drive me out to the Isle of Man where she fed me copious amounts of pasta lathered in tomato sauce and bread for dipping. It was exquisite. I still remember the satisfaction of those meals. She did this because I was sick. She didn't really worry about Annie packing her face with McDonald's sloppy crap and the fact that my brothers were fending for themselves at home.

The recuperation process on the Isle of Man was short lived. It wasn't because I got better; it was because I couldn't stand it any longer, not even for all the pasta and sauce in the world. Every day at the cottage was thick with booze, excessive profanity, and fighting. My mother fought with my father and my father fought with everyone.

It was on one particularly hostile evening that I took my leave. I asked my cousin Darren to drive me to my house. He was also tired of the bullshit that night. Nanny Ida was spilling her whiskey while screeching out Johnny Cash tunes and my Uncle Darren Sr. was trying to hold my father back so that he couldn't give my mother a swat. When Darren and I left, not one person noticed.

Back at home, my brothers and I scraped the cupboards for food. We practically licked them for crumbs. Annie had been gone for days, working her McDonald's job and staying at a friend's house. She was the lucky one; she had a car, a little money, and a friend's family willing to let her stay with them indefinitely. She wasn't about to remain at home eating squishy vegetables. Wally, Sean, and I found a packet of Clubhouse dried turkey gravy; we mixed it with water and ate it, taking turns with a spoon. Our parents didn't call us or provide groceries. I still couldn't go back to work and I missed my daily popcorn. We scoured the basement for old potatoes and plucked what we could from the garden. We ran our fingers around jam jars and drank pickle juice. Eventually, Wally cracked. He had had enough fried zucchini.

"Fuck this," Wally says. "I can't take this anymore. I'm fucking starving." He isn't wearing a shirt and his ribs protrude grossly, like the bars of an otherworldly cage.

"W-what's the problem?" Sean asks smirking. "W-what's wrong with a h-h-hot, sun ripened tomato? Just needs a little salt."

I start laughing. "Hey, I could make us some more zucchini."

"Fuck zucchini," Wally yelps. "I've had it. We need some fucking meat or something."

This was in the early days before my brother discovered that squirrel meat tasted like chicken.

"I have an idea," Wally continues. Wally's ideas were almost always mischievous and blameworthy.

"What idea?" I ask, my voice registering clear skepticism.

"I'm not telling you. You'll just have a shit fit. C'mon Sean, let's get our bikes."

"Wally," I tell him, "please don't do anything stupid. If Dad finds out, he'll make hamburger out of your ass and make you eat that."

"Look, are you hungry or not? I'm just trying to find a way to get us some decent food. Dad doesn't give a fuck. Do you see him bringing us a lousy loaf of bread?"

Hours later, my brothers walked into the house with two bags of groceries. They had bread, bologna, cheese, pop, cookies, and tiny cakes. It was a genuine banquet and we gorged ourselves. Not one word was uttered until our tummies were full. Upon my final swallow, I asked, "So Wally, how did you get all this stuff? You obviously paid for it. Where did you get the money?"

"Just don't worry about it," Wally said. Sean looked at the table and continued chewing, chocolate icing smeared on one cheek.

Within a couple of days, the entire family became aware of how Wally obtained the cash for the groceries. He had forged a cheque and had somehow managed to cash it at the bank where our mother worked. Because she was on holidays, it took time for the bank to discover my brother's crime. With Wally's theft revealed, our parents raced home from the cottage. Father burst through the door and instantly forced his hot, stinky alcohol breath into Wally's face.

"You stupid fucking little bastard," he shrieked, one white-knuckled fist fastened like a clamp on the collar of Wally's shirt.

Wally's face went purple. "B-but Dad, just wait a minute. I was just trying to get…"

"Shut your motherfucking hole! What the fuck were you thinking? You forged a fucking cheque where your mother works. Are you fucking crazy? This could affect her job, you worthless idiot. Did you even think about how much deep shit your mother would be in after what you'd done?"

"I'm really sorry," Wally squealed weakly and desperately. "We were hungry. We needed some…"

"Shut your fucking face,I told you! Now get your filthy ass out that door!"

I don't recall where my mother was at that moment. I only know that she did not witness what came next. Father shoved Wally out the door, causing him to fall down the stairs into the garage. He swiftly followed the boy, thrust his hand into his hair, raised him to his feet, and laid a powerful strike onto the side of his head. Like me, Sean had followed the activity into the garage. He exploded. With one wild scream, he dove at our father's waist and almost succeeded in knocking him to the floor. As Father turned on him, Wally managed to scramble to his feet and run down the driveway.

Sean was next. His face distorted by his rage, our father snatched a rake from the wall of the garage and moved toward him. The look on Sean's face was one of sheer terror. He looked like a cornered animal as his eyes darted in all directions, searching for a way out. There wasn't one. Sean was blocked by Father's large, red Snap-On toolbox on one side and the enormous pile of black, prehistoric looking car parts on the other. He did the only thing he could do: he dropped to the floor and covered his head with his arms. Our father raised the rake into the air.

"DAD! DON'T!" I screeched. He was beyond hearing or listening.

The monster in the garage brought the rake down onto Sean's back. My brother curled up into a ball and began screaming. "STOP! DAD! STOP!" It was no use. He continued to raise the rake and slam it down, never missing his target.

Then it was my turn. I took a virtual swan dive off the stairs and grabbed the fiend around the neck. Together we fell to the floor. The rake had been knocked free; I crawled toward it, picked it up, and used all my strength to throw it across the garage. I stood and faced the monster as my youngest brother writhed and wept with pain. The beast huffed and puffed and cuffed me with an open hand. At that point, he was finished. He looked at us, made a guttural sound of disgust, turned, and walked slowly up the stairs and into the house.

At the dinner table that evening, our father laughed and called us a bunch of stupid, snivelling pussies. Mother said nothing. Wally didn't take his eyes off of the table and Sean ate his sauce-less spaghetti with a shaking hand, never letting his body touch the back of his chair. I called my father a prick over and over again in scarcely audible whispers. That night in bed, like so many other nights, I prayed to my grandmother, my grandfather, and to God to help me find a way out. I started to think quite seriously about dying. The thought of suicide was not uncommon to me. I had pondered its beauty and ugliness since the age of thirteen. Plagued by visions of hanging in my closet or doping myself with my mother's medication, I searched for reasons not to do it. At seventeen, the reasons were dwindling. Two things kept me breathing. I wanted to somehow protect my sister and brothers, and I wanted to go to school. Really. There I was, with a self-centered attitude, thinking that I could make a real difference. My siblings were there, croaking for love and nurturing, and school was something that I was good at. I wanted to believe what my teachers told me. When I weighed the pros and cons of living and dying like an accountant deciding on an investment, I figured that if I worked hard, I might escape the noose and stand a chance at a good life.

X X X

MANY LOOKING AT THIS PHOTOGRAPH MIGHT THINK THAT I didn't stand an icicle's chance in an inferno at a good life. It is Christmas again at the Hellers house. Dull, gray light comes through the picture window of the living room and rests heavily on the tree that stands to the right, sparsely decorated with ornaments but loaded with gobs of tired tinsel. Annie sits beside me on the Couch of Piss. Wally, with his scraggly hair and mismatched pyjamas, is sitting on the floor at my feet, grinning with excitement. They watch as I pull a log out of a decorated box; it is a ruse to the true contents of the package. I have absolutely no recollection of the gift, but I loathe this picture. I cannot stand to look at myself. I am visually hideous. My hair hangs in fine, fuzzy, curled strands and every ring of my bony trachea is visible along my neck, a neck that swims like the leg of a heron in the middle of a large crewneck sweatshirt. There sits a troll with bulging eyes and bony hands, wrinkles beginning to develop. The troll appears to be terminally ill. This photograph I want to burn. Torching it might save some future embarrassment, but would erase part of the history, the story, revealed. I am torn.

After all, 'twas the season to merry, fa, la, la, la, la,--- la, la, la, la. That last Christmas that I lived in my parents' house was the worst. Santa was long gone and the elves followed with a big "fuck you". The aged ceiling decorations had lost their lustre and the streamers never seemed to meet. Scotch tape held most things together.

Christmas Eve festivities began as usual. Mom set out platters of sliced cheddar cheese, vegetable crackers, canned smoked oysters, pickles, and olives. She made her famous dip with chipped ham and mustard. The table was loaded with her homemade zucchini bread, sugar cookies, and lemon squares. We sat there drooling, waiting for her to give us the okay to partake of the delights. Sean leaned over the table, eyeballs bulging.

"God, Mom, th-this looks amazing," he said.

Father, opening his fifth beer, said, "Get your fucking hands off of that table until your mother tells you that you can have something. Go into the living room, sit down, and wait until everything's ready, you little pig. Holy fuck, the things I deal with." He let an explosive fart.

Sean's face flushed red, his head dropped, and he shuffled into the living room. He parked himself on the carpet beside the three of us who knew better than to hang over the Christmas Eve table. The Hellers kids sat there, staring catatonically at the television, waiting for any version of *A Christmas Carol*. Without taking his eyes from the light of the TV, Wally hissed, "What a fucking dick he is."

Minutes later. "Okay guys, the feast is ready!" Mother chimed from the kitchen. "Come and get it!"

We didn't need a second invitation. We four rushed for the table's edge, like chickens running across a coop, so afraid that we would miss even one treat. Our father screamed at us to settle down and to take our time; meanwhile his large, oil-stained gaff hooks had already rifled through the cheese and gherkins.

Mom turned down the TV and put a record on the stereo that had Jiminy Cricket reciting "'Twas the Night Before Christmas," before joining us at the table. The squeaky, freaky voice of that cartoon bug filled the room as we tried to eat as much as we could, as slowly as possible. After a few minutes of gob stuffing, Father directed his attention toward Wally. He stared with eyes unblinking, disgusted.

Setting his beer down, he said, "Would you slow the fuck down, you goddamned pig? If you ate pussy like you're eating that food, you might get somewhere. What do you need all that for anyway? You don't play hockey anymore. You're a pathetic waste. You know I saw your cousin playing hockey the other night and he certainly hasn't lost his touch. And there you are, stuffing your fucking face, nothing but a drain on the bank account."

Wally ignored him, stared ahead, and continued munching on crackers and ham dip.

"That's enough," Mother said. "There's plenty here for everyone."

"Not with him around," Father continued. "My mother is right. He's nothing but a hungry gutted little bastard." He picked up his beer bottle and opened his throat for a huge gulp.

"Why don't you leave me alone?" Wally said, eyes on the table. "I don't know what you're worried about. You always make sure that you get your fair share." Annie gasped. She knew what was coming next. Father slammed his bottle down onto the table and backhanded Wally across the face, sending his head into the kitchen wall and causing his chair to slip out from under him.

"Jesus Christ!" Mother squealed. "What the hell are you doing?"

"What do you think I'm doing? I'm teaching this mouthy little fuck a lesson!"

"Oh my God, you're fucking crazy," she said. "Why can't we have a nice Christmas Eve for once? I've had it with you. Fuck this shit!" With that, she grabbed her black vinyl purse, tucked it roughly under her arm, and marched to her bedroom in tears. Wally pulled himself to his feet and staggered into the living room, whimpering.

Jiminy Cricket chirped on:

> *And what to my wondering eyes should appear,*
> *But a miniature sleigh and eight tiny reindeer.*

"Nice, Dad, really nice," I said.

He pointed his finger at me and told me to keep my fucking mouth shut or I would get worse. On his way out to the garage, he stopped at the refrigerator to load his arms with beer. The door slammed, shaking the walls.

Annie and Sean went sickly white. I walked to the other side of the table and picked up my brother's upended chair, looked at it, and hurled it across the room. It shattered into about five pieces. The rage that I had felt was immediately replaced by terror. The wooden kitchen chair, one of a set, lay in chunks on the floor. I couldn't believe that it had busted up so easily. My father was going to kill me.

Wally stopped crying and walked over to the pile of splintered pine. Sean and Annie joined and we formed a circle around the wreckage. "You're dead," Sean said without hesitation or stutter.

"Oh my God, what am I going to do?" I asked of no one in particular. I fought the urge to cry as my heart sprang for my throat.

"Well we have to do something," Annie said. "Dad will flip if he sees this. So will Mom. Lynn, you're in deep shit with this one."

I began to weep. I wept out of fear of my father and out of disappointment at the destroyed Christmas Eve. Wally bent down and examined the pieces of wood. "We can fix this, guys," he said.

"How?" I snivelled. "It's smashed to shit."

Wally held a chair leg in his hand, eyeing it carefully. "Dad has some wood glue in the basement. I'll go get it and we'll put this back together and that drunk bastard won't know the difference." It was one of those wonderful moments when we banded together to help each other in lieu of busting each other's skulls.

The four of us sat in the privacy of the enclosed front foyer while Wally and I glued and Annie and Sean held the pieces together to dry. To lighten the situation, Annie joked about how, on Christmas Eve, it was usually parents putting together play kitchens for their kids while we sat there gluing a chair that was smashed to smithereens, the festive result of a family argument. As soon as it was reconstructed, it was placed back in its rightful spot at the kitchen table. Mom hadn't left her room and Dad continued sucking pints in the garage.

"Well, I hope this works," I told them. "And we really shouldn't let all this great food go to waste." Wally and Annie looked worriedly at the remaining feast, but Sean smiled.

"W-why not?" he said. He dug into the ham dip with a vengeance. We all laughed passionately and joined him at the table. The oysters were a little dried out and the cheese was sweating buckets but we didn't care. We were learning to take what we could get.

The following morning all was to be forgotten and that hideous photo was taken. Between my scruffy brother's wide grin and the skinny, smiling troll on the Couch of Piss, no one could know about the misery of the night before. After all, everything was there. A tree. Decorations. Smiles. A log.

X X X I

THAT NEW YEAR BLEW IN ON A PARALLEL STORM. THE YEAR OF 1984. For me, Orwell had definitely hit the mark. I was a member of The Party and my father was Big Brother. I was guilty of so many thoughtcrimes that I was in danger of becoming an unperson. Hate week went on for far more than seven days.

I became aggressively determined to get out. The thought police would not get the best of me. Without even consulting my parents, I completed applications to attend Queen's University in Kingston. Science was among my considerations but I opted for my true love, the visual arts. The first choice on my application was the fine arts program, which accepted only thirty out of a possible six hundred applicants after a portfolio interview. I thought that my chances were pretty slim but I was encouraged by many teachers, guidance counsellors, and by the memories of my grandparents' praises.

My interview was scheduled for March. Marc was supportive but seemed a little jealous at the attention I received from our high school art teachers. They helped me prepare my portfolio with matting, photographs, and slides. I could not afford a real portfolio case and kept my work in two raggedy, torn, Bristol board sleeves.

My art teacher that year, Jan Peterson, had entered Regi on a year's contract to replace my mentor, Mrs. Hagen, while she went on sabbatical. Ms. Peterson was lovely and assisted me in every way that she could. Before my interview, she presented me with her black leather portfolio case to take my work to the panel at Queen's. I almost wept at her act of kindness after spending many nights fretting about walking into the art building, Ontario Hall, with my well-used Bristol board.

I worked feverishly on that portfolio. For weeks, I assembled pieces, sprayed fixative, matted drawings, touched up paintings, and photographed sculptures with my teacher's camera. I used so much fixative that I got high every time I opened my portfolio case. Sketchbooks were arranged in chronological order. Awards and certificates were set neatly in a binder.

The only reprieve I had from swimming in my portfolio and other school-work were my contacts with Marc, Tammy, and Aisling. Marc spent every Friday night at our house, much to my father's chagrin. Though Marc slept on the Couch of Piss, clearly willing to do anything to spend time with me, my father paid my siblings to spy on him and to keep one eye on my bedroom door throughout the nights. To Tammy, I wrote letters and waited painfully for her replies; I couldn't wait to start working in the summer so that I could see her more often. As for Aisling, she was a constant humorous distraction while I was at school. Her witty and amusing stories always carried me to another realm, a place where pimply faced boyfriends drove her to Harvey's for a nice burger and fries luncheon and then convinced her to skip school to have sex on someone's couch. Aisling continued to stylishly describe her home, a place where mothers convinced their daughters that it was make-up genius to put green eye shadow on their blistering red zits.

At home, the siblings and I reached new heights of idiocy to alleviate frustra-tion, intense anger, and boredom. It was common for one of us to chase another with a hatchet. One day I shot Wally in the face with a BB gun. He later shot me in the back with a bow and arrow. We took turns hog-tying Sean and throwing him into the swampy, algae ridden above-ground pool to see if he could escape; Sean thought that he was literally the reincarnation of Houdini. Sometimes he managed to wriggle free and other times we had to dive in, fish around for his hump, and pull his choking carcass out of the green mire that was infested with water beetles. Eventually we would tire of our antics to prove our fearlessness and would pound the shit out of each other.

When the day of my portfolio interview arrived, I worked frantically on my thin hair to cover a fresh, oozing scab acquired when Sean slammed my forehead against the concrete basement floor a few days prior. As usual, I had nothing appropriate to wear. My Dress Gordon tartan kilt and white Oxford shirt were out of the question. I ended up in an outfit that looked like it had been stolen from an unfashionable geriatric patient at Providence Manor. I donned a pink and grey billowy blouse complete with a wide bow at the neck and a pair of grey pleated pants that could not conceal the ankles that connected my growing limbs to my monkey feet.

Annie drove me to the interview in her red Duster, the vehicle that afforded her so much valuable freedom. The radio boomed with a song I still remember and, to this day, I cannot listen to without breaking out into a nervous sweat:

> *Panic bells, it's red alert.*
> *There's something here from somewhere else.*
> *The war machine springs to life.*

Opens up one eager eye.
Focusing it on the sky.
Where 99 red balloons go by.

Nena, *99 Luftballoons (99 Red Balloons)*

I could see myself as one of the ninety-nine balloons, floating across the horizon, not over the Berlin Wall that inspired the song, but out of my family prison onto the beautiful rolling greens of the university, if my father didn't shoot me down first.

As Annie stopped the car in front of Ontario Hall, my bowels gurgled. I was a nervous wreck and wanted to tear the bow from around my neck. As she wished me luck, I pulled my portfolio from the back seat and turned to face the three gorgeous stone arches of the structure's façade. I waved back at her and put one tentative foot in front of the other, ascended the curved stairway and pushed mightily on the enormous wooden door of the Queen's art building.

Once inside, I was immediately intoxicated by the smells, the odours of creation: solvents, linseed oil, paints, inks, wood, plaster, and charcoal. I took a deep breath and knew that this was where I wanted to be. My skin prickled.

A small handcrafted sign with a black pastel arrow pointed the direction to the interview room: *Student Candidates This Way.* Upon entry to the large classroom, lined with chairs around its perimeter, my bowels turned to mush and I fought the gorge rising in my throat. With one look around the room, I knew that I stuck out like an ostrich on an ice floe. Everyone there was dressed in varying degrees of black: black turtlenecks with jeans, black jeans with grey sweaters, black jackets, black slacks, and black boots. The odd splash of colour came from a fashionable scarf around the neck or a thick belt around the waist. With one exception, the smell of money was all over that room. I cursed my shitty, pathetic wardrobe.

Taking a chair, I felt countless eyes on me. Some smirked, some stared, then looked away, and others ignored my presence and wrung their hands waiting for their turn on the chopping block. I could only imagine what the grinners were thinking. *Look at that dork wearing her grandmother's clothes. What can she be thinking with that fucking bow?*

I agonized for half an hour before my name was called. There was an audible snicker as I lifted my portfolio and walked toward the interview room. *Fuck you, dick,* I thought.

There were three professors in the room, all male, stern, and serious. Each welcomed me to the Queen's University Art Department and shook my hand. I laid my portfolio on the table and unzipped. My cursed intestines rumbled and

I hoped that they couldn't hear the sounds. I completely forgot about my unsuitable outfit.

The three men leafed through my portfolio saying very little; there were questions about a few pieces, about inspiration, media, and influence. They were most impressed by a fitness manual I had illustrated for a community organization. I gave terse answers and longed to escape. I knew that it was only a matter of time before I soiled my pants.

There was one last question. It was from a bearded professor with the tiniest blue eyes I had ever seen.

"On your application, I see that you only applied to Queen's for Visual Arts. You have left spaces blank. You could have applied to other schools as well. Why didn't you take this opportunity?"

Oh shit, I'm not going to get in and I wasted my other chances. "Well sir," I answered, "this is where I want to be, where I need to be." The professor with the thick, smoky coloured glasses smiled. *Christ, he probably thinks I'm one of the most pitiful sights he has set those eyes upon.*

The panel of three men exchanged glances. The bearded one, the clear leader of the pack, eyed me and said, "Well, Miss Hellers, you will hear from us by mail and I would like to say that your chances of entering this program are very good."

Very good. Not excellent. Fuck. "Thank you very much for your time, sirs." I stood up, shook each hand, and ran, dragging my now five hundred pound portfolio, to the nearest bathroom I could find. My bowels emptied and I fought the urge to puke. *Calm down,* I told myself, rubbing the sides of my face. *It's okay. Why are you such a shaking nerve bag?*

I exited the stall and shoved my hands under the faucet of one of the sinks. I let the water get as hot as possible and scrubbed my hands until they were red and raw. Leaving the washroom, I turned and glanced at my image in the mirror. What the hell *was* I thinking wearing that blouse? A lump constricted my airway and my eyes uncontrollably filled with water.

With my ass stationed on the cold stone steps of Ontario Hall, I waited patiently for Annie to pick me up. I stared at the chiselled limestone and thought about the questions during my interview, wishing I had said more; wishing I had said nothing. By the time Annie arrived, I couldn't wait to leave a cloud of dust behind me.

"How'd it go?" she asked after I threw my portfolio into the back seat.

"Oh fuck all of that," I said. "I'm starving. Do you think that you can get us some grub from your friends at McDonald's?"

"Yeah, sure. But how did the interview go?"

"It was bloody painful," I said. "I was a wreck. I had to crap so bad, I could taste it."

Annie heaved with laughter. "No way! That's terrible. Did you make it through?"

"Oh sure. But then I destroyed one of the toilets in that pretty stone building."

She laughed even harder. I loved to hear her laugh, always straight from the depths of her belly.

It was more than a month before I received news from Queen's University. Not one day passed since the interview that the mailbox was left unchecked as soon as I disembarked the school bus.

The day finally arrived that I pulled the long white envelope, bearing my name and the Queen's emblem, from the black aluminum box across from our house. I walked slowly, almost catatonic, down the driveway and into the house, never taking my eyes off the big Q. My brothers ran by me, poking each other in the ribs, screeching.

My legs became jelly as I loped down the hallway and eventually came to rest on the floor in the privacy of my bedroom closet. I turned the envelope over and looked at the paper seal; the moment had arrived. This would be the difference between doom and future for me. I ran my thumb under the seal and removed the letter. I stared at my shabby clothes hanging in the closet and then lowered my head to see the matter revealed.

Dear Miss Hellers,

We are pleased to inform you...

I gaped at the words. The page blurred and cleared and then blurred again. *Oh my God. Oh my dear God! I made it! I've been accepted!* I screamed so loud that Wally and Sean ceased their antics and rushed into my bedroom just as I was rising out of the closet shelter.

"What the hell is wrong with you?" Wally asked, looking quite frightened.

I grinned at the two of them. "I got in," I said slowly. "I got into Queen's University for Art." I would be the first person, not only in my immediate family, but as my Aunt Bea later pointed out, the first person in the entire extended family to attend a university.

"Big deal," Wally said. "Are you coming out to play road hockey or what?"

"Yeah, sure," I said, laughing. Nothing could take this moment away from me. Soon I would be free.

X X X I I

"SO, YOU GOT INTO QUEEN'S." IT WAS MY FATHER'S VOICE breaking the silence at the dinner table, topped with fried bologna and Rice-A-Roni. I knew that he had already bragged to his friends; his kid got into a university. His drunken ass found its place on a chair under the phone as soon as he had heard the news. He didn't leave his perch until dinner was served.

"Yes," I said, as I laid my fork across the crusty surface of the scorched bologna.

"Well, good for you," Father said. "What do you plan to do with that kind of education?"

I stopped digging at the meat and stared ahead. "Well, I think that I might like to teach art. Maybe at a high school."

Annie jumped right in. "Oh, Lynn, you'd make a great teacher! You know, Dad, Lynn got me through my math exam. I wouldn't have got the credit if it hadn't been for her. She taught me more in one week than that asshole Mr. Dunlop taught me in a whole year!"

That was my sister. Always positive. Always finding the good and excellent in everyone and everything–except for Mr. Dunlop. Always preparing for damage control. I blushed at her compliment.

"Is that a fact?" Father said. He leaned back in his chair and placed his slit eyes on me. "You must think you're pretty hot shit, aye?"

I wanted to bolt from the scene; wanted to leave my greasy meat and rice in the true hot shit that was about to fly. "Not really," I answered.

"You know, you're not the only talented one in this house. I'm pretty good at math and I used to be one hell of an artist," he continued before stuffing a healthy chunk of bologna in his mouth.

He was baiting me. He wanted me to contest, to ask him why he had done very little with these gifts.

"I'm sure that you are good at those things, Dad," I stated decisively. His lure proved ineffective.

He stopped chewing and his face softened. "Well, maybe you did get some of your talent from the old man, aye."

"Probably." I played with the rice on my plate, sculpting the form of a flying bird.

"You're damn right you did," he said with a snort. "Now, what are the rest of you goofs going to do with your lives?" He tipped his beer bottle back and waited for the fearful and desperate responses.

Annie, Wally, and Sean all dropped their heads and continued with dinner.

"Well?" he said. "I asked a simple question." He had turned his attention toward Annie.

"Dad, I'm going to St. Lawrence College. You already know that."

"Well, ya, sure, but what for?" Father asked, eyes half closed again. His head was starting to wobble on his wiry neck.

"I already told you. Accounting."

He dropped his fork. "Accounting, right. But at a college, right. St. Lawrence isn't a university."

"No," she said, beginning to fidget.

"Well what the hell do you plan on doing with that? Accounting at a college. Jesus Christ. I guess that your great aspiration is to poke the keys on a cash register at the A&P."

Annie rubbed her forehead. She was clearly on the margin of a breakdown. Our mother sat silent, sucking the end of a Player's Light in front of the glow of the television. Her place at the dinner table became increasingly vacant. She would sit in the living room, stupefied, close to unconscious, smoking her cigarettes, twisting her wedding ring, now so loose on her finger. She needed something that not one of us could give her.

I felt myself losing control, the familiar prickle behind my neck, the drop of my gut. *Don't you fuck with her. Not Annie.* I didn't even think before my lips started moving.

"It's certainly nothing like your achievement, Dad. Was it grade nine or grade ten that you actually managed to finish?" This was becoming my familiar retort. I knew that saying those words was like squeezing his balls in a vise.

His orbs bulged and his lips curled into a snarl. He picked up his fork and flicked my Rice-A-Roni bird off my plate and into my face. I called him a pathetic drunk and told him to crack open another beer. He lashed out with the back of his hand causing me to spin off the kitchen chair. Refusing to cry, I picked myself up, dusted off the Rice-A-Roni, and calmly retreated to my bedroom.

Once again in the safe vault of my closet, the door left ajar for light, I flipped open a book from the school library about the prints and watercolours of Albrecht Durer. I followed the curved lines of a knotty tree and wondered at his marvelous technique. I wanted to see the real thing, not just a reproduction in a book.

I longed to visit an art museum. My teacher, Mrs. Hagen, had taken me to see a Van Gogh exhibit in Toronto when I was in grade ten. I hated myself in retrospect for not appreciating what I was seeing at the time. I was more concerned with impressing Katie and Terri with my immature antics than enjoying the spiralling brushstrokes and brilliant colours that exploded before me. I stood behind viewers and held a finger to my chin, tilted my head, and pretended to be a gallery snob, full of mocking. Getting a laugh out of Terri and Katie was far more important than those fiery sunflowers. Idiot.

Now, in the tiny gallery of my closet, I would know how to view them, appreciate them. I could escape into those yellow fields, safe and elevated. I stared at Durer's *Adam and Eve*, his *Great Piece of Turf.* All elements worked together like a fine orchestra. The perfection of line and colour, perfecting nature. Durer had certainly left his mark, the pressure of his existence. I suddenly realized that these artists were becoming saviours for me. They weren't going anywhere and would teach me everything I wanted to know.

I pulled out my sketchpad and a charcoal pencil. I wanted to leave the closet and find a tree that would inspire Durer, but I didn't dare. I couldn't get through any of the doors in our house without my father noticing. Instead, I opted for observational studies of the objects littering my closet floor. I drew an old, withered boot with salt stains, a balled-up t-shirt, the reel-to-reel tape deck. Then I drew myself looking into a compact mirror. It didn't look right at all. I added a carefully rendered clock to my forehead, a clock without hands.

X X X I I I

JUNE CAME. LUCKY FOR ME, TIME JUST COULD NOT STAND
still. Graduation was around the corner and I worked feverishly to maintain the
entry standards required by Queen's University. I found employment with my
usual job at Lake Ontario Park, complete with pals Aisling and Tammy and my
boyfriend Marc. We saw each other every weekend and revelled in our carnie
existence. "We should take this shit on the road, ladies," Marc joked. "All we
need is a Tilt-A-Whirl, a Merry-Go-Round, a pig on a spit, and cotton candy
for dessert."

Thankfully, I no longer had to ride my red Raleigh to work. After my illness,
Annie, my parents, and Marc's father took turns ensuring that I had transpor-
tation. This provided for far more time and energy to work on my art. I was
engaged with two important pieces.

In the first piece, I pondered aging. I used a mirror and excerpts from reflec-
tive poetry on a wood background topped by three pencil portraits that were
scattered about, as if found haphazardly on a desk. The soft, subtle lines and
gentle tonal range of one drawing of youth stood in dramatic contrast to the firm
dark lines and arcs of the portrait done in old age. The most beautiful of the
portraits by far was the one I conceived for middle age. She was a gorgeous, ener-
getic blend of the other two—just enough shadow, just the right pressure from
the pencil, strong but delicate lines. I wanted to be her. I wanted that chance.

The second piece was to be my showcase painting for graduation. Copious
studies were done with a variety of media. In the end, I opted for oil paint and
created a triptych composition, three large stretched canvas panels with three
trees, each at a different level of the picture plane, growing with flowing roots
from the earth to reach the highest sky. Both the ground and trees were formed
from twisting human bodies. My teacher told me that it was "genius" and wanted
to buy it. I don't know about it being genius, but I do know that I went at it
with an unprecedented ferocity and that it kept me distracted from my impotent,
imprisoned life in Inverary.

* * * * *

Marc and I sat in the kitchen on that dreary Sunday. There was no work at Lake Ontario Park; with such dismal weather, we were given the day off. The two of us worked on our sketchbooks and I kept one eye on my biology textbook in preparation for final exams. He continued with his Dark Man series and a flock of eerie ravens done with a 6B pencil. I did a quick sketch of a blue heron. I could rarely concentrate on anything when he was around. I either wanted to rub myself against him or was afraid that my father knew that I wanted to rub myself against him.

Marc's father was due to pick him up at any moment. We hadn't had a second of privacy all day. Dad was in and out of the garage endlessly, drinking beer, cursing about missing tools, and how he would fry Wally's ass for using them and not putting them back.

When Mr. Gatien arrived, I walked Marc out to the car. Mr. Gatien said hello to me with a huge smile and asked me how the studies were going.

"Oh, pretty good," I answered. "I think biology is going to be my toughest exam."

"You're going to do just fine, young lady," he said, winking. "I just hope this son of mine takes some of your influence."

"Gee, thanks for the vote of confidence, Dad," Marc said, laughing.

At that point, Marc did something to make my blood crystallize. He gently put his arm around my waist and pulled me toward him. It was that simple. I knew that Mr. Gatien didn't mind and that Marc was showing his pride and affection. *Oh, but what if Wade S. is watching?*

"Well, gotta go!" I said, loosening Marc's grip. "My biology text is waiting."

"Okay, sweetie. I'll call you later," Marc finished, giving me a peck on the lips. *Oh shit, please God, don't let my father be watching this!*

"Goodbye, my dear," Mr. Gatien said.

I mustered a strained grin and waved goodbye. I was acutely aware of gravel crunching under my feet. The garage was empty and I made my way to the door.

Entering the house, I was greeted with an unnerving silence. *Where are you, you freaky bastard?* An electric shock traveled the length of my spine when I suddenly realized that there was no one there but him and me. *Where are you? Where are you?*

I could hear the loud *tick tock* of the kitchen clock. I touched the cool surface of the refrigerator. *Where the hell are you?*

I slid my sock feet along the kitchen floor, keeping as quiet as possible, and lifted my biology text up and tucked it into my chest. *Chill out! Maybe he's been down in the basement this whole time. Get a grip.*

I walked softly along the carpeted hallway toward my room, feeling some sense of relief at the possibility that he was engrossed in some project. I had just passed the bathroom when he stepped out of his bedroom and stood square in front of me.

"Well, wasn't that fucking cute," he says.

I gasp and my head spins. "What do you mean?" I ask.

"That! That fucking display in the driveway, you little slut."

"I don't know what you're talking about," I say.

His black eyes bore into me, even through skin slits. The cords in his neck are starting to swell and pulsate.

"You! You… with that little jack-off! I saw you kiss him, you pig." His words are slurred; he staggers into the wall.

"Oh God, Dad, it was just a peck!"

"Right in front of his fucking father! What do you think that tells me about the times that you're alone with that pock-faced arsehole?"

"You know what, Dad? I'm not listening to this. I have to study for exams. I don't have time for this bullshit." I move to push past him.

"You don't have time for this, aye. I'll fucking tell you what you have time for, you little whore!" He grabs me by the arms and pushes me with full force into my bedroom. I fall to the carpeted floor and the textbook goes flying from my arms and flutters open beside my bed. I notice the detailed diagram of the animal cell before he lifts me up by the back of my shirt and pushes me onto the bed.

I have the chance to scream one thing. "You crazy asshole, what are you…"

He is on top of me; his knees are on my arms and his hands are around my neck. "You cock-sucking little whore! You have no respect! I could kill you, you fucking bitch!" Spit spray from his mouth lands on my face. His hands squeeze tighter.

I can't get air. I see his screwy face and his clenched teeth and they begin to blur. He is the scariest monster I have ever seen. My eyes fill with black spots and I have enough time to think: He's killing me.

With that thought, I suddenly remember something Grandpa taught me. In a forceful instant, I raise my right knee up and slam him between the legs from his ass end.

The monster groans loudly, loosens its grip, and rolls off the bed.

Choking and fighting for every breath, I use the rest of my strength to pull myself up. As I hit the floor, he is already on his feet and hissing, saliva flying everywhere, "You cunt! You bitch! You're gonna be sorry for that."

I lean forward and rush him like a pro linebacker. My shoulder lands in his gut and he falls dramatically backward, smashing his head on the doorjamb. He drops like a sack of grain. No movement, not even a slight twitch.

Blood. Oh God, so much blood. There is blood on the doorjamb, blood in his hair, blood soaking his shirt, blood on the carpet.

I stand there looking at him, a big lump on the floor. I notice the green and blue plaid shirt he is wearing only because blood is changing the pattern. His blond hair is turning red. I have an indescribable urge to touch it, to feel the wet stickiness of it.

I poke him on the shoulder. Nothing.

I ran. I didn't call for help. I didn't seek assistance from the neighbours. I didn't administer any amateur first aid. No pressure on the wound. No taking of pulse. No checking the airway. None of what I had learned from books and TV.

I ran. I ran out of the house and down Latimer Road. I ran to the woods that shouldered the highway. I sought sanctuary and buried myself in the cathedral of trees as deeply as I could. I had killed my father.

XXXIV

I STAYED IN THE SANCTUARY FOR COUNTLESS HOURS AND WAS remarkably comfortable and fearless. I pictured the flight of John Wilkes Booth after he had assassinated President Lincoln, hanging out in the woods of Virginia and moving only under the cloak of night. I felt like I had killed someone as big as a president. The difference was that my father deserved it and Lincoln didn't. Would I be cornered in a shack and shot down?

Darkness fell and I crawled under a tree, covering myself with a fresh green blanket of brush that I had gathered to give some warmth. Grateful for the lack of thirst, I was dreadfully hungry and did not possess the survival skills to figure out what berries or leaves were edible. Fortunately, I had grown rather accustomed to being hungry.

I amazed myself with my short supply of feeling where my father was concerned. I actually contemplated my self-defence for trial purposes. There would be no outcry from me if he were dead. Who was it that had wished him dead so many times before? In the subterranean pockets of my mind, I considered that something that evil could never die anyway.

I slept only briefly and woke up to leaves tickling my lips. It was time to check out the territory. The rest of my family would have to be home by now. I wondered who would be the one to discover his body. Like the main character in an espionage novel, I deftly worked my way through the wooded areas, outlining farmers' fields, toward my house. I kept a safe distance from the road and discovery.

On approach, the lights glowed dimly out the living room picture window. There were no police cars, no ambulances, not one inch of yellow tape. I was almost disappointed. I peered inside and saw Sean and Wally watching television, laughing. They certainly wouldn't be doing that if their father was dead, would they?

The chance was taken. I walked up to the side door and entered the kitchen. Mom was making a pot of tea and wiping the counter. She turned and looked at me curiously.

"Where have you been? Supper has already been served, you know," she said.

"Oh, uh, I went for a long walk. It was such a beautiful night. Where's Dad?" I didn't waste any time.

Mother waved one hand in the air and said in an exasperated tone, "He's asleep in bed. He must have fell when he was drunk because he cut his fucking head pretty bad. That asshole will never learn. I had to clean blood off the goddamned carpet. It took me over an hour and you can still see the Christly stain."

"Well, are you sure that he's okay?" I inquired, still unsure of the nature of my future jail sentence.

"That idiot? He's fine. He ate two pork chops and kept poking at the scab on his head wondering how the hell he had hurt himself."

I couldn't believe what I was hearing. *Not only is that son of a bitch still alive, but he can't remember what happened.* I laughed loudly and uncontrollably.

Mother stared at me. "What the hell has got into you? What's so goddamned funny?"

I couldn't answer her. I held my stomach through the strain of my laughter. I waved my hand over my face, a gesture to indicate that I couldn't speak, and walked to my room. My mother certainly must have realized at that moment that she was living in a hellish house full of lunatics.

Gasping for my next breath, I entered my bedroom and saw the biology text still lying there, open to that squishy animal cell. This incited a whole new barrage of hilarity and I wondered if anyone ever died from laughing too hard.

Nothing grandiose, no greater tragedy ever came out of that incident with my father; yet, it was the most violent of our confrontations. Our epic conflict was escalating. I knew that if I stayed in that house much longer, one of us would die. After all, he had rifles and plenty of ammunition. Attempted strangulation could only be the beginning.

X X X V

IT WAS A GOOD TIME TO MAKE MYSELF SCARCE FOR A COUPLE of days. Tammy called me quite unexpectedly and suggested that we hang out together for the weekend at her house as a reprieve from our slavery to Lake Ontario Park. We would work during the day, and I could spend the night at her place. She said she really needed to talk to someone. It was important. I involuntarily bounced in the kitchen chair and nearly dropped the phone. She was inviting me to her house. Blood rushed through my body so rapidly that I thought the top of my head was going to blow off.

I tried to imagine what was so important. With all the time we spent together at work and on breaks, she had never invited me to go anywhere before, let alone to her house. Then it struck me with sudden icy avalanche force: *what if she likes me as much as I like her?* My skin prickled with both exultation and sheer terror. *That couldn't be it...could it? Oh dear God, why am I feeling like this? I'm not a lesbian. Am I?*

This thought petrified me but I didn't have time to waste considering it. I had to figure out which of my shitty clothes I was going to wear and what I was going to wear to bed. The thought of her seeing me up close and personal in any of the sloppy t-shirts I wore to work every day was inconceivable. Bedtime garments instilled equal dread. How could I wear the threadbare, grungy *Little House on the Prairie* nightgown that I had draped myself in for the past couple of years? *Oh my God, and I can't possibly borrow any of Annie's prissy shit!*

The next day, that fateful Friday, I had Annie drop me off downtown on her way to work. I had a couple of hours before my shift at the Park and figured a little shopping needed to be done. I withdrew $20 from my meagre tuition savings and made my way to Zeller's. I found what I thought was a cute collared t-shirt with orange and blue stripes that I would change into after work and settled for a cheap pair of cotton pyjamas, lemon yellow. I finished my purchase with a bottle of gardenia scented body spray. I removed the tags and carefully folded the garments and placed them neatly in my knapsack. I was energized and ready for my visit with Tammy.

I practically skipped my way over the miles to the Park and gleefully entered the candy floss booth ready for my shift. Adrenaline filled my veins and my exhilaration created shock waves. I whistled as I made a fresh load of popcorn and quickly became the paragon of customer service. My usual flat "Can I help you?" turned into, "Hello there, what delight can I get for you today?" I even propelled myself into suggestive selling by recommending candy bars, licorice, or a nice Slush Puppy to go with the popcorn. My smile was infectious and my customers left very happy. Some of them even graced me with a tip, which was not the norm.

When Tammy stopped by before her shift, she leaned into the service window with a huge smile. As she placed her hand over mine on the counter, she asked, "Hey, are we still on for tonight?" My heart leapt to my throat and I felt the familiar pressure of blood filling the small vessels of my face.

"Oh most definitely," I said grinning. "Can't wait. Should be fun."

"Cool," she replied. "Well, I'm off to sling some grease. See you in a couple of hours." And then she winked.

Oh my God, she winked at me. I think I might die.

"See ya," I said as my heart exploded in my chest.

The rest of the workday was a blur. Coke and Sprite was shakily poured, candy floss flew through the air in spidery wisps, and I frequently spilled the popcorn that never tasted better. When Tammy finally came to meet me after work, I was close to spontaneous combustion or a stroke.

"Let's get the hell out of here my friend," she said boisterously.

"I'm with you," I replied, grinning from ear to ear.

As we walked to her house on that beautiful June evening, we bantered, laughed, and drank Dr. Pepper—and I fell more madly in love. I watched her perfect smile, the pushing back of her long hair, and I almost slipped into a trance. When we arrived at her townhouse, I swear that every cell in my body was hotly charged with electricity. *Oh please God, let her feel the same way I do.*

I had to ask. "So Tammy, I have to say that I'm very curious about this important issue that you want to talk about."

"Oh that can wait a little bit. I have to work up the courage," she said, giggling.

Oh my God.

"Well the suspense is killing me," I replied, laughing.

"We can talk about it after dinner. My mom is making her famous lasagne." I could smell its gourmet quality as soon as we walked through the door.

"How heavenly," I yelped. Tammy bent over laughing.

"You use some of the funniest words sometimes," she said.

"I'm going to have a quick shower and change before dinner. I need to get rid of the smell of grease," Tammy said. "Do you want to do the same?"

"Oh yes," I replied, "I've got candy floss stuck in my arm hair." Laughing, she told me to go first.

It was luxurious, every part of it—the soap, the shampoo, the conditioner. It was grand not being told to get out because my two minutes were up or that I had to reuse my sibling's swampy, grey bathwater.

After finishing, I changed into my new striped t-shirt and a fresh pair of jeans. I peered hesitatingly into the mirror at my flushed face and I thought I looked okay. I certainly smelled better with my gardenia spray.

"Nice shirt," Tammy said when she saw me. "It's really cute."

"Thanks. It's new." *Oh why did you say that?*

While Tammy had her shower, I greeted her mother as she prepared dinner in their kitchen. Mrs. Collins sliced bread and I noticed how rough and lined her hands were. They matched her creased face. Somehow, this made me feel at ease with her.

"That dinner smells amazing, Mrs. Collins," I said, opening the conversation.

"Why thank you…Lynn, isn't it?"

"Yes. I must tell you that lasagne is one of my favourites," I told her cheerfully.

"Well it looks like you could use a couple of pieces," she said smirking. "My dear, you are thin."

"Ya, my mom says the same thing. I eat like a pig and don't gain an ounce."

She cackled. "That just might serve you well in old age."

"Tammy tells me that you are an excellent artist," she continued, thankfully changing the subject.

"I don't know about that. I like to draw and paint. And I've been accepted into art school," I told her in a low voice, blushing.

"Congratulations to you, Lynn," she said with a smile. "I would love to see your work sometime."

What struck the greatest chord with me was that Tammy had talked about me with her mother. My heart flitted and flipped. When Tammy walked into the kitchen, I felt my blood rise. Her chestnut hair was wet and hung neatly over her shoulders; her face was clean and smooth and she smelled far better than my gardenia spray.

During the magnificent lasagne dinner, I couldn't help but periodically stare at her. While she was in conversation with her mother, I was studying every angle, every line, and every contour of her face. I wanted to draw her. I wanted to buy the best paper and use my best set of pencils to create a portrait worthy of her unique beauty.

Following dinner, Tammy and I thanked her mother for her efforts as we cleared the table and washed dishes. The three of us made small talk as I worried about what was going to happen next when there was nothing left to do in the kitchen.

"Let's go up to my room," Tammy said. "We can play some music."

I replied rather tentatively, "Sounds great." *Can she hear my heart pounding?*

We climbed the stairs to Tammy's room and I noticed all the portraits and framed snapshots adorning the wall. Her family photos weren't sloppily stuffed into a plastic bag like mine. She was a cute little girl, cuter than her sister, but her parents were clearly very proud of both of them. There were no more images of one than the other. The first day of school, Halloween, Christmas, sports outings; no event seemed to be missed.

When we entered Tammy's room, I appreciated her even more. The room was impeccably tidy and clean. She had a desk! *I so wish I had one of those,* I thought with complete envy. Her walls were adorned with posters of her favourite musicians and bands—Rick Springfield, Billy Squires, Journey.

"I love your taste in music," I told her.

"Hell ya," she replied, scanning the posters. "You can't beat these guys."

"I completely agree."

She pulled out the Journey *Escape* record from a sleeve on her neat pile and placed it on her turntable, another luxury I didn't have. The room filled with sound:

> *Just a small town boy*
> *Living in south Detroit*
> *He took the midnight train going anywhere*

She turned on a small lamp and flicked off the overhead light. "Far more relaxing, don't you think?" she asked.

"Um, yes, for sure," I agreed.

"Here, have a seat," she said, patting the space on the bed beside her.

With blood pounding between my ears, I gently sat down.

> *Don't stop believin'*
> *Hold onto that feeling*

I stared straight ahead at Billy Squires on the wall. I couldn't believe I was with her, in her house, in her bedroom. I gasped.

"So, Lynn, I need to talk about something," she started.

Oh my God, finally, here it is. "What's up," I asked, trying to sound as nonchalant as possible.

"Well, I want to talk to you about this problem because I think you will understand. I figure we have become pretty good friends, don't you?"

"Sure," I replied.

"I really respect what you think. You are really smart. You're not full of bullshit like so many girls I know." She turned away at that point.

"Okay," I said, "I'm happy you feel that way. I am here for you no matter what it is."

"This isn't easy," she said. "I'm having a hard time even saying it."

"It's okay, Tammy, really." *I'm attracted to you too. If you want to kiss me, I promise I won't stop you.* I gulped, loudly.

She carefully placed her hands on her knees, took a deep breath, and said, "I'm pregnant."

My eyes immediately dropped to her stomach. "What?" I asked in a barely audible voice.

"Oh Lynn, don't make this any harder than it already is," she pleaded.

Sorry, but I cannot oblige. "Are you fucking kidding me?" It was close to a shout.

"You seem angry," she said, clearly shocked.

I took several deep breaths trying to control my urge to bolt from her house. It was implausible. *This cannot be true.* I stared at Billy Squires and wanted to fling the Journey *Escape* album down the staircase.

"Are you going to keep it?" I asked her as I slowly turned to look her in the eyes.

She glared at me as if I had just told her that the baby she was carrying was the anti-Christ. "Uh, YA, I'm keeping it. How could you even ask that?"

"Because, you said that we have become good friends and yet you never told me that you were seeing a guy, let alone that you were fucking one."

She gaped. "What has gotten into you, Lynn?"

"Oh I don't know," I replied. "Maybe it's like you said and I'm just not big on bullshit."

"Why the hell are you so angry? You're not the one who is going to be cranking out a kid in seven months!"

That did it. She was right. Tammy had turned my guts to paste but she didn't even know it. She was in a different place and had far bigger problems.

"I'm sorry," I said as convincingly as possible. "You just really caught me off guard. Maybe I'm upset because I thought I knew you and now I realize that I know so little about you. I'm sorry...really."

I wasn't sorry. I wanted the night to be over. If she wanted support, she was going to have to look elsewhere.

"Jesus, what about school? You've got two years of college left. What are you going to do? Who the hell is this guy anyway? Oh shit, please don't tell me he's one of those losers that works at the park!" In an instant, I felt the heat creep through me with the realization that my very own boyfriend worked there.

"No, you don't know him," she replied. "His name is Ron. He is twenty-three. He works downtown as a mechanic. I've been seeing him for a couple of months. He has asked me to marry him." She grinned broadly.

A cleaver sliced through my heart. A mechanic, like my father. I pictured her living the life of my mother. *Oh Tammy, do you have any idea what you're in for?*

I focused on a pushpin that held up one of her posters and let my vision blur. I wasn't being a good friend to her. I couldn't.

"Wow," was all I could say. "Wow."

"I'm tired," Tammy finished. "Maybe we should get some sleep."

"Yep," I replied.

"Maybe we could talk about this tomorrow?" she asked.

"Sure," I answered, trancelike.

She left the room so that I could change into my new pyjamas. *What a waste of money,* I thought. I laid beside her that whole sleepless night, tortured, heart-broken, and finished.

X X X V I

THERE - ANOTHER IMAGE OF ME FOREVER SEALED ON PAPER IN the S&R bag. It is a true portrait, posed and devised, my school graduation photo. I am wearing a white shirt and one of those ghastly bowties I so fancied in the eighties. Over top of that is a black gown. In my hands is a white tube, a false version of the paper I was croaking to get. I hate this picture like all pictures of myself. The only pleasant features are my eyes. I know I am not mistaken. I see something in them. Hope.

Despite my broken heart and my father's repeated attempts to sabotage my studies during his drunken rants at all hours of the night, I graduated from Regiopolis-Notre Dame High School in June of 1984. I somehow managed a final average of 89% and won highest academic standing in Grade 13 for visual arts, biology, and French. I also received a community award from the Kingston Arts Council for excellence in the arts. No one was more surprised than me.

It was time to move on, in more ways than one. Just before graduation, I ended my relationship with Marc, not convinced that he or any other boy was going to be a part of my future. Though he was the kindest boy I had ever met, he couldn't shake his yearnings for a growing list of artificial stimulants. By that time, he was taking absolutely anything he could get his hands on. He even stole some of my mother's blood pressure pills and chased them with a pint of whiskey. I had grown tired and bored of his perpetual numbed state and certainly didn't want to end up with someone that reminded me of my father. The decision wasn't even all that difficult for me. Losing him stirred me far less than Tammy. I was getting rather used to hardening my heart like a stone.

Weeks before graduating, I started pouring over the *Whig Standard*, searching for an apartment to rent. I wanted to be out of my father's sight as quickly as possible. *Just hang on for a little bit longer.* I used a red pen to carefully circle all potential prospects.

Pedaling my Raleigh around Kingston, exactly one day after graduation, I visited Home Locators and viewed countless bachelor and one-bedroom apartments. Most were revoltingly filthy and well beyond the limits of my meagre pocketbook. Fear and frustration began their terrible chokehold and I wept while sitting on the stone steps after arriving back at Home Locators.

The sun beat down and the heat was punishing. Cars, buses, and bikes whizzed by. Everyone had somewhere to go except me. My shoulders heaved under the weight of my self-pity. I watched a string of ants carry bits of crud into a crack on the step. Even they could locate a home. As I sat, trying to muster the energy to get up and walk back into the offices of that familiar white building, a gentle voice caught me from behind.

"Excuse me, Ms. Hellers, can I have a word?" It was the nice lady from Home Locators, whose name I cannot recall. She knew me already, an indication of how many times I graced her with my presence and pleadings for any reasonable apartment.

I rubbed the tears from my eyes before standing and turning around to face her.

"Yes," I said.

She smiled the sweetest smile. "I think I have something you might be interested in. This one just came in. It's a one-bedroom apartment on lower Princess Street. It sounds like it could be the thing for you. It's in your price range; it's $300 a month, all-inclusive. I saw you out my window and brought it right to you. No one else has seen this apartment yet. Isn't that great?"

I wanted to kiss her. "That's amazing," I screeched. "Thank you so much! I've had the hardest time today."

"Well, I guess you were in the right place at the right time," she said. *If you only knew how rare that is,* I thought.

She handed me a piece of paper with all the details. I needed to speak to a Mr. Greenwood for an appointment. "Come on in and use our phone," she said, holding the door for me. I knew in that second that if there really could be angels walking among us, like my geography teacher Sister O'Shaunessey insisted, then this woman certainly had to be one of them.

"Thank you," I said simply.

Mr. Greenwood was willing to see me right away. My jubilation could not be contained and I clumsily dropped the phone. The nice lady laughed and picked it up for me.

"He can see me right now," I blurted excitedly. "Thank you so much for helping me!"

"Good luck to you, Ms. Hellers." She winked at me and turned back to her desk. I wanted to hug her, but was much too shy.

I bolted down the stairs, hit the wall of heat, unlocked my Raleigh, and pedaled harder than I ever had. I weaved in and out of traffic and jiggled my ass in anticipation at every red light. Mr. Greenwood, true to his word, met me directly outside the century old limestone building at 46 Princess Street.

Mr. Greenwood was an elderly man with thin wisps of white hair that seemed to struggle to hang onto his head in the breeze of the alleyway. I could tell that his smile was fashioned from overly white false teeth. He wore a short-sleeved, light blue shirt, and beige pants. I liked him immediately.

He ushered me up the crooked stairs of the building and opened the door of apartment 3. The rooms had been freshly painted, beige of course, and an enormous window looked down onto the bustle of Princess Street. It was one of those windows that one could climb into and sit for hours. I loved it and almost crawled into it right there in front of him. I barely heard any words he said as I excitedly checked out the bedroom, the kitchen, and the tiny bathroom.

I noticed that absolutely everything had been cleaned and that absolutely everything was crooked. There wasn't one straight line in that place. The floors sloped dramatically and were separated from the walls by at least three inches on one side. The doorways were askew and only the bathroom door could be completely closed. I had to tilt my head to make any vertical line appear perpendicular. It was perfect.

"I would really like to rent this apartment, Mr. Greenwood," I told him.

"Would it just be you on your own, dear?" he asked.

"Yes sir. I'm going to Queen's University in September."

He grinned and said, "That is one fine school, I must say." I nodded, still taking in every facet of the space.

"Well, my dear lady, the apartment is yours if you want it."

I gasped. "Really?"

He laughed heartily. "Really. Now all I need from you is a cheque for first and last month's rent; that would be a total of $600. All utilities and heat are included in that price."

My heart sank immediately and bile found its way to my mouth. Mr. Greenwood must have noticed the change because a look of concern crept over his face.

"What's the matter, dear?" he asked.

Fighting tears, I said, "I don't have $600. You see, I get an OSAP grant in September, so everything will be fine then, but for the summer I have to rely on my job. I could give you $400, but that would be all that I have. I've saved almost every penny from my pay cheques." It felt like every cell in my body weighed a thousand pounds.

Mr. Greenwood put his spotty hand to his chin and hummed, considering how to let me down as easily as possible. I thought I might vomit. Freedom was so close.

"Well, you seem like a really nice girl," he said. "I'll take $300. Would you be able to write a cheque today?"

I near fainted. "Really? You're sure? Of course I can write a cheque right now! Oh, thank you, thank you, thank you!" I screamed, pulling my chequebook from my back pocket.

Mr. Greenwood giggled and gave me his clipboard so that I could write it out. I scrawled the thing with so nervous a hand that my normally impeccable penmanship now resembled the work of a cat's paw.

"When would I be able to move in?" I asked.

He giggled again. "You can move in today, dear, if you would like."

I leapt into the air so high that I almost fell with my uneven landing on the crooked floor.

My new landlord laughed as I blabbed nonstop about how I would take such good care of the place, how I would keep it clean and tidy, how I would decorate it as best as I could.

"Enjoy yourself, Lynn," he said as he handed me the key. "Now here is my address and phone number. Call me if there are any problems at all. And remember that the rent is due on the first of every month. You can mail it to my address, okay?"

"Of course! I won't be late with it, sir." Mr. Greenwood shook my hand and left. He walked out of *my* apartment. I couldn't believe any of it. I had found myself a home. I spun around in a full circle before locking the door of *my place* and biking to Lake Ontario Park in time for my shift.

Upon arrival, I wasted no time in telling everyone who would listen about my good fortune. I even hit the payphone to call Annie at McDonald's. She screamed, "No fucking way!" into my ear and told me that she would meet me after work to see the place. Marc wasn't near as happy for me. When I told him, he walked away from me in a huff, his widening ass jiggling like Jello in his Sergio Valentes.

When I put the key into the lock of my apartment door, Annie and I clucked and chuckled like two little girls doing something wrong. I turned on the lights and we entered the empty expanse of the living room.

"Oh, Lynn, this is fantastic," Annie said. "Look at the size of that window. It's beautiful."

"I know," I said, "And look at this!" I grabbed her by the arm and pulled her into the bedroom.

"So, what am I supposed to be seeing?" she asked. "It's just a bedroom."

"Just a bedroom?!" I shrieked. "Do you know that most places for students are bachelor apartments? Do you know what that means? It means that you live, eat, sleep, piss, and shit pretty much in one room. Getting an apartment with a bedroom in it isn't easy, or cheap."

"Wow, this is amazing, Lynnie. You're so lucky. Have you told Mom and Dad?"

I lowered my eyes to stare at the floor. "No. Not yet. I'm going to tell them tonight and I really don't care what they think. I want to get all of my clothes and stuff into this place in the next day or two. I have to get out of there, Annie."

"I know," she said.

"Will you help me bring my things here with your car? You could stay over with me anytime you want."

"Of course I'll help. What are sisters for?"

"Thanks."

We both glanced around one more time and moved toward the door. "Hey, Lynn," Annie said. "Do you realize that these floors are really slanted?"

"Yes, I know. Isn't it fabulous?"

"You're weird," she said.

X X X V I I

TELLING MY PARENTS THAT I WAS MOVING OUT WAS FAR EASIER than I thought it would be. My mother went silent and took her purse to her bedroom to smoke the night away. My father cried. Really. I figured he was saddened over the loss of his favourite punching bag. My brothers fought over which one would get my bedroom after I emptied it of my "crap and shit". My father screamed that nobody was getting that room.

Annie helped me pack up what little belongings I had. My parents would not allow me to remove any furnishings, utensils, draperies, or bedding. They even refused to turn over several pieces of my framed art that hung on some of the walls of the house. I was allowed to have one towel and a bookshelf from my grandfather, the one that he had made with his own hands. Other than that, my clothing, books, and art supplies fit into two garbage bags. I was grateful that I had been taught by my grandparents that the value of a person's life should not be measured by their possessions.

With everything ready, I waited until the following evening to take formal leave of that house on Latimer Road in Inverary. Annie and I loaded my bags and the bookshelf into her car. I said goodbye to my parents who were sitting, stone-faced, at the kitchen table.

"Take care of yourself," Mother said flatly.

"Sure," I said.

My father took a slug off his beer bottle and started crying again. "Our first child is leaving, Margaret," he said through sobs. He rose from his chair and staggered toward me. I was stricken, terrified, and rooted to the spot. *What the hell is he going to do?*

"You take good care of yourself, sweetheart," he said. Then he hugged me. *He's fucking nuts.*

"Bye, Dad," I said before turning abruptly and walking out the door. I had no idea when or if I would ever walk through that door again.

Annie, who had the displeasure of witnessing the whole event, began the drive with a careful, almost clinical assessment of our father's behaviour.

"I think Dad is full of regret, you know. Deep down inside, he really respects you. He just has no idea about how to show it."

"Come on now, Ann. The man hates my guts."

"No he doesn't. He just doesn't know *how* to show love until it's way too late."

I turned and looked at her like she had suddenly decided to pick her nose.

"Have you gone brain-dead or something?" I said. "That asshole loves nobody but himself and the big brown bottle."

With her eyes fixed on the road ahead, she said, "That's not true."

I worried about her but not as much as I worried about our brothers. She had a car and was accustomed to staying with her friend Lisa. Wally and Sean would have to complete their growing pains under the roof of my father. I couldn't take them into my small apartment but maybe they could stay over sometimes once I got some furniture.

At 46 Princess Street, it took us about twenty minutes to move everything in and hang my clothes in the bedroom closet. We carried my Raleigh bike up the topsy-turvy stairs and stationed it along the wall of the small hallway at the entrance of the apartment. The two of us sat on the cold bedroom floor, peered around, and began giggling ferociously.

Through my laughter, I said, "Hey, I don't have much, but this is the best, isn't it?"

"Oh, you bet," Annie agreed.

"Hey, do you want to stay overnight?"

"Lynnie, there's no goddamned bed here! Thanks for the offer, but I'm expected over at Lisa's house for the night. Her parents rented a couple of movies. Do you want to come?"

"No thanks. I've got to get this lavish palace in order." We both split our sides and rolled around on the floor.

"Where the hell are you going to sleep?" she asked, eyes bulging.

"Oh, I don't know. I'll figure something out. I've slept in worse places."

"Isn't that the truth," she said, shaking her head.

After she left, I layered some of my clothes on the bedroom floor and laid myself down for the night. I stared at the room's empty corners and I could hear the constant drone of the cars and human energy from the street below. I was comforted by this sound, such a change from that eerie silence of my bedroom in Inverary, always waiting for my father to explode through it.

The following morning, I awoke to a loud rap on the apartment door. *Who the hell can that be,* I thought, *I just moved in here for Christ's sake. Nobody knows I'm here yet. If it's a Jehovah's Witness, I'm going to commit homicide.*

I pulled my weary, aching bones up off my bed of clothes and was suddenly conscious of how hungry I was. My stomach was making animal noises before

I even got to my feet. I wiped my bangs away from my eyes and peered out the tiny peephole in the door. I thought that it was so cool to have one of these. I had never looked through one before, and here I had my very own. I squinted one eye allowing the other to focus on the person outside my door. It was my uncle.

"Uncle Darren?" I asked as I opened the door. "What are you doing here?"

"Hi Lollipop! I guess I woke you up, aye. Well, I've got something for you. I wanted to make sure that you were home before I lugged it all the way up here. Your dad called me and told me that you had found a place, but that you didn't have a bed. We figured that one of the cots from the old farm might do you just fine, so I brought one for you. I found a couple of curtains that you may be able to use too. They're not pretty, but they'll do the trick, I think."

"Wow, thanks so much, Uncle Darren. Come on in."

"Actually, I'll get you to come on out and help me carry this thing up here. Your uncle is gettin' old, you know."

"Sure. I'll just throw on some shoes and I'll be right down."

We carried the folded cot, which was far heavier than it looked, up into my bedroom. Uncle Darren opened it up and a substantial amount of mice turd, like chunky brown rice, spilled onto the floor.

"Oh, don't worry about that, Lollipop," he said matter-of-factly. "You might find a few of those but they ain't gonna hurt you."

"That's okay," I said. "It's nice to have something to sleep on."

"Well, your dad was a little upset that you wouldn't have a bed. He's worried about you, you know." *Not worried enough to let me have my own bed from home.* I looked out the window and said, "I'm sure that he is."

"Anyway, I'll go grab those curtains out of the truck and then I have to head off to work."

"Thank you, Uncle Darren."

"Make sure you thank your dad too, okay Lollipop?"

"Right." *Oh God, cut me a break with this one, would you?*

After he had left, I walked into the bedroom to survey the cot more closely. It was in pretty good shape, except for the odd grain of mouse shit. I looked at the floor and suddenly realized that I didn't even have a broom and a dustpan for cleaning; in fact, I had absolutely no cleaning supplies.

As chance would have it, S&R Discount Department Store was directly across the street from where I now lived. Even though most people nicknamed it "Shit and Rubbish", it was well known that the three floors of this enormous stone building contained the best deals on any retail item in town, from a can of Beefaroni to window caulking. What I couldn't afford there, I might be able to get at The Salvation Army.

With the whole day off to myself, I took a quick bath, since there was no shower, thankful that I hadn't forgotten my coveted Alberto VO5 in Inverary. I put on the cleanest and best clothes that I could find in my new closet. I opted for a pair of greying white cotton pants made dull by too many hard water washes, and a yellow, V-neck t-shirt. Glancing in the mirror, I thought I looked better than I had in a very long time. I looked relaxed.

Before leaving the apartment, I checked my blue plastic wallet. I had a twenty-dollar bill and a five tucked in behind. I had to do things the right way. I needed food, cleaning supplies, a plate, and a fork, before I could get a phone. There was no way that I could even consider a stereo or television.

My adventure began at The Salvation Army. I found a toaster for two dollars, a plug-in kettle and teapot for fifty cents each, a set of four plates, bowls, cups, and cutlery for a few bucks. I uncovered a dented portable transistor radio in a bin of mixed house wares. I turned it on and it instantly tuned into the signal from the CKLC radio station as clear as a bell. The generous woman at the register threw in a broom and dustpan for nothing. The Salvation Army was a gold mine. It took two determined trips with a cardboard box, but finally I dropped my great find at the apartment before making my journey to S&R.

"Shit and Rubbish" was also filled with treasures. I bought cans of no-name spaghetti, beans, Econo-Tea with a hundred teabags for a dollar, Kraft Dinner, a loaf of bread and a jar of peanut butter. I found a tea-cozy that I couldn't resist with colourful knitted flowers surrounding it. I found inexpensive cleansers for the bathroom fixtures, the floors, and for dishes. I could barely contain my glee when I discovered a stack of dishcloths banded together for $1.50. I grabbed a small saucepan and a can-opener.

I also looked at things that I couldn't afford. The bedding looked luxurious and the patterned curtains hung perfectly on display rods. I even visited the third floor, which housed the toy department, the same place that attractively shelved the Barbie bicycle I had yearned for so many years earlier while my Nanny lay dying. Now I lived right across the street. I stopped in my tracks with a sudden thought flooding my brain: *Maybe I should try to get a job here.*

It made perfect sense. My job at Lake Ontario Park would end in August and here was an opportunity so close to the place that I now called home. Besides, it was becoming increasingly painful to be around Tammy. I took my items to the nearest checkout and asked the clerk if the store was hiring.

"Are you a student?" she asked, tilting her head to one side.

"Yes. I'm going to Queen's in the fall."

While bagging my treasures, she said, "Well, they're always hiring students for the summer and for part-time positions. You should go see the manager. He's in his office on the second floor. It's the one with stairs going up to it and glass that looks out over the whole floor."

"Thanks a lot," I said as I raced for the stairs. *This is turning out to be a great day. I have to keep going with it.*

On the second floor of S&R, the manager's office was easy to find. The cashier was right: You really couldn't miss all that glass. I had a brief thought about Orwell's Big Brother but quickly dismissed it. I needed another job.

I bravely climbed the stairs and stared at the writing on the door of the office: *Mr. Roberts.* Simple and scary. I took one deep breath and knocked. The man who opened the door was of mid height, chubby, balding, and wore a suit that didn't seem to fit very well. His striped tie was as lopsided as his dark-rimmed glasses.

"Yes?" he said, peering at me with his tiny eyes.

"Mr. Roberts?" I inquired. I couldn't be sure that this man was indeed the manager of this gargantuan department store.

"Yes?" He looked irritated.

I stuck my hand out toward him, forcing him to shake it. "My name is Lynn Hellers. I'm very interested in applying for a job here at S&R." I sounded like a pathetic geek.

"Okay, come on in and I'll get you to complete an application," he said a little more good-naturedly. He was probably relieved to find that I wasn't just a disgruntled customer. He handed me a long sheet of paper and a pen. I could complete the application at the other desk in his office.

"Thank you, sir." I set my bags down on the floor and put the pen to the paper. Within a few minutes, I handed him the form and thanked him for his time.

"Now, just wait a minute," he said. "Let me take a look at this application before you go. Here, have a seat." I sat across from him and watched as he scanned the paper.

"So you're going to Queen's University in September."

"Yes, sir. I just graduated from Regi-Notre Dame High School a few days ago."

"We have several Queen's students working here," he stated without lifting his head.

"Your application looks pretty good, Miss Hellers. I'll look over your references and call you."

"Um, I'm sorry sir, but you won't be able to call me. I don't have a phone," I told him, embarrassed.

"What do you mean, you don't have a phone?" he asked, as if he had just heard news of an alien landing on the roof of the store.

"I mean, sir, that I don't have one *yet.* I just moved into an apartment right across the street. The job I have right now is only a summer job. I need more regular employment."

He stared at me above the rim of his glasses; his mouth gaped. "You live across the street?"

"Yes. At 46 Princess Street," I said proudly. *You sound like a desperate goon. Shut up!*

"I guess you'd never be late for work then," Mr. Roberts said, laughing.

"No way."

He flipped the paper back and forth in his hand and read its contents again. "When can you start, Miss Hellers?"

"What?" I was astounded.

"Do you want me to write it down for you? When – can – you – start?"

I laughed. It didn't seem like he was really making fun of me.

"I could start right away," I told him eagerly.

"What about your other job?"

"Oh, they'll understand, Mr. Roberts. They're aware that I'm looking for another job. They've been very good to me and they know how far I have to travel to get there. They'll see how far more convenient this is for me. My boss is a really nice man."

"That's nice to hear. Well, you talk to your boss and come back in and let me know exactly what day you can begin work for me. Does that sound like a deal?"

"That sounds fantastic," I said, grabbing his hand to shake it. "You've made my day, Mr. Roberts." I picked up my bags of groceries.

He smiled broadly. "That's not something I hear very often," he said, leading me to the door.

I raced across the street to my apartment so fast that I'm not sure if my feet actually touched the pavement. I wanted to tell somebody, anybody. I blasted into my space and searched for a phone that wasn't there. *Next step: get a phone.*

I unpacked my booty and salivated at the sight of the tins of spaghetti. I hadn't had a thing to eat since midday prior. Taking out my brand new can-opener, I placed it to the lip of a can and had a very unexpected urge to pee. All senses were heightened and I was consumed by the sheer joy of it all. I gleefully emptied my bladder into my own toilet and left the door open! *Oh God, have you let me die and brought me to Heaven? Where's Nanny and Grandpa?*

After feasting on canned spaghetti, I cleaned my bedroom first. I swept the mouse poop, checked for pedestrians and threw it out the window. I cleaned everything from top to bottom and set up the small appliances. I tried out the kettle and made a pot of tea, covering it with my new decorative cozy. I was having the best time of my life.

The dented transistor radio found its place on the shelf of a rectangular opening in the wall between the kitchen and living room. I thought some small plants would look great there too, when I could afford them. I turned the dial and a crisp, tinny sound filled the room:

> *If only you believed like I believe baby,*
> *Like I believe, we'd get by,*
> *If only you believed in miracles, baby*
> *So would I*

Jefferson Airplane, *Miracles*

I sang along and sang loudly. There was an echo to beat any in the Swiss Alps. Everything I had purchased was situated and still the place looked pretty bare. The living room was wholly vacant; the kitchen had a few appliances, and the bedroom had a cot. Still, I didn't want to be anywhere else.

Each of the plastic S&R bags was carefully folded and placed on a shelf in my closet. *They'll be useful. You never know when you might need one of those, for trash or whatever.* I unfolded the curtains that Uncle Darren had given me. There was a large pattern of blue roses on white. One I placed on the cot as a sheet and the other would cover me as a blanket. The cot actually looked inviting with a garden of blue roses covering it.

In the miniscule bathroom, I brushed my teeth and washed my face. I leaned closely into the mirror. For the first time, I wasn't trying to blur my image. For the first time, I really studied my own face. No longer afraid of what I was going to see, I looked carefully and smiled. The braces that had been removed months earlier had done wonders for my teeth. *Thanks, Mom.* My large brown eyes appeared fiery and alive and my skin tone was flushed. Blood rushed through my veins and arteries. *I'm going to make it. I'm going to school and I'm going to be a teacher. Watch this, Dad.*

"I'm going to be a teacher," I said out loud. Suddenly there were no maybes about it.

I changed into a fresh t-shirt and crawled between the curtains on my bed. A dull light from store signs below filtered in through the tall narrow window of my room. There were those sounds again, the voices, the horns, the engines, tires over wet asphalt, clicking shoes on concrete. It was the comforting racket of Princess Street. Those street noises lulled me as they did years ago in the home of my grandparents. The constant whirring, humming, and buzzing was like a welcome symphony with my Nanny's voice rising above it:

> *Twinkle, twinkle, little star*
> *How I wonder what you are.*

EPILOGUE

"SHE LOOKS PREGNANT, MS. HELLERS." IT IS ONE OF MY STU-
dents in the Grade Eleven advanced art class. I smile and turn toward the
large screen. Filling the front of the classroom is Jan Van Eyck's Arnolfini
Wedding Portrait.

"Yes, Janet," I say. "Excellent observation." I wait to see if anyone can find the
incongruence. Silence.

I smile slyly. "Consider the reason for the portrait and the date, 1434," I
tell them.

Matthew raises a hand. "Well it's a wedding portrait, right?"

"Yes it is." We had already talked about the portrait being painted before mar-
riage became a sacrament, but still the candle in the chandelier above reflected the
light of God in the presence of this union.

Matthew continues. "Well, that would mean that she is pregnant before the
marriage. Wouldn't that be scandalous?"

I love this class. Grinning, I say, "Very clever, Matthew. Yes, it definitely would
have been scandalous." I refrain from telling them that a woman who got pregnant
out of wedlock at that time would have been stoned to death, or forced into a river
with rocks in her pockets. I settle for the least traumatic of possible outcomes. "She
would certainly have been sent away from her family and possibly sold into slavery,"
I say. "Perhaps she would become a prostitute to save herself and her child."

There are gasps. "That's awful," Janet says, "and completely unfair."

"So is she pregnant or isn't she?" asks Matthew. "Why would the artist make it
look that way?"

"Great question. Look carefully. What has the artist done with her position to
make her look pregnant?"

The whole class stares, even the ones who weren't interested at first.

Hands fly into the air. "Yes, Laurie?" I ask, pointing to her.

She rarely participates. I can't believe she has raised her hand. "The artist has
her holding her cloak out in front of her with her hand. It's like she's pulling it away

from her body. That's what makes her look pregnant. Maybe the artist is telling us what's in her future."

"Yes, Laurie!" *I almost yelp,* "You are very intuitive."

She smiles and looks down at her notebook and I can see that she is blushing even in the low light coming from the screen. I know what kind of shyness that is. Hang in there, kid. I'll help you in any way that I can.

*   *   *   *   *

Yes, I became a teacher, which fulfilled my childhood desire and any motherly instinct I had left, while my sister Annie completed a year of college and embarked on a career in retail prior to her marriage at the young age of twenty-one. Though it was filled with love, her marriage was volatile, mirroring my parents (minus the black eyes). She longed to be a mother and it took her several years and a miscarriage before she had the first of my two beautiful nephews. Despite what she endured as a child, she has always appeared to be the best adjusted out of the four of us, even though she cannot sleep without a light on. She was, and always will be, my best friend and greatest supporter.

Wally became his own worst enemy. As the oldest boy in the family, he constantly tried to please our father. He still has not come to the realization that it's impossible. Crippled by his abuse, his resulting insecurity, substance abuse, and a diagnosis of bipolar disorder, Wally's life has been a topsy-turvy surreal world interrupted by several terms in jail. Though physically beautiful, artistic, and poetic, Wally has always been a mess inside and could rarely hold a job for very long. He never married, but has sired several children from different women, some of whom I have never met. Craving love and security, he has had multiple relationships trying to find one woman who will put up with his bullshit. He always has a hard time when they decide to leave him. This fear of loss led him to beat and tie one woman to a woodpile until a SWAT team arrived. His unpredictability, a penchant for violence, and always erratic behaviour reminding me of my father has made me keep a healthy distance from him over the years and continues to inspire a disquieting measure of guilt.

Sean outgrew his stutter, but not what caused it. Though he finished the top of his class at St. Lawrence College in Instrumentation and Engineering, he has often felt the need to protest about the depth of his knowledge over any university student in the field. Just like the rest of us, he has had a constant need to prove his worth. He married and had two lovely children. The pressures of marriage and fatherhood soon took their toll and Sean needed to be medically treated for severe anxiety disorder. He thought he was having a series of heart attacks. The best treatment he received, he conceded, was from a psychiatrist who asked him how he could survive a heart attack that lasted over a year.

Our parents, Margaret and Wade Hellers, are still together. My mother always said that she stayed with him through the years because there was little recourse for a woman who had four kids and not enough money to sustain her family. She said, "It's not like today, when a woman can take her kids to a shelter." I have always found this interesting because the four of us have been long gone from the household and she is still with him. My inability to forget the crimes of my parents has left us estranged. They have never wanted to hear any part about the past, even if it meant that one of us could find some peace and healing. In my need to tell the truth, they have pledged to sue.

After several law-imposed treatment programs, my father eventually quit drinking, well after we had all left home and the damage was done. This does not mean that he learned to control addiction. He merely replaced alcohol with something else. Wade Hellers became addicted to painkillers like Percocet known on the street as poor man's heroin. He had his ways of finding a steady supply. My mother continued to express her frustration about babysitting an addict and it wasn't uncommon for her to come home from work to find him unconscious with his head buried in a plate of spaghetti. Presently, he is undergoing chemical treatment and she insists that he is a changed man. His persistent threats toward me have left me in doubt.

As for me, I failed at a medley of relationships with men before marrying the one I saw as the perfect man, an event that coincided with the beginning of my teaching career. I thought that I had it made and for a couple of years I really did. It took the perfect man, with empathy, understanding, and patience to show me that I should be with a woman. To this day, I wish I had known definitively and could have spared him that pain.

Finding the truth about myself, about my gifts, my limitations, my creations, my destructions, and my true love, became a long, torturous yet rewarding journey.

But that's a whole other story.

CPSIA information can be obtained
at www.ICGtesting.com
Printed in the USA
LVOW10s1045160217
524478LV00001B/132/P